目录
Content

- 4 广州白云机场铂尔曼大酒店
  Pullman Guangzhou Baiyun Airport
- 14 广州富力丽思卡尔顿酒店
  The Ritz-Carlton®, Guangzhou
- 26 广州天誉威斯汀酒店
  The Westin Guangzhou
- 38 广州香格里拉大酒店
  Shangri-La Hotel, Guangzhou
- 50 中国大酒店
  China Hotel, A Marriott Hotel
- 62 彭年酒店
  The Panglin Hotel, Shenzhen
- 72 深圳华侨城洲际大酒店
  InterContinental® Shenzhen
- 84 深圳马哥孛罗好日子酒店
  Marco Polo Shenzhen
- 96 深圳威尼斯皇冠假日酒店
  Crowne Plaza® Shenzhen
- 108 深圳大华兴寺菩提宾舍
  The Mahayana OCT Boutique Hotel, Shenzhen
- 114 深圳茵特拉根房车酒店
  Parkview O·City Hotel, Shenzhen
- 120 深圳茵特拉根华侨城酒店
  The Interlaken OCT Hotel, Shenzhen
- 132 深圳茵特拉根瀑布酒店
  Otique Aqua Hotel
- 138 阳光酒店
  Sunshine Hotel
- 150 三亚凯宾斯基度假酒店
  Kempinski Resort & Spa Sanya
- 162 重庆洲际酒店
  InterContinental® Chongqing
- 174 成都索菲特万达大饭店
  Sofitel Luxury Hotels Wanda Chengdu
- 186 雅鲁藏布大酒店
  Brahmaputra Grand Hotel
- 198 甘肃阳光大酒店
  Grand Soluxe Hotel Gansu
- 204 新疆海德酒店
  Hoi Tak Hotel, Xinjiang
- 216 参编单位

广州白云机场铂尔曼大酒店坐落于白云国际机场的中心位置，是机场内唯一的国际五星级酒店。据悉，酒店在建设之初便按照五星级标准打造，机场集团共投资5亿多元，建筑面积近6万平方米。自2007年9月开业以来，酒店取得了不俗的业绩，与中国国际航空、美国联邦快递等大公司相继签订了长期合约，2008年酒店平均入住率达到70%以上，同年11月还成功成为第16届亚运会指定接待饭店。从机场出发大厅步行3分钟即可到达酒店大堂，驾车10分钟便可到达九龙湖高尔夫球场。方便到达广州各大商业中心，如天河城、北京路步行街等。距酒店仅3分钟步行路程的地铁站将在2010年内建成通车，届时，搭乘地铁只需15分钟便可直达广州市中心。

460间铂尔曼客房是真正的宁静之所，为那些跨时区旅行的客人提供优质的旅居体验，特殊的"铂尔曼床（Pullman Bed）"，根据人体力学功能原理而设计，配有新工艺的记忆枕及拱枕，有助于放松因长期旅途劳顿而紧张的肌肉及保证周身血液循环畅通；此外，房间还配备了iPod播放器、便捷实用的"插座系统（Docking System）"和个人专属瑜伽垫，在部分房间内还提供摩登咖啡机。考虑到临近机场，所有房间都安装了双层隔声玻璃以降低噪声，确保宾客在安静舒适的环境下得到良好的休息和睡眠。

以时尚餐饮理念打造的5个餐厅和酒吧

为客人带来卓越不凡的美食体验，让客人们充分领略铂尔曼的"餐桌艺术"。

全天候的U8自助西餐厅提供各国的美食佳肴和园林美景，"活力美食"概念的融入，让客人们近距离欣赏料理的全过程，发现每个厨师不同的烹饪风格与技术诀窍；恬园创意中餐厅以精致的粤菜见长；麟一日式铁板烧餐厅，让您感受"和"式风情；相聚大堂吧空间开阔，拥有3层楼高的室内瀑布，并提供浓香的咖啡和各式特调饮品驱散客人的旅途疲倦。

460平方米的无立柱式协和堂多功能厅和10个会议室，均配备高端会议设施：投影仪、高保真音响系统和投影屏幕等，此外所有会议场所均覆盖因特网，保证沟通无阻。会议活动经理可根据不同客人的需求量身订制各种会议及活动策划，并对其进行全程跟踪。IT经理也从幕后走到台前，变身为IT信息技术经理，直接与客人接触，提供各种专业的多媒体技术的支持和建议。

独创的铂尔曼"休憩空间（Chill-out Space）"配有按摩垫、咖啡机、iPod、电脑及各种娱乐设施，而量身订制的各种主题茶歇活动，（Coach à La carte）让与会者放松身心，恢复活力。

广州白云机场铂尔曼大酒店致力使每位客人都在舒适愉悦的环境中充分放松身心。酒店拥有设备齐全的健身房、网球场、篮球场、泳池、瑜伽房和桌球等休闲娱乐设施，为宾客的健身活动提供最大的便利和最有效的协助。水疗中心提供舒缓的瑞典精油按摩，传统的泰式瑜伽理疗和古典的中式指压，客人都可以在轻松惬意中达到舒心的美妙境界。

1. 酒店外观夜景
   Hotel Exterior View (Night)
2. 酒店外景
   Hotel Exterior View (Day)

Strategically located in the central area of the Guangzhou airport complex, only a 3-minute walk to the departure terminal, Pullman Guangzhou Baiyun Airport is the only 5-star international hotel in the airport area, which offers easy access to the Guangzhou railway station and numerous shopping malls. The metro station within 3-minute walk will be established in 2010.

460 Pullman rooms are a genuine oasis of calm, offering customers a quiet place to work and communicate. Special "Pullman Bed" is the fusion of new technologies and quality products, which includes generously sized bolsters, pillows and cozy comforters, to ensure all guests not only have a good nights sleep. Rooms are equipped with Docking System, yoga mat and espresso machine. Considerations of nearby the airport, the rooms are fitted with sound proof windows and sound-absorbing soft surfaces to maintain peace and quiet.

The hotel offers unforgettable "Pullman dinning" experience. U8 Action Cuisine, with a courtyard view, providing innovative global cuisine and a creative open kitchen buffet. Tianyuan Chinese Restaurant provides classical Cantonese cuisine with the ambience of the traditional Lingnan culture. Lin-Tepanyaki offers refined Japanese set menus; Société Lobby Lounge offers a range of coffee, tea and cocktail to "chill out" from the stresses of travel.

460sqm pillar-less Concord Ballroom and 10 meeting rooms are equipped with flat screens, A/V system and internet access to ensure efficient connectivity. Professional expertise is available at all times with a dedicated Event Manager ready to handle every detail with creativity and precision. An IT Solutions Manager

1. 铂尔曼欢迎大使
   Pullman Welcomer
2. 大堂
   Lobby

1

will recommend and deliver all multimedia and technology requirements.

Pullman "Chill-out" spaces for breaks, with modern coffee machines, massage cushions and I-Pods, are perfect venues to make participants comfortably relaxed during a meeting. A range of creative Pullman "Pause" breaks are available to choose from.

Guests can maintain regular workout routines while staying at Pullman Guangzhou Baiyun Airport. The hotel offers the contemporary Fitness Centre, the outdoor tennis and basketball courts, swimming pool.

Rejuvenate with an exquisite SPA experience, designed specifically to provide you with a total sense of purity, tranquility and peace of mind.

2

1. 大堂吧
Lobby Lounge
2. 行政酒廊
Executive Lounge
3. 麟日本餐厅
Tepanyaki Japanese Restaurant
4. U8风味餐厅
U8 Action Cuisine
5. 协和堂——宴会厅
Concord Ballroom

1. U8 餐厅自助餐
   U8 Buffet
2. 恬园中餐厅——包厢
   Tianyuan Chinese Restaurant-Private Room
3. 都市厅——会议室
   Metropolis-Meeting Room
4. 伊甸厅——会议室
   Eden-Meeting Room
5. 网球场
   Tennis Court
6. 水疗——舒适情侣房
   SPA-Couple Room

1. 游泳池
   Swimming Pool
2. 健身房
   Fitness Center
3. 水疗
   SPA
4. 蜜月房
   Honeymoon Room
5. 铂尔曼床
   Pullman Bed
6. 行政套房
   Executive Suite
7. 宁静的铂尔曼房间
   Pullman Room

广州富力丽思卡尔顿酒店是广州首家国际级奢华酒店，拥有351间客房，91套豪华公寓。酒店地处广州中央商务区珠江新城的核心，临近珠江，毗邻广州新地标——广东博物馆和广州歌剧院，与广交会新馆和广州电视观光塔隔江相望，是珠江边上最璀璨的明珠。

酒店拥有351间客房，位于建筑的第二十到三十八层，坐拥迷人江景和璀璨城景。最基本的房型有50平方米，每间客房均拥有入门走廊、步入式衣帽间等贴心设计，原木板搭配柔软细腻的羊绒地毯让旅途之家倍感温馨。58间行政楼层客房及35间套房拥有一系列尊贵设施和服务，如888支纱的床上用品和个性化唤醒服务等，将奢华的享受进一步提升。行政酒廊位于酒店的第三十三层，270°珠江美景和CBD新地标的迷人景致尽收眼底，被誉为广州"最美的空间"。在这里，行政楼层客人可以于每日5个时段享受精致餐饮及众多个性化服务。

位于酒店三十八层的丽思卡尔顿总统套房占据中央商务区珠江新城的核心高空。400平方米的宽敞空间、270°无敌江景、私家健身房、步入式酒窖、两个面积达40平方米的超大露台，分别配置了户外按摩池和烧烤炉等专属设施，使其成为城市中央和璀璨珠江边上的奢享空间。

酒店的水疗和健身中心泳池置于酒店中央的四层，是一站式的休息绿洲，为宾客提供个性化休闲体验。25米×10米的室外恒温泳池在罗马式大理石柱的围绕下分外湛蓝，超大号的休闲太阳椅让人格外放松，在池中畅泳或按摩池中放松身心，是城中达人的休闲首选。

广州富力丽思卡尔顿酒店拥有设计各具特色的餐厅，承传了岭南文化的精髓又紧贴国际饮食潮流。

1. 酒店大堂
   Hotel Lobby
2. 酒店外观图
   Hotel Exterior Shot

Located in the heart of Pearl River New City area of Tianhe District, the 40-storey Ritz-Carlton, Guangzhou is the jewel in the crown of this new regional central business development, introducing new heights of luxury service, elegance and sophistication to the city and the region.

Occupying the 20th to 38th floors of a stylish, modern building, the hotel offers 351 luxurious guestrooms featuring elegant European design, distinctive amenities and premier views of the Pearl River. The entry level guest rooms, at 50 square meters/540 square feet, are the largest in the city and set the style for luxury in Guangzhou.

The Ritz-Carlton Suite is located on the top floor of the hotel and features a walk-in wine cellar-which can be customized to suit the guest's individual requirements and tastes-a private gym, and two 40-square-meter/430-square-feet patios, including an outdoor Jacuzzi and barbecue grill.

Food is taken very seriously in Guangzhou and The Ritz-Carlton, Guangzhou has a variety of dining options in keeping with the traditions of a city that made Cantonese food widely known throughout the world.

A 24-hour fitness center with state-of-the-art Technogym equipment is available to guests who wish to exercise, while The Ritz-Carlton SPA® with 11 treatment rooms is available for those who wish to pamper themselves in luxurious style.

1. 丽轩月牙门,每晚现场古筝演奏
   Lai Heen / Chinese Restaurant
2. 豪华宴会厅迎宾区
   Ballroom Foyer

1. 意轩餐厅
   LIMONT/Italian Restaurant
2. 餐厅
   Restaurant
3. 餐厅室外餐区
   Foods Outdoor Seating
4. 珍珠吧
   Pearl Lounge

1. 中式婚宴细节
   RCGZ Chinese Wedding Detail

2. 婚宴
   Wedding Set-up in Ballroom

3. 丽轩中餐厅
   Lai Heen

4. 丽轩中餐厅VIP房
   Private Dining Room in Lai Heen

5. 茶艺角
   Tea Corner

6. 行政酒廊
   Club Lounge

1、2.邱吉尔吧
　　The Churchill Bar
3.豪华宴会厅迎宾区
　　Ballroom Foyer
4.豪华宴会厅
　　Ballroom with Meeting Set
5.会议室
　　Meeting Room

1. 室外恒温泳池
   Outdoor Heated Swimming Pool
2. 水疗中心
   The Ritz-Carlton Spa
3. 健身中心
   Fitness Center
4. 邱吉尔吧
   The Churchill Bar

5. 行政套房
   Executive Suite
6. 总统套房
   The Ritz-Carlton Suite
7. 卡尔顿套房
   Carlton Suite
8. 豪华客房
   Deluxe Guest Room
9. 总统套房/浴室
   Bathroom of the Ritz-Carlton Suite
10. 公寓客厅
    Residences Living Room
11. 公寓厨房
    Residences Kitchen Room

广州天誉威斯汀不只是提供住宿的酒店，更是集所有消闲设施及服务于一体的度假胜地，为追求宁静舒缓或焕发身心的必然之选。

酒店位置得天独厚，坐落于市中心天河商业区，毗邻中信广场，云集大部分驻守广州的世界500强企业。此外，酒店距离穗港直通车总站广州东站仅咫尺之遥。

酒店共拥有448间特大客房及华丽套房全部设有Westin Heavenly Bed®，让宾客压力全消、安睡入梦；酒店亦备有设施高端、服务优质的一系列活动室及会议室，可举行任何会议及聚会。此外酒店备有设施完善的健身室WestinWORKOUT®及水疗中心Heavenly SPA®，透过各项疗程，让宾客身心松弛，神采飞扬。

威斯汀行政会所位于39层，有一间可容纳十位宾客的会议室。

448间客房及套房都以"让您达到最佳状态"为设计理念，每间客房的装潢都现代时尚，让宾客在最舒适环境下休息。威斯汀普通客房面积达50平方米，呈献各项顶尖舒适科技，包括威斯汀星级睡床品牌Heavenly Bed®、令人精神一振的淋浴与浸浴Heavenly Bath®、高速无线上网、平面电视以及无绳电话。宾客亦可选择全新推出的WestinWORKOUT®客房，在绝对私密的环境下进行日常健身操练习惯。酒店大约四分之一客房及套房均在60平方米以上，并提供额外消闲设施及服务，包括特大书桌的

行政工作区、Herman Miller座椅及博世波浪式收音机。

皇家套房面积达150平方米，配上时尚现代的装潢，令宾客俨如化身帝王。总统套房面积达250平方米，拥有极尽豪华的顶尖装潢设计。

大型户外及室内游泳池、按摩浴池、蒸汽室、桑拿室及Heavenly Spa by Westin®让宾客尽情松弛，保持健康体态。酒店预留整个楼层供宾客作保健之用，是都市焕发活力的避世天堂。先进的健身房WestinWORKOUT®每天24小时开放，让宾客可以随时操练，保持身心健康。宾客亦可以享用Run Westin服务，在专业的跑步教练陪同下，早晨于市内跑步或步行，强身健体之余又可漫游广州的大街小巷。

酒店备有顶级中菜、意大利菜及欧陆佳肴，并设有拉丁美洲餐厅吧及酒廊。

Prego意大利餐厅位于酒店最高层，宾客可欣赏到无与伦比的城市景观，并细品美酒佳肴，享受正宗的意大利特色美食。无论是简餐，还是休闲的午餐、晚餐，甚至来一场"味觉的盛宴"，Prego都能满足不同的需求。饮品系列网罗款式繁多的各地佳酿，由传统名酒到新兴品牌都一一兼备，包括糅合顶级咖啡豆、烈酒和香草的正宗意式咖啡、由最佳葡萄蒸馏而成的意大利格拉巴酒、还有全部以最新鲜进口及本地水果精制而成的各款鸡尾酒。Prego设有四个私人意式厅，餐厅的Graziano Pia大厨将带所有宾客踏上美味之旅。

无论早午晚间，Taste全日供应自助餐及自选国际美食。餐厅环境开阔、光亮。开放式厨房及现代时尚的自助风格使烹饪专家与宾客得以实现各种食材的最佳配搭，体验自助带来的多样选择的乐趣。Taste的一系列鲜制果汁更是必试怡神佳品。

红棉中餐厅网罗正宗时尚的粤菜及中国其他各地名菜。装潢耀眼夺目的餐厅设有十个私人宴会厅，宾客可乐享私宴。

到Qba感受烧烤热力及拉丁salsa魅力吧！这间拉丁餐厅精心从全球选取各式鲜嫩肉类，堪称城中最佳。炽热火焰、鲜美热荤，再加上一杯接一杯的Mojito，宾客将焕发无限活力，并完全沉浸于欣赏现场南美

1. 酒店大堂
   Lobby
2. 电梯间
   Guest Room Floor Foyer

乐队的精彩表演中。至于雪茄狂迷亦大可品尝上等雪茄及优质干邑。

大堂酒廊特别营造明亮自然的格调,让宾客在舒适休闲的环境下,品尝精挑细选的各式名茶及天然小食,活力重现,精力充沛。

酒店设有多个会议及宴会场地,设计先进完善,无论举办行政级会议、中型至大型会议或特别活动,广州天誉威斯汀酒店都可满足不同要求。光洁明亮、广阔宽敞的会议室坐拥有广阔都市景致,在此举行会议及社交聚会均事半功倍。室内设有精心安排的投射荧幕、内置式投影仪,行政会议室更配备Herman Miller星级座椅、独立音响及灯光控制系统及可召唤Service Express服务的IP电话。

The Westin Guangzhou is more than a hotel. It is a retreat offering a full spectrum of amenities and services that provide everything from tranquility to rejuvenation.

Located in the heart of the business district-the Tian He District, our hotel is adjacent to the CITIC Plaza, which is home to the majority of the Fortune 500 companies in Guangzhou. We are also within a short walk of high-end retail shopping and the Guangzhou East Train Station-a major access point into Guangzhou from Hong Kong.

448 oversized guest rooms and beautiful suites will help you find total relaxation and a peaceful night's sleep in the Heavenly Bed ®. State-of-the-art technology, superior service, and a variety of function and meeting rooms will enable our hotel to cater to any conference, event, or function. Fully-equipped gym and Spa facilities, with a wide range of treatments, will help you relax and rejuvenate both body and mind.

Westin Executive Club is located on the

1. 酒店夜景
   Hotel Exterior
2. 酒店外观
   Hotel Facade

39th floor. 1 meeting room accommodates 10 persons.

Our 448 rooms and suites are designed to allow you to "Be at your best". Each room offers you an environment which is modern and contemporary. Our Westin rooms which are 50sqm in size offer you the ultimate in comfort and technology including Westin's signature Heavenly Bed ®, invigorating shower and bath, access, flat screen television and IP Phones with cordless handset. Or choose our new Westin WORKOUT ® Room to maintain your wellness routine and fitness regime in the privacy of your room. Approximately one quarter of our rooms and suites are larger than 60 sqm and offer additional amenities and services including an executive work area with oversized desk, Herman Miller chair and BOSE wave radio. Our 50-square meter Deluxe Rooms are Guangzhou's largest deluxe rooms, with a modern interior and the ideal facilities for business travelers. Our Executive Deluxe Rooms offer all the features of the Deluxe Rooms, as well as additional benefits for the most discerning travelers. Generously sized Grand Deluxe Rooms are on the corners of the Hotel boasting garden views. Feel renewed in our spacious 71-square meter Westin Renewal Room, the ideal choice for those seeking total relaxation. WestinWORKOUT ® Room is 69 sqm. with workout equipment. Our Executive Suites offer 96-square meter of spacious and understated chic accommodation. The Royal Suite Feel like royalty with 150-square meter contemporary designs. The Presidential Suite is

250-square meter with premier designs for luxury living.

Large outdoor and indoor swimming pools and jacuzzis, steam and sauna rooms and the Heavenly SPA by Westin™ allow guests to keep fit and to relax. With a whole floor dedicated to your well-being, expect a generous and gracious urban sanctuary where guests will feel renewed. State-of-the-art WestinWORKOUT® is accessible 24-hour to keep help you keep your commitment to fitness. Explore the city's streets and keep fit at the same time with Run Westin, designed for guests who want to run or walk in the morning with a "running" guide.

Chinese, Italian and Continental Cuisines dishes are served Latin-American Bar and a Tea Lounge are built.

Wine and dine with gusto with our authentic Italian specialties surrounded by unrivaled panoramic views of the city's skyline on our top floor. Whether it be for a quick bite, a leisurely lunch or dinner, or a gastronomic "degustation", Prego can do them all.

Day, noon and evening … Taste offers an all-day buffet and à-la-carte dining of international favourites in a light, airy and open atmosphere. The open kitchen and modern buffet style give our culinary experts and guests the chance to sample the best combination of cooked ingredients, enabling them to savour a wider selection of personally served delicacies. Try Taste's rendition of the freshest and invigorating juices.

Hong Mian brings the best of evolved, traditional

1. 大宴会厅
   Grand Ballroom Wedding
2. 咖啡厅
   Taste
3. 意大利餐厅
   Prego Italian Restaurant
4. 红棉中餐厅
   Hong Mian Main Dining

Cantonese and popular national dishes to enliven your body, mind and spirit. The impressive and modern Chinese restaurant also includes 10 dining rooms if you opt for privacy.

Feel the heat from Qba's hot grills and Latin salsa beat! This Latin bar and restaurant has the city's best succulent meats from around the globe. Fiery flames, fleshy meats and a Mojito create energy you will need to mambo the night away to a live South American band. And for cigar "aficionados", nurture your Cognac with the finest selection of cigars.

Refresh and be invigorated at White Scent with our High tea of carefully steeped tea leaves accompanied by natural and light nibbles in a cozy and relaxing atmosphere.

Advanced and well-designed facilities in various and modular meetings and banquet space, whether it is for board meetings or for medium to large conferences and corporate or social events like weddings, The Westin Guangzhou's facilities are equipped and designed to meet your needs. Light and airy rooms have fantastic city views making it conductive to meetings and social events. All meeting rooms are fitted with strategically placed projection screens, overhead built-in projectors, Herman Miller signature chairs in our board meeting rooms, independent audio and light control systems, and IP phones making Westin's services accessible with Service Express®.

1.会议室
Board Meeting Room
2.大宴会厅课堂式
Grand Ballroom Conference
3.意大利餐厅
Prego Italian Restaurant
4.日落仪式——茶道
Lifestyle Unwind
5.婚宴
Grand Ballroom Wedding
6.酒店40层空中花园
Garden at 40th Floor

1. 意大利餐厅包房
   Prego Italian Restaurant Private Dining Room
2. 拉丁美洲餐厅吧
   Qba Bar & Grill
3. 天梦水疗室外按摩池
   Heavenly Spa Outdoor Jacuzzi
4. 威斯汀健身房
   Westin WORKOUT
5. 天梦之浴
   Heavenly Bath
6. 天梦水疗护理房
   Heavenly Spa Treatment Room

1. 室内游泳池
   Indoor Swimming Pool
2. 行政超豪华房
   Executive Grand Deluxe
3. 总统套房
   Presidential Suite
4. 行政套房
   Executive Suite
5. 威斯汀活力客房
   Westin Renewal Room

廣州香格里拉大酒店
Shangri-La hotel
GUANGZHOU

广州香格里拉大酒店毗邻广州国际会议展览中心，该中心已经连续举办了两届举世闻名的广交会，有望成为世界第二大会展中心。广州香格里拉大酒店的地理位置优越，位于新商业区的黄金地段，俯瞰中国第三大水系——珠江的美丽景致。在广州的数家豪华酒店当中，香格里拉距新白云国际机场最近，仅需30分钟车程。

酒店拥有城中最宽敞的客房704间，面积均在42平方米以上，而最大的套房面积更达到305平方米。楼高36层的广州香格里拉大酒店是目前广州最高的酒店之一，成为该市的新地标。

酒店的豪华阁行政楼层，设有108间客房，占地面积达6层楼。入住行政楼层的客人可在他们专属的、同时也是广州面积最大的酒廊享受一系列的个性化服务，其中包括快捷办理入住、退房手续，免费享用早餐。全天免费享用软饮、下午茶以及傍晚鸡尾酒等。

酒店坐拥5,800平方米的幽雅花园，是城市中的一片绿洲。这里有露天泳池、散步小径，以及2,000平方米的户外活动草坪。

酒店设有8间餐厅和酒吧。其中，妙趣咖啡厅设有开放式厨房，提供来自世界各地的丰富美食。夏宫是香格里拉的招牌中餐厅，供应各色精致粤式点心，并有18间包房，宾客可在此欣赏珠

江的美丽景色。这里还有备受客人喜爱的滩万日本料理餐厅，这是滩万品牌在中国南方的首次亮相。在爱弗罗意大利餐厅轻松愉快的气氛中享受精致意大利美食，香泰餐厅享受传统和新颖的泰国料理。此外，大堂酒廊、交点酒吧和池畔烧烤吧也提供各色餐饮选择。

「氣」Spa是香格里拉独有的Spa品牌，其设计灵感源自《消失的地平线》一书中的香格里拉传奇，各种疗法都基于中医和喜马拉雅健康理念、仪式和传统设计而成。「氣」Spa拥有广州最大的理疗场地，最大的理疗室面积可达到70平方米，具有"Spa中的Spa"的氛围。另外，客人可以享用专属的浴室、更衣室、休息区和淋浴、沐浴等设施。11间理疗室中有8间拥有超大浴室，提供色彩治疗等独特疗法。

酒店的健身设施包括1间健身房、2间有氧运动室、2个露天网球场，以及室内游泳池（广州最大的室内游泳池之一）。

广州香格里拉大酒店目前拥有该集团旗下最大的会议和宴会场所，总面积达6000平方米，包括2间大宴会厅，8个多功能厅，1座礼堂，3个贵宾室和1间新娘房。其中珠江大宴会厅面积达到2240平方米，而且整个厅内没有一根支柱。它是目前香格里拉集团内，也是广州城内最大的宴会厅之一。

Shangri-La Hotel, Guangzhou is strategically located adjacent to the Guangzhou International Convention and Exhibition Centre, home to the world-renowned, twice-yearly Canton Fair and slated to become the largest exhibition centre in Asia and second largest in the world. Shangri-La Hotel, Guangzhou is in the heart of the new Guangzhou business district, overlooking the Pearl River, the third longest waterway in China. Of the city's deluxe hotels, the Shangri-La offers the shortest drive to the Guangzhou Bai Yun International Airport, at 30 minutes drive away.

The 704-room hotel offers the largest guest

1. 酒店正门
   Hotel Main Entrance
2. 酒店大堂服务
   Hotel Lobby Service

1. 室外游泳池
   Outdoor Swimming Pool
2. 酒店外景
   Hotel Exterior

rooms in the city with a minimum size of 42 square metres and up to 305 square metres for suites. Shangri-La is the newest landmark on the city skyline; at 36 floors, it is Guangzhou's tallest hotel.

The 108-room, six-floor Horizon Club, includes the most expansive executive lounge in the city, with panoramic views, personalised check-in, complimentary breakfast buffet, all day refreshments, afternoon and evening cocktails with canapés.

Hotel grounds provide an oasis of 5,800 square metres of landscaped gardens, including a free-form swimming pool, walking paths and a 2,000-square-metre lawn area for open-air events and functions.

Eight dining and entertainment venues include WOK TOO Café, serving international cuisine from an exhibition kitchen in a cozy setting. Summer Palace, Shangri-La's signature Chinese restaurant, serves fine Cantonese cuisine and offers 18 private dining rooms, many with Pearl River views. The popular Nadaman Japanese restaurant opens its first South China restaurant at the hotel. Italian casual fare is offered at il Forno and a traditional and fusion Thai menu in coolThai. Dining choices are supplemented by the Lobby Lounge, Lift Bar and Poolside Bar & Grill.

Chi, The Spa at Shangri-La – Shangri-La's signature Spa brand – is inspired by the legend of Shangri-La in the Lost Horizon novel, offering treatments and therapies based on Chinese and Himalayan wellbeing rituals and traditions. Treatment rooms are the largest in Guangzhou at up to 70 square metres and provide a "Spa within a Spa" environment, complete with private bathroom, dressing room, relaxation area, shower and bathing facilities. 8 of the 11 treatment rooms include infinity baths with healing colour therapy.

Health Club facilities include a gym, aerobics rooms, two open-air tennis courts and the city's largest indoor swimming pool.

The opening of Shangri-La Hotel, Guangzhou heralds the largest portfolio of meeting and banquet space of any Shangri-La Hotel, with two ballrooms, eight function rooms, an auditorium, three VIP greeting rooms and a bridal room, totaling 6,000 square metres. The 2,240-square-metre, pillar less Pearl River Grand Ballroom is the largest in Guangzhou and for the Shangri-La Group.

1. 大堂
   Lobby
2. 珠江大宴会厅——中式喜宴
   Pearl River Grand Ballroom—Chinese Wedding Setup
3. 夏宫私人包房
   Summer Palace Private Dining Room
4. 夏宫大厅
   Summer Palace Main Hall

1. 珠江大宴会厅——西式政府会议
   Pearl River Grand Ballroom—Western Government Setup
2. 珠江大宴会厅——讲座式
   Pearl River Grand Ballroom—Classroom Setup
3. 功能厅(莲花)——圆桌式
   Function Room (Lian Hua)—Round Table setup
4. 功能厅(圭峰)——U形台
   Function Room (Gui Feng)—U Shape Setup
5. 功能厅(鼎湖)——中式政府会议
   Function Room (Ding Hu)—Chinese Government Setup

1. 交点吧
   Lift Bar
2. 羊城套房会客厅
   Yang Cheng Suite Living Room
3. 健体中心健身房
   Health Club Gym
4. 室内泳池
   Indoor Swimming Pool
5. 商务中心
   Business Centre

1. 「氣」Spa
   Chi, The Spa
2. 豪华轿车服务
   Limousine Service
3. 宴会服务
   Banquet Service
4. 礼宾专员
   Concierge
5. 妙趣咖啡厅
   WOK TOO Café
6. 豪华阁尊荣套房
   Horizon Premeier Suite
7. 酒店外景
   Hotel Exterior

中国大酒店是一个传奇，一个根植于中国改革开放沃土的传奇。因为酒店的兴建，使南越国第二代王赵昧的陵墓被发现，这让中国大酒店从诞生之日起便拥有一种神秘的王者之气。

中国大酒店是中国首家中外合作经营的大型五星级酒店，由万豪国际酒店管理集团管理。酒店坐落于风景怡人的越秀公园与流花湖公园的环抱中，紧邻历史悠久的西汉南越王博物馆，地处广州市繁华的中心地带，正对广州锦汉展览中心，距新白云国际机场仅35分钟车程，位居地铁2号线越秀公园站旁，宾客可乘地铁轻松直达中国进出口商品交易会琶洲展馆及广州火车东站，交通便利，环境舒适。

中国大酒店拥有850间客房，均配备舒适的万豪新床褥、雨洒按摩浴设备、可与iPod及电脑连接的高清晰度视听设施等，务求为广大商务客人展现出时尚、精致及极具活力的崭新面貌。同时，为突出健康环保的居住理念，酒店在空调系统中增设光催化氯化净化装置，在排水系统中增设全热回收设备，在外立面改装上采用中空节能防噪声玻璃，全力打造一个绿色环保，提升人居环境的酒店。

酒店的饮食设施一应俱全，设有7间中西餐厅及酒廊，宾客置身其中可品尝到世界各地的美味。扒房为宾客提供独特的现代欧陆美馔，奉上来自世界各地的顶级牛扒和龙虾。除了正宗顶级西餐外，更创新地将东方元素加入欧陆风味菜肴，实现了欧亚风格的相互融

合,加以极品美酒相伴,向宾客提供帝皇般的享受。在马天尼吧内,屡获国内调酒比赛殊荣的专业调酒师现场调制马天尼酒和供应顶级品牌酒水,酒吧与泳池毗邻,宾客在品尝各式创意、新颖的马天尼酒之余更可欣赏怡人的池畔美景。在四季厅宾客可品尝到色香味俱全的高级粤菜;丽廊餐厅供应品种丰富的环球自助美食;在展现古老西关风情的食街,宾客则可尽享大江南北的风味小食。大堂吧及雪茄香槟吧也绝对是一个让宾客开怀舒缓,享受轻松时光的好去处。另外,龙野城日本餐厅、星巴克等著名饮食巨头也选择于中国大酒店开设分店,使中国大酒店真正成为世界名馔佳肴的汇集之地。

除饮食住宿外,店内还设有汇集多家国际顶级名牌商铺的名店城、银行、邮局和美容美发室、洗衣、24小时客房送餐服务、豪华轿车服务等也一应俱全。全新的健康中心配备完善,器材先进,环境舒适。24小时健身房拥有超过30套的高级多功能训练器材,跑步机、划船机、健身车等高级多功能器械应有尽有,让宾客在随心所欲的健身体验中迸发活力与健康。室外阳光泳池全年为宾客开放,宾客可一边畅泳,一边欣赏蓝天白云,更可远眺越秀山的景致,开阔的视野令人们心情无比舒畅。在环境幽雅的更衣室内,蒸汽室、桑拿室和水力按摩池等设施一应俱全,为宾客营造一个舒适放松的私密空间。更衣室内更配备了两台24寸的液晶电视机,有多达35个电视频道可供选择,宾客在放松身心的同时也可以收看喜爱的节目。

在会议设施方面,豪华的丽晶殿及15间多功能厅房总面积达2,300平方米,能同时容纳1,500余位宾客,有多种座位布置可供选择,更可根据会议的不同需要和规模进行分隔,这些都使中国大酒店成为市内首选的大型会议、展览及宴会场地。商务中心、行政楼层设有的高速宽频上网接入,可让客人随时通过国际互联网收发电子邮件及进行网上信息交流,随时随地掌控全球资讯,时刻与世界同步。

从1996年起,酒店连续多年荣获由美国酒店服务科学学会颁发的"钻石五星奖"。自1984年6月10日全面开业至今,中国大酒店已获国内外奖项逾500项,始终保持酒店业中的彪炳地位。

1. 酒店外景
   Hotel Exterior
2. 下午茶套餐
   Afternoon High Tea Set

1. 扒房
   Prime
2. 酒店大堂
   Lobby

China Hotel, A Marriott Hotel is a legacy hotel that dates back to the early opening of China to the Western world. The mausoleum of Nan Yue King of the Western Han dynasty was unearthed as the very foundations were being laid for this hotel, which gives the hotel its inherent greatness.

China Hotel, A Marriott Hotel, is the first Sino-foreign cooperative five-star hotel in Mainland China. It is also one of Marriott International Corporation's flagship hotels in the Asia-Pacific region. Surrounded by the verdant greenery of Yuexiu and Liu Hua Lake Parks—and within walking distance to the world-famed Museum of the Western Han Dynasty Mausoleum of the Nanyue King—the Hotel enjoys a prime location in the heart of Guangzhou, directly opposite the Guangzhou Jinhan Exhibition Centre, with easy access to China Import and Export Fair (CIEF) Pazhou Complex and Guangzhou East Railway Station by Metro, and only thirty-five minutes drive from Baiyun International Airport.

China Hotel, A Marriott Hotel features 850 guest rooms providing the ultimate in comfort for the discerning guests. The new guest rooms, reinvented in fusion style, boast high-definition LCD TV with easy connectivity to iPods (MP devices) and computers, separate rain shower and tub, extra large working space for business travelers. Environmentalism is also a significant concept. The new hotel air-conditioning system has installed a recently developed oxygen purification system – Special Photo Catalytic Oxidation Air Treatment, for higher efficiency and cleaner air. In addition, double glazing windows have been installed for spatial energy conservation and noise reduction.

A selection of seven restaurants, bars and lounges provides a diverse range of casual and fine dining featuring Eastern and Western cuisine. Savor hand-carved Australian and

Kobe grilled steaks and international cuisine at Prime. Accompanied by a glass of Cabernet or Chardonnay, every guest can dine like royalty. Sapphire Lounge houses China's award-winning bartenders, prepared to shake up the best drinks right before guests eyes. The poolside view, transparent sliding glass doors and inverted martini glass ceiling gives an extra gloss and shimmer to this romantically luring venue. Café Veranda features lavish international buffet. Four Seasons provides the finest, authentic Cantonese cuisine, teas and wine selection found anywhere in Guangzhou. Food Street offers a wide range of appetizing cuisine from throughout China – prepared "open kitchen" style. Bar and Champagne & Cigar Lounge, featuring live music and fine wines, are also the perfect place to relax and savor good life. Within our Shopping Arcade, we additionally offer you Starbucks Coffee and Japanese cuisine at Tatsunojo Restaurant to add to your dining enjoyment.

Covering a wide range of services and facilities, China Hotel, A Marriott Hotel also features a Shopping Arcade with top brand shops, in addition to a HSBC Premier Branch, Post Office, Beauty Salon, Valet and limousine and 24-hour room services. Its brand new Health Club, the largest in all of Guangzhou's hotels, provides just enough exclusivity so guests can enjoy a fully-focused and undisturbed workout on more than 30 machines – eight of which are treadmills alone … so no waiting is necessary. There's an extensive range of Star Trac cardio and

1. 丽晶殿
   Crystal Ballroom
2. 丽廊餐厅
   Cafè Veranda
3. 美食阁"鲜"
   Fresh
4. 食街
   Food Street

weight equipment. The outdoor swimming pool is available all year round as well. Behind the sanded glass locker room doors exists a personal space of pampered luxury. Not only are there spacious, full-service, digitally-secured lockers but a four-square meter Jacuzzi; state-of-the-art steam room and beautifully designed sauna. The Hotel's 35-channeled flat-screen HD television is also available to keep guests entertained any hour of the day.

The Crystal Ballroom and fifteen adjoining function rooms can accommodate up to 1,500 guests. All venues, feature state-of-the-art audio-visual equipment and facilities together with the Hotel's exceptional service, are the perfect place to hold meetings, cocktail parties and exhibitions. Internet service is available at the Business Centre and Executive Lounge. Express check-in/check-out service is also available for domestic flights improving the efficiency of our guests' business day.

Since its inception, China Hotel, A Marriott Hotel, has won more than 500 awards, marking its remarkable achievement in all areas of service. Since 1996, China Hotel, A Marriott Hotel has been selected to be the recipient of the "Five Star Diamond Awards" for consecutive years.

1. 水晶轩
   Centenary Room
2. 马天尼吧
   Sapphire Lounge
3. 行政楼层会议室
   Executive Lounge-Conference Room
4. 行政55
   Executive 55
5. 四季厅
   Four Seasons

1. 水晶轩
   Centenary Room
2. 吧
   Bar
3. 雪茄香槟吧
   Champagne & Cigar Lounge
4. 茶艺轩
   Tea Terrace
5. 健康中心
   Health Club
6. 室外泳池
   Outdoor Swimming Pool

1. 健康中心水力按摩池
   Jacuzzi
2、3、5. 服务员
   Waitress
4. 厨师
   Chef
6. 尊豪房
   Premier Room
7. 行政套房
   Executive Suite

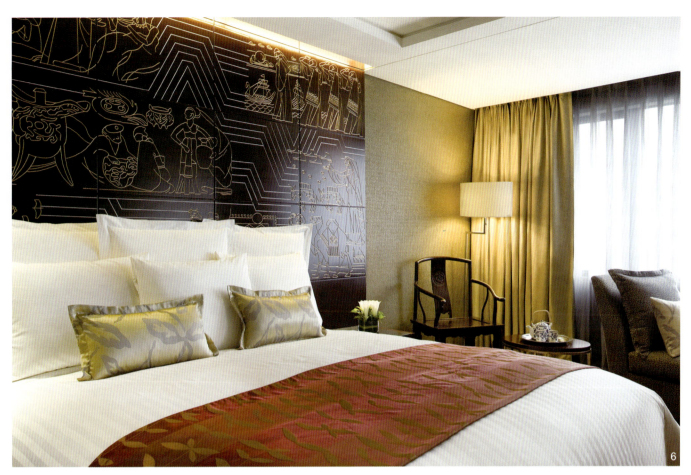

深圳彭年酒店位于深圳罗湖区心脏地带。彭年酒店所在的彭年广场有57层楼高，由酒店及写字楼两部分组成，外表雄伟壮观，是罗湖区标志性的建筑物之一。

深圳彭年酒店为深圳商业和经贸中心区内最好的五星级酒店，举步可至深圳各主要商务办公中心区和购物、餐饮、娱乐中心，距罗湖口岸仅5分钟车程。

深圳彭年酒店设有专为您的舒适及便利而设计的527间客房（包括48间行政楼层客房及87间套房），并设有全国信号连接、通过卫星及电缆接收的电视频道，如：HBO、CNN、ESPN、NHK以及多个东南亚地区的频道。

深圳彭年酒店客房宽敞舒适、装饰豪华、设备先进，所有房间均配备免费宽频上网，独立淋浴间、私人保险箱、卫星电视应有尽有，残疾人士专用房、非吸烟楼层更能于细微处见关怀。

深圳彭年酒店二十二层的皇朝会为尊贵的客人度身订造了一系列个性化服务，提供一系列专业设施，包括可容纳6～10人不等的小型多功能会议室，同时更有独立接待大厅可供您餐饮小憩，适合私人聚会和商务洽谈。

深圳彭年酒店设有中餐、日餐、咖啡厅、扒房等各式风味餐厅，还拥有可俯瞰深港两地美景的深圳最高的旋转餐厅，提供国际自助餐，现已成为国内外人士光临深圳的必到之处。

深圳彭年酒店四层的彭年殿气势恢宏，尽显宾主尊贵，桂花厅、茶花厅、荷花厅三间多功能厅可自由连通，同声传译及一流视听设备，专业策划助您宴会、会议圆满成功。所有会议厅配备最先进的会议设备，是您举行新闻发布会、研讨会、周年庆典或婚礼等的首选之地。商务中心提供各种商务服务并设有独立会议室与私人办公室，为您拓展商机助上一臂之力。

酒店还设有卡拉OK厅、健身室、桑拿浴室、桌球室、阅览室、棋牌室、贵宾赏乐室、豪华影院，同时更有独立接待大厅可供您餐饮小憩。二层的咖啡厅荟萃中西美食，古典独特的环境，满足各界商旅人士的不凡品位。红酒雪茄吧温情洋溢。

另外，该酒店也是中国目前唯一一家将营业利润悉致捐献给慈善事业的酒店，并享有"慈善酒店"的美誉。

1.外景
Exterior View
2.四层彭年殿
4/F Panglin Ballroom

1. 酒店夜景
   Hotel Night View
2. 一层大堂
   1/F Lobby Lounge

Centrally located in Lowu District of Shenzhen, Panglin Hotel stands right Panglin Hotel is in the over 57 floor Panlin Plaza, which constitutes hotel and office building, a magnificent landmark in the heart of Shenzhen.

As the best five-star hotel amidst the thriving business and commercial district, Panlin Hotel is walking distance to shopping center and entertainment area, 5 minutes' ride to Lowu Border.

527 rooms designed for guests' comfort and convenience, including 48 rooms on the Executive Floor and 87 suites, feature separate shower stall, in-room safe, internal data hook-up, TV with satellite and cable receptions i.e. HBO, CNN, ESPN, NHK and various Southeast Asian channels. Rooms for handicapped and non-smoking floors deliver the Hotel's most customized care and attention.

The CLUB LOUNGE on the 22nd floor provides a series of customized services, including professional facilities like 6-10-men small multi-functional conference room, personal butler service suitable for both private gatherings and commercial meetings.

There are Chinese restaurant, Japanese restaurant, café, grill-room; sky paradise -the city's highest revolving restaurant- presents a fantastic panoramic view of both Shenzhen and Hong Kong, featuring an innovative buffet concept with a live band playing through the night. Now the sky paradise is a place attracting both domestic and international tourists.

Ballroom on the 4th floor is with capacity up to 600 attendees, including three function rooms: Laurel, Camellia, Lotus, which can open up into one. All equipped with the most advanced facilities, including simultaneous interpretation system, audio-visual system, broadband internet access, etc. The commercial center provides various kinds of services and has individual conference room and private offices, which helps a lot while you're staying at the Hotel. It is the perfect venue for press conferences, seminars, anniversary celebrations, wedding ceremonies.

People could leave behind the fast tempo of city life and release themselves in the Littoral Health Centre, Karaoke, gym, sauna, massage, solarium, billiards room, reading room, chess and card room, separate sections for VIP and Ladies, luxurious theater and individual lobby lounge for catering. The café on the 2nd floor outdoor serves Chinese and western food, and its elegant atmosphere can satisfy guests' every need.

It's the only hotel who donates all its profit to the charity and enjoys the reputation for "charity hotel".

1. 一层嘉宾吧
   1/F Jiabin Bar
2. 二层咖啡厅
   2/F The Cofé
3. 三层钓鱼台中餐厅
   3/F China Garden
4. 四层荷、茶、桂花厅
   4/F Lotus, Tea and Laurel Chamellia
5. 四层宴会厅
   4/F Ball Room
6. 四层中式婚宴
   4/F Chinese Style Wedding

1、2、3. 五十层云景轩旋餐厅
　50/F Sky Paradise
4. 五十一层渡月桥餐厅
　51/F Togetsukyo

1. 四层荷花厅
   4/F Lotus Hall
2. 六层泳池
   6/F Swimming Pool
3. 六层浴池
   6/F Bathhouse
4. 六层健身室
   6/F Health Center
5. 六层桑拿浴室
   6/F Sauna Massage Jacuzzi
6. 总统套房局部
   Part of Presidential Suite
7. 洗手间
   Rest Room
8. 公寓房
   Apartment Room
9. 10. 套房
   Suite
11. 总统套房
    Presidential Suite
12. 单房
    Single Room
13. 二十一层行政楼层
    21/F Executive Floor

深圳华侨城洲际大酒店是国内首家以白金五星级标准建造的西班牙风情主题酒店。酒店位于集文化、艺术、金融于一体的华侨城片区，优越的地理位置和便利的交通使宾客在半小时内可抵达深圳国际机场、火车站及蛇口码头。步行10分钟可到达各大主题公园、华侨城创意园、购物中心、酒吧街等城市热点。

540间豪华装修的客房，其中总统套房面积达688平方米。七、八层为行政楼层，房间大都有独立阳台。25套酒店式公寓，面积从77平方米到200平方米不等，有现代行政、经典绅士和时尚精英三种风格可供选择。房间均配备液晶电视、Bose音响系统和DVD播放器、iPod播放连接，舒适的工作台提供高速网络接入，宽敞的浴室设有水疗式浴缸和液晶电视。酒店近万平方米的户外花园，集水疗、健身、瑜伽于一身的悦源优健水疗会所，提供多项专有服务。

8间风格各异的主题餐厅和酒吧提供全天候特色美食新体验。环球厨师团队给客人带来正宗地道的法国、巴西、西班牙、德国、中国、东南亚等特色美食和文化风情。其中横空停泊在酒店三楼的船吧延续了哥伦布航海的梦想，以桑塔玛丽亚号为原型，扩大了2倍，历时2年时间建成。提供400个露天坐席和室内现场乐队表演，宾客可享受自酿德国啤酒和西班牙美食。

位于酒店一层总面积达2,800平方米的宴会活动场地，包括可容纳逾千人的无柱大宴会厅，其宽敞的入口设计便于汽车直接通达；还有一间充满欧陆风情的小宴会厅和7间多功能会议室，均配备先进的智能灯光音响配置；另外，环绕各个宴会厅的高迪花园为您的活动增添一抹绿色的清新。

城中首创的婚礼中心，为渴望拥有浪漫婚礼的人们提供一站式服务，不仅可以量身定做顶级的婚戒、礼服、蛋糕，还配有美容美发及婚纱摄影等，更有代表圣洁爱情的结婚礼堂和玫瑰花园，为希望拥有纯西式婚礼的人们提供多种选择；2008年9月1日开业的华·美术馆使酒店成为国内首家拥有美术馆的酒店，提升了酒店的艺术品位，为国内先锋艺术设计、展览、活动和人才搭建了交流平台。

1. 酒店外观
   Hotel Exterior
2. 1982 廊
   1982 Corridor
3. 华·美术馆
   OCT Art and Design Gallery

1. 婚礼中心小教堂
   Chapel of Wedding Ceremony
2. 华·美术馆外景
   Exterior of OCT Art and Design Gallery

The award-winning InterContinental Shenzhen is the first Spanish-inspired luxury business hotel in China with platinum 5-star standard. Located in the upscale Nanshan district of Shenzhen, the hotel is within half an hour driving distance from Shenzhen International Airport, the Railway Station, Shekou Ferry Terminal and only 10-minute walking distance from city attractions such as theme parks, OCT Loft, shopping malls, and bar street. Perfectly located for travelers and business visitors.

The hotel provides 540 luxuriously designed rooms with a presidential suite at 688 square meters. Two executive floors from level 7 to level 8, most rooms are equipped with private balcony. There are 25 Serviced Apartments varying from 77 square meters to 200 square meters with three decoration styles: Executive, Studio and Classic for different taste. All rooms, suites and serviced apartments have complimentary high-speed broadband and wireless Internet access, LCD televisions, Bose sound systems and extravagant bathrooms. Despite the luxury of the rooms, don't be tempted to stay in. The Hotel's fitness center is state-of-the-art with a SPA and indoor heated pool, and the landscaped outdoor pool has a natural sand beach to relax on.

Each of the eight thematic restaurants and bars offers innovative and exciting dining experiences. An international team of Chefs present real authentic flavors and cultures from France, Brazil, Spain, Germany, China to Southeast Asia. Amongst all, the Galleon Restaurant and Bar that parks atop the hotel's car park is an replica of Santa Maria, which was the galleon that sailed to the Americas with Christopher Columbus, this unique venue hosts 400 outdoor seating with live band performance and home-brewed German beer…everything to creative the night scene of the city.

The hotel's pillar-less grand ballroom seats up to 1,200 guests and is divisible by thirds, while a customized ramp access is ideal for hosting more spectacular events such as automobile launches. The advanced audio visual and intelligent lighting systems enhance the visual impact of events. Seven smaller event rooms and a landscaped poolside with natural sand beach are available to serve programs with varying needs, while their full service Wedding Center completes with chapel-styled service and menus created in consultation with our chefs take the stress out of your big day.

On September 1st 2008, the OCT Art and Design Gallery was launched as the first art gallery that promotes pioneer contemporary arts from design, exhibition, event to many forms, which is the platform for talents from all around the world.

1. 广场咖啡厅
   Café of Square
2. 大宴会厅
   Banquet Hall
3. 华善中餐厅
   Huashan Chinese Restaurant
4. 巴塞罗那小宴会厅
   Barcelona Little Banquet Hall
5. 芫香·东南亚餐厅
   Wuxiang Southeast Asian Restaurant

1

2

1. 华膳中餐厅醉翁厅贵宾厅
   VIP Room of Zuiweng Hall
   Huashan Chinese Restaurant
2. 马德里会议室
   Madrid Conference Room
3. 宴会精美摆设
   Exquisite Bibelot of Banquet
4. 法国餐厅
   French Restaurant
5. 洲际俱乐部行政酒廊
   Club Lounge
6. 马德里会议室
   Madrid Conference Room

1. 室外泳池憩栖区
   Resting District of Outdoor Swimming Pool
2. 室外泳池
   Outdoor Swimming Pool
3. 悦源优健水疗会所瑜伽室
   Yoga Room of Waterfull SPA & Wellness
4. 悦源优健水疗会所健身房
   Fitness Room of Waterfull SPA & Wellness

1. 行政走廊
   Executive Corridor
2. 总统套房
   President Suite
3、5. 中式主题套房
   Chinese Style Suite
4、6. 豪华房
   Luxury Room

深圳马哥孛罗好日子酒店

深圳马哥孛罗好日子酒店是一家国际五星级商务酒店，坐落于繁华的福田中心区。酒店邻近深圳国际会议会展中心及地铁站，宾客前往罗湖火车站仅需20分钟，前往蛇口港和深圳宝安机场仅需25分钟，到达皇岗口岸及福田口岸仅5分钟车程。

391间豪华客房和套房均设有豪华浴室、宽频上网及先进的通信、娱乐设施。贵宾行政楼层位于酒店的三十五层至四十一层，是专为高端商务客人所设计的，可提供顶级的个性化服务，其全部采用欧洲现代装饰风格，以舒适的设施和专业的服务为客人提供超凡的感受。总统套房拥有267平方米的超大空间，位于酒店顶层，占据了酒店的最佳位置，拥有最好的视野和景观。套房内每个单独的活动区域都有独特的功能设置，并配备了相应的设施，兼备会客、用餐、商务活动及休闲等多种功能。

酒店拥有便捷的地理交通位置，为配合这一优势，满足大量商务会展的需求，酒店设有31间多功能会议厅，总面积达3,136平方米，共可容纳3,000多人，是您安排大型会议、研讨会及宴会的理想场所。马哥孛罗宴会厅面积达760平方米，净高7米，宽敞气派，可同时接待600人就餐、800人开会、1,000人举办鸡尾酒会。其他大、小会议厅都以国内外著名城市的名字命名。所有宴

会厅均配备先进的设备，如同声传译系统及耳机、电视监控系统等。酒店专业的宴会运作团队还可以为您设计不同主题的会议。

马哥孛罗咖啡厅内设有开放式厨房，提供亚洲特色的自助餐和各式中、西美食服务。北角露台咖啡厅为您精心搭配各种让您口齿留香的美味佳肴。佳宁娜中餐厅是深圳首屈一指的中式餐厅，设有多个独立的私人贵宾房，以提供特色潮州菜系为主。西村日本餐厅内设大厅和私人贵宾房，并设有铁板烧房、榻榻米房及吧台，提供正宗日本寿司、铁板烧和日式风味食品。大堂雅座内幽香的咖啡、传统的茶及精美的健康小食，是您休闲聚会的好去处。华尔街会所提供上等佳酿葡萄酒和极品雪茄，是高级行政人员休憩和商务客人聚会的最佳选择。宾客可在玛格丽特吧享用各种玛格丽特酒及精美小食，尽享人生瞬间惬意。

健身中心面积达320平方米，为热爱运动的您提供完善的运动器材、专业瑜伽课程及私人教练服务。远离城市的喧闹，于美丽的池畔沐浴阳光，室外游泳池是您放松心灵，与亲朋至爱享受清凉饮料、美味小食的最佳去处。蔓达梦水疗源自于泰国，专业的水疗中心拥有11个贵宾房，其中包括2间双人房及1间豪华套房，同时提供一系列放松身心的水疗护理，并设有美容、美发及足浴、美甲区域。蔓达梦是人们追求美，放松身心的宁静天堂。

1. 酒店外观
   Exterior
2. 酒店大堂
   Lobby

Marco Polo Shenzhen is located in the business, commercial and entertainment area of Futian (Shenzhen's new CBD), with close proximity to the Shenzhen City Hall, new Shenzhen International Convention & Exhibition Center and Metro Subway Station. The hotel is a 20-minute drive from Luohu Railway Station, 25 minutes from Shekou Ferry Terminal & Shenzhen Baoan International Airport, and 5 minutes to Huanggang and Futian borders.

The 391 well-appointed rooms and suites are equipped with broadband Internet access, The Puesideutial Suite is luxurious bathrooms, state-of-the-art communications and entertainment facilities situated on the 35th to 41st floors of the Hotel, The Continental Club provides the most luxurious accommodations for travelers. Decorated with a Euro-contemporary style, it provides the grandest environment, combined with additional services and facilities. Located on 41st floor, this suite is 267 square meters of contemporary elegance. It offers the most luxurious and impressive accommodations, with marble bathroom equipped a Jacuzzi and sauna.

Marco Polo Ballroom, 30 multifunction rooms and one auditorium can accommodate up to 3,000 persons, and provide the ideal venue for meetings, seminars and social events. All of our meeting rooms feature state-of-the-art AV equipment and wireless broadband internet access. The 760 square meter Marco Polo Ballroom has been a venue for exclusive and important events. We have also been the meeting hotel of choice for numerous multi-national companies and governmental organizations.

Café Marco is a All-day dining restaurant with open kitchen, featuring Asian & International Buffet and à la carte menu.Terrace is adjacent to Café Marco and welcomes afternoon tea lovers to escape the blistering stress

1. 西村寿司
   Nishimura Sushi
2. 酒店大楼
   Hotel Exterior

1. 酒店大堂
   Lobby
2. 马哥孛罗宴会厅（中式）
   Marco Polo Ballroom (Chinese Banquet)
3. 华尔街会所
   Wall Street Club

of the day. Carrianna Chinese restaurant is Shenzhen's premier Chinese restaurant. Nishimura Japanese Restaurant serves sushi, teppanyaki and other authentic Japanese specialties. For pleasure or business entertainment, the restaurant features elegant dining rooms, teppanyaki counters, traditional tatami rooms and a sake bar.

The Gym measures 320 square meters and offers a wide range of professional services and facilities to cater for today's health-conscious travelers. Yoga classes and personal training are available. Outdoor Swimming Pool is an ideal venue for guests to enjoy refreshments and light snacks on the sun deck while soaking in the rays. Mandara Spa The renowned has 11 exclusive treatment rooms, including two couples rooms and a luxurious VIP suite with spacious Jacuzzi. The Mandara Spa offers a wide range of relaxing Spa therapies, a beauty salon, and a specialized pedicure / manicure area.

1. 悉尼演播厅
   Sydney Auditorium
2. 巴黎罗马厅
   Rome & Paris Function Room
3. 伦敦厅
   London Room
4. 马哥孛罗宴会厅(课桌)
   Marco Polo Ballroom (Classroom)
5. 北京厅
   Beijing Boardroom

1. 马哥孛罗咖啡厅
   Café Marco
2. 玛格丽特吧
   Margarita Bar
3. 健身中心
   The Gym
4. 泳池
   Pool
5. 蔓达梦水疗
   Mandara Spa

1. 豪华客房
   Deluxe Room
2. 高级客房浴室
   Superior Room Bathroom
3、5. 马哥孛罗套房
   Marco Polo Suite
4、6、7. 总统套房
   Presidential Suite
8. 贵宾楼层豪华房
   CCF Deluxe Room
9. 蜜月套房
   Honeymoon Suite

深圳威尼斯皇冠假日酒店（CROWNE PLAZA SHENZHEN）位于深圳湾畔风光秀丽的华侨城，是中国首座以威尼斯文化为主题的国际品牌五星标准商务酒店，酒店由华侨城集团公司投资兴建，聘请洲际酒店集团(InterContinental Hotels Group)进行管理，使用国际连锁的五星级品牌皇冠假日(CROWNE PLAZA)。酒店在2001年10月28日开业，于2003年3月21日正式挂牌，成为五星级涉外旅游饭店。

深圳威尼斯皇冠假日酒店位于深圳的西南部，紧邻著名的主题公园世界之窗、欢乐谷、锦绣中华和民俗文化村。交通便利，酒店距市中心和西部通道10分钟车程，距蛇口码头15分钟车程，距罗湖口岸和深圳国际机场仅20分钟车程。

深圳威尼斯皇冠假日酒店是中国第一家以威尼斯文化为主题的酒店。金光闪烁的圣马可狮屹立在主体建筑之顶，昂首向天，雄姿英发。圣马可狮是威尼斯城的象征。狮子所持的书上写着传统的拉丁文是威尼斯由圣马可狮守护的声明。圣马可翼狮的后腿站在水里，前肢站在土地上，标明了威尼斯共和国统领陆地和海洋的力量。矗立在广场标志柱上的威尼斯守护神圣西奥多脚踏鳄鱼，一手执长矛一手执盾牌，日夜守护着驻足威尼斯皇冠假日酒店的尊贵客人。

酒店建筑及艺术设计聘请国内外著名大师联手精雕细凿而成，充分体现了威

尼斯的文化风格。酒店赭红欧式建筑之顶，怀抱福音书的威尼斯城徽金色翼狮雍容华贵，熠熠生辉；广场罗马柱上威尼斯守护神雕塑傲然屹立。穿过取材于圣马可广场公爵府的一排威严高大的哥特式柱廊，走进高贵典雅的室内装饰空间，恍如置身于威尼斯的艺术宫殿。

威尼斯皇冠假日酒店的室外景观堪称中西合璧的佳作。"水"是威尼斯皇冠假日酒店园林景观的灵魂。蜿蜒如威尼斯运河的水渠以及玲珑的石桥，张扬起美丽白帆的空中泳池，随风轻摇的"贡多拉"船，各式的叠水与涌泉如梦如幻，威尼斯的"水"恰如一串灵动的音符。"绿"是威尼斯皇冠假日酒店园林景观的主旋律。层次丰富色彩明艳的花坛、曲径通幽的绿色走廊、树影婆娑的竹林、意境幽远的"生态岛"和充满意趣的明净沙滩等，为深南路的如画美景增添了浓墨重彩的一笔。

酒店总投资4亿多人民币，建筑面积5.8万平方米，地下2层，地上17层。酒店拥有舒适客房375间，其中套房47间，为商务客人特设有3层威尼斯行政楼层。还设有无烟楼层和残疾人房间。酒店高级客房面积达40多平方米，套房面积达50多平方米，且多数有观景阳台，宽敞温馨。

酒店客房主要设施均按照商务客人的需要以及皇冠假日（CROWNE PLAZA）国际品牌标准配备。所有客房均有宽频互联网接口，客人可以坐享超速上网的迅捷服务。打开卫星接收电视，客人可以收CNN，NHK，HBO，CNBC，ESPN，FASHION等电视节目，了解全球最新资讯。客房配有国际国内直拨电话、语音留言信箱，有独立淋浴间，单独空调、迷你吧、保险柜、吹风机等设施，并有当日洗衣／熨烫、免费咖啡／茶、24小时送餐服务。

酒店威尼斯行政楼层为繁忙的商务客人提供更为便捷的服务。客人可以直接在行政楼层办理快速入住和离店手续；所有客房均配有多功能传真机，独立的商务中心及会议设施。行政楼层的客人可免费使用两小时行政楼层的会议室；全景式豪华行政酒廊为客人提供免费早餐、全天咖啡／茶和傍晚"欢乐时光"的酒水。各种不

1. 外观
   Hotel Exterior
2. 大堂入门
   Lobby

同的专职服务尽显体贴与尊贵。

酒店内各餐厅精心制作世界各地美食佳肴,让各位客人任意品尝。意华轩中餐厅拥有24间包房,您可以尽情品尝地道的粤式大餐;典雅的意大利餐厅提供一流欧陆传统美食;风格清雅的日韩料理令人难以抗拒;在酒店的咖啡厅,透过巨大的玻璃窗可尽情玩味水乡泽国把酒品茗的优雅,在浪漫的威尼斯氛围中舒缓工作的压力;酒店大堂穹顶是彩绘的蓝天白云,灯光的变幻使穹顶呈现早、中、晚的不同景象,尤其是星星点点的夜空效果,充满威尼斯的浪漫与温馨。在大堂吧咖啡广场小憩其乐融融,在V吧欣赏现场乐队表演,充满异域的激情,在威尼斯池畔吧与三五知己把盏更觉心旷神怡。

酒店商务中心提供24小时服务,包括小型办公室、秘书翻译、复印传真、互联网资讯、邮寄速递、国际性报纸杂志、机票预订等,务求令各位商务旅客犹如有私人助理随伴左右。另外酒店还提供外币兑换、儿童托管、医务室、精品店、旅游服务等。

酒店提供中央视像会议系统、宽频高速上网、液晶投影仪等先进会议设施。酒店的大宴会厅源自1709年一幅反映威尼斯贵族沙龙生活的油画,置身其中,彰显贵宾身份的尊严与高贵。685平方米的威尼斯宴会厅可容纳700人,并可根据需要分隔、组合,并配有活动舞台和同声传译系统,8个多功能会议厅,可满足不同会议的需要。酒店为各种中西宴会、小型展览、座谈会、发布会及商务会议提供一个理想的空间。

位于威尼斯皇冠假日酒店内,由著名建筑师John Chan 匠心演绎的健身水疗美体中心,为您献上一个梦寐以求的舒适、悠闲的生活新境界。

健身水疗美体中心主要分为三个部分:水疗美体区、健身区以及总面积超过1,000平方米的特大户外园林泳池和全天候室内泳池。健身水疗美体中心引入"水疗法护理",水疗法是利用水之冲力促进健康及康复的古典护理方法,功效包括舒缓精神紧张、消除身体疲劳、平衡血液循环、促进新陈代谢、增进体力、加强免疫系统,以及有效塑造体形、达到护肤瘦身的效果等。

酒店高高悬建的泳池映衬拉起的白

帆，像酒店怀抱里一艘扬帆欲航的船。全天候室外游泳池和室内温水池旁拥有2,000平方米的超大空间，旁边还设有儿童嬉戏的小水池，足见酒店服务的体贴入微。设施完善的健身中心、时尚的美容美发以及在深圳独一无二的温情SPA，让人在紧张的商务活动之余，轻松拥有一份身心的舒逸。

华侨城是深圳最美丽的城区。酒店东临福田中心区，西接高新科技产业园区。凭窗眺望，世界之窗景区一览无余，欢乐谷尽收眼底，透过深圳湾海景可见对岸香港元朗。

著名的主题公园锦绣中华、中国民俗文化村、中国国家级美术馆何香凝美术馆、高雅艺术的殿堂华夏艺术中心，华侨城高尔夫俱乐部等，使深圳威尼斯皇冠假日酒店更具有不可比拟的环境优势。

1. 旋转楼梯 Staircase
2. 大堂 Lobby
3. 咖啡厅 Cafe Zentro

The Crowne Plaza Shenzhen is owned by the premier property group in Southern China, the Overseas Chinese Town Group (OCT) and managed by InterContinental Hotels Group under the Crowne Plaza brand. Invested by Overseas Chinese Town Group and Overseas Chinese Town Real Estate Company with approximately cost of RMB 400,000,000. The Hotel opened on the 28th October 2001, and was awarded Five Star status at a ceremony on the 21st March 2003. Located in the southwest of Shenzhen city, right next to the famous Window of the World, Happy Valley, Splendid China and China Folk Culture Villages theme parks, the Crowne Plaza Shenzhen is 10 minutes away from City Centre and West Corridor accessing Hong Kong border, 15 minutes away from Shekou Harbour Passenger Terminal and 20 minutes away from Luohu Port and Shenzhen International Airport.

Being the first international Venetian style hotel in China, the hotel represents a unique and distinctive Venetian theme. The Winged

1. 威尼斯宴会厅
   Venice Ballroom
2、3. 意华轩中餐厅
   Marco's Chinese Restaurant
4. 日韩餐厅
   JK Restaurant

Lion of St. Mark, sitting above the Hotel, painted in 1516 by Vittore Carpaccio for the Magistrato dei Camerlenghi in Rialto is exhibited today in the Doges' Palace in Venice. Following religious accounts, the body of the apostle St. Mark, was smuggled from Alexandria to Venice in 828 and laid to rest in the new church – at the same time the lion became the emblem and symbol for the city of Venice. The lion is holding up the book with the traditional Latin inscription, a declaration that Venice is protected by the apostle St. Mark, acting as patron saint of the city. The Winged Lion of St. Mark illustrates the power on land and sea of the Venetian Republic, symbolized by the lion standing with its hind legs in the water and its forelegs on dry land.

With a total area of 58,000 square meter, the Hotel boasts 375 guest rooms and suites, each affording luxury and privacy, including 47 suites and 3 floors of Crowne Plaza Club rooms for discerning executives. Most of the guest rooms feature private

balconies and all feature deluxe amenities like satellite reception; separate shower in bathroom; spacious working area; personal in-room safe; IDD / DDD and voice mail; in-room coffee / tea maker and hair dryer; fully stocked mini bar and high-speed Internet access. Guests staying at the Crowne Plaza Club, can enjoy the all-in-one fax/copier/printer unit in room, complimentary breakfast, evening Cocktail, all day Coffee/Tea in the Club Lounge, minibar soft drinks (up to 6 bottles daily), pressing service (up to 4 pieces daily), 2 hour complimentary use of the Club Meeting Room, late check out till 1,630 subject to room availability and express check-in and check-out.

You would expect Shenzhen's premier hotel to offer the finest restaurants and bars in the city and you won't be disappointed. Marco's (Chinese Restaurant) with 24 VIP private rooms presents outstanding Cantonese cuisine along with a mix of regional Chinese specialties. Blue (Italian Seafood & Grill Restaurant) is known for its fresh live seafood and excellent selection of steaks. The elegant JK (Japanese & Korean Restaurant) offers the traditional Japanese sushi and Korean pickled vegetables (Kimchi). La Piazza (Lobby Lounge) combined "Espresso Bar & Newspaper Stand" in one area, a place to see and to be seen. Café Zentro (Coffee Shop) features the best Pizzas in town and best international buffet. It also offers Asian/

1. 池畔
   Poolside
2. 咖啡厅
   Cafe Zentro
3、4. 意大利餐厅
   Blue Italian Seafood & Grill Restaurant

Chinese dishes, fresh bread and Italian Ice Cream specialties. V-Bar and Poolside Bar & Restaurant are the perfect rendezvous for evening entertainment and live performance. Supported by enthusiastic and friendly staff, the food and beverage outlets provide a warm welcome and efficient service to guests.

The hotel's 24-hour Business Centre offers a comprehensive range of translation, secretarial and administrative services, ticketing, international newspapers, mailing service as well as private meeting rooms. Other facilities include foreign currency exchange, baby-sitting service, clinic, shopping arcade, limousine / shuttle service and travel / tour service, etc.

Leisure facilities include a fully equipped Fitness Club, indoor and outdoor swimming pools and an up-to-date Health Spa. Whether at play or at work, guests at the Crowne Plaza Shenzhen can take full advantage of the activities on offer.

Whether it is for an elaborate banquet, a demanding conference or a cozy private gathering, the Crowne Plaza Shenzhen offers eight function rooms and a Ballroom. The Venice Ballroom features a 685 square meter pillarless ballroom, accommodating up to 700 people for a reception and can be split into two smaller sections for private functions. All function rooms are fully equipped with the latest audio/video system to suit all types of meetings or conferences.

1. 池畔
   Poolside
2. 日韩餐厅
   JK Restaurant
3. 咖啡广场
   La Piazza
4. V吧
   V Bar
5. 威尼斯宴会厅
   Venice Ballroom

1、2. 泳池
　　 Swimming Pool
3. 总统套房
　　 Crowne Suite
4. 客房
　　 Guest Room

深圳大华兴寺菩提宾舍，是以佛教文化为主题的精品酒店，坐落于东部华侨城华兴寺景区内，它将"禅宗"理念融入酒店设计当中，呈现"闲寂、自然、幽雅、朴素"的精神内涵。菩提宾舍倡导关注心灵文化，表现对人性的尊敬态度，更将山海之间独有的禅意世界呈现在都市人的眼前，让每一位客人感受妙在高顶、不可言传的精神体验。

菩提宾舍精心打造22间禅意客房，其中包括4间高级房、12间豪华房及6间套房，让您的修行之旅，静谧无忧。同时为潜心修行的客人量身订制礼佛、请法、灵修等体验课程，并有东部华侨城华兴寺住持印能法师定期举行的禅聚活动。

在大华兴寺内，以汇聚大江南北精美素食而闻名的香积斋，将斋菜也做得"活色生香"。内部以质朴、自然为设计风格，全部采用原木餐桌与座椅，极力突显实用与功能性。蒿草编织而成的镂空屏断，巧妙、完美地划分出一个个静谧的空间，而画有精致花纹的灯罩，将整个馆内的气氛烘托得恰到好处，韵味十足，让客人在此尽享人间美味，品味自得悠然。

Located in the breathtaking Wind Valley of OCT East, The Mahayana OCT Boutique Hotel, sanctuary of Zen, within Hua Xing Temple, offers a brand new level of tranquility, elegance, peace and nature for the soul searching being.

Equipped with 22 Zen-inspired guest rooms which including 4 superior rooms, 12 deluxe rooms and 6 deluxe suites, the Mahayana OCT Boutique Hotel provides a sanctuary and home for you to study, investigate and listen to Buddha Dharma especially for those require privacy. Regardless of novice, experienced layperson, senior cultivator, or any monks, we are at your service. The Mahayana OCT Boutique Hotel provides liaison service for arranging Buddhist activities, hierurgy service and lessons with Hua Xing Temple.

With a conducive and Zen-filled ambience, our vegetarian restaurant offers you delicate food, reflecting vegetarian food's history as a cultural crossroads for you from China. Apart from pampering your sense of taste, the restaurant also features a conducive and Zen-filled ambience for diners: the dining table and chairs made of original timber log perfectly integrated with functionality and a touch of simplicity; and the hollowed-out screen woven with wormwood stick partitions, contrast with the modern lampshades, and ragged stone walls, that brings you a different level of vegetarian dinning.

1. 大华兴寺菩提宾舍
   The Mahayana OCT Boutique Hotel
2. 紫砂茶具
   Yixing Tea Set

1

1. 大华兴寺
Hua Xing Temple
2. 四面观音
Guanyin Sitting on Lotus
3. 深圳大华兴寺菩提宾舍大堂
The Mahayana OCT Boutique Hotel Shenzhen–Lobby
4、5. 豪华房
Deluxe Room

1.斋菜
Vegetarian Food
2、3、4.深圳大华兴寺菩提宾舍套房
The Mahayana OCT Boutique Hotel Shenzhen-Suite Room

深圳茵特拉根房车酒店坐落于深圳东部华侨城云海谷的茵特拉根房车酒店，是以房车文化为主题的精品酒店。它将房车的动感与随意融入酒店的设计理念中，依托东部华侨城独有的湖光山色、云海奇观，将最休闲生态的空间呈现，带给客人洒脱与自然的全新居住体验。

酒店拥有159间概念客房与4辆豪华房车，其中客房包括标准房、高级房、豪华房、豪华套房、温馨家庭套房，各式房型都为您的入住提供最满意、舒适的选择。从德国引进的豪华房车采用环保航空材料制造，内部线条明快流畅，视听、餐吧、淋浴等生活设施一应俱全，让您的郊野之行随心所欲。

3间多功能会议厅，将最先进和开阔的会议空间呈现在您面前，让您在会议期间高枕无忧，成就精彩。Cabin2咖啡厅、Oil Bar-KTV酒吧，连名字都散发着汽车的味道，让您在品味上乘美食的同时，犹如置身于车中，体验心随律动的澎湃。棋牌室、放映室、室内泳池、保龄球馆、网球场等为您带来缤纷的娱乐享受。

Parkview O·City Hotel Shenzhen, located in the Wind Valley of OCT East, is flexibly composed of guest rooms in main building which are designed following the Motorhome concept, and luxury caravans. Guests can enjoy leisure life and appreciate the unique lake and mountain sceneries.

Parkview O·City Hotel Shenzhen is equipped with 159 guest rooms in main building and 4 Motorhomes, including standard room, superior room, deluxe room, deluxe suite and family suite, which will dazzle you. Motorhomes from Germany are equipped with all kinds of traveling, living, entertainment and audio & video facilities, environment-friendly aeronautic materials and feature a fashionable exterior design and a streamlined interior style.

Three well equipped multi-function rooms to meet your needs. Professional service team will give extra effort to make your meeting successful. It contains an all-day-dining (Cabin 2), KTV (Oil Bar & KTV), recreation room, cinema, indoor swimming pool, bowling alley and tennis court for entertainment.

1. 茵特拉根房车酒店
   Parkview O·City Hotel
2. 进口房车
   Motorhome

1. 茵特拉根房车酒店大堂
Parkview O·City Hotel Lobby
2、3. 进口房车
Motorhome

1. 咖啡厅
   Cabin
2. Oil Bar-KTV酒吧
   KTV (Oil Bar & KTV)
3. 豪华套房
   Deluxe Suite Room
4. 标准房
   Standard Room

东部华侨城茵特拉根主题酒店群坐落于中国深圳大梅沙，占地近9平方公里，由华侨城集团斥资35亿元精心打造，是国内首个集休闲度假、观光旅游、户外运动、科普教育、生态探险等主题于一体的大型综合性国家生态旅游示范区（中国国家旅游局和国家环境保护部联合授予），主要包括大峡谷生态公园、茶溪谷休闲公园、云海谷体育公园、华兴寺、主题酒店群、天麓大宅等六大板块，体现了人与自然的和谐共处。

深圳东部华侨城茵特拉根主题酒店群，落址在深圳东部最美丽的海岸线和梧桐山森林氧库之间，由深圳东部华侨城与华侨城国际酒店管理有限公司历时4年倾心打造，目前包括：茵特拉根华侨城酒店、茵特拉根房车酒店、大华兴寺菩提宾舍、茵特拉根瀑布酒店，共拥有600间客房，每个酒店各具特色，其设计理念、建筑风格以及整体氛围都是特定文化的集中体现，将经典浪漫、大乘境界、自由肆意和艺术品韵等个性演绎得淋漓尽致。

深圳茵特拉根华侨城酒店，是以瑞士文化为主题的超豪华五星级酒店。它坐落于深圳东部华侨城茵特拉根小镇，秀丽的湖泊、茂密的树林不仅为酒店营造出不可多得的自然景观，更为它带来终年清爽的宜人气候。酒店建筑设计独具匠心，艺术元素渗透每个小细节。一

流的设施设备、一流的服务品质，尽展茵特拉根酒店的好客之道。

酒店拥有豪华客房308间，特色套房61间。茵特拉根酒店主楼、池畔别墅、连排别墅、商业街公寓、总统别墅等各类建筑交相辉映。24小时私人管家为入住酒店至尊俱乐部及套房的宾客提供最贴心、周到的服务。舒适畅快的入住体验尽在酒店娱乐、餐饮、休闲观光等服务项目中。酒店的餐饮娱乐设施包括：哥特吧、茵特拉根咖啡厅、湖逸轩中餐厅、日本秋叶餐厅、意大利花园餐厅、湖畔酒吧及烧烤、雪茄厅及知识堂。

酒店的会议设施为客人提供商务会议、宴请宾客的宽阔空间。健全、高端的会议设施，使茵特拉根的星级服务更上一级。茵特拉根宴会厅以古典唯美设计为主，是举办婚宴、大型会议、新闻发布、商务庆典及产品介绍的绝佳场所。会议厅包括：硫森湖、比尔湖、布林湖、曼德湖、图恩湖等。茵特拉根大剧院，具有晚会表演、大型宴会、商务会议和展览等多种功能。近300平方米的LED舞台背景屏幕是"中国第一屏"，其多媒体技术为游客带来绝无仅有的视觉震撼。

Four exclusive theme hotels in OCT East, a 3.5-billon-yuan investment supported by OCT group, is located at DaMeisha, Shenzhen. Occupying about 9 square kilometers, OCT East is the first eco-tourism and scenic spot in China. The project offers adventures education and fun-field experiences. Besides, theme parks, four theme hotel are at you disposal.

OCT East Theme Hotel Cluster, a new property–a theme hotel group and unique hotel experience that promote an exceptional lifestyle supported by OCT East and OCT International Hotel Management Co. Ltd., is located between Dameisha and Wutong

1. 深圳茵特拉根华侨城酒店夜景
   The Interlaken OCT Hotel Night
2. 深圳茵特拉根华侨城酒店全景
   The Interlaken OCT Hotel Panorama

Mountain, Shenzhen. With 600 finest rooms, OCT East Theme Hotel Cluster contains Interlaken OCT Hotel, Parkview O·City Hotel, Mahayana OCT Boutique Hotel and Otique Aqua Hotel, delivering four sought-after hotels with distinctive style in this secluded paradise of the OCT East region to create a soul of life to this precious wonderland.

The Interlaken OCT Hotel Shenzhen provides an unparalleled European-style 5 star experience within Interlaken Village at East OCT in the eastern part of Shenzhen. Situated in a perfect panoramic position between lovely lakes and forest, the area enjoys a mild and stable climate throughout the year. Our 308-room luxury hotel offers a perfect blend of sleek design, state-of-the-art facilities, and OCT's legendary hospitality.

The Interlaken OCT Hotel features 308 guest rooms, including 61 suites, reflecting the comfort and luxury of chic Swiss-European design. Guests staying in any of the Interlaken Hotel's Premier Club Rooms and Suites will enjoy 24-hour Butler Service, the pinnacle in service quality. Other service includes Interlaken entertainment, restaurant and leisure reservations. Dining and Entertainment Facilities include: Gothic Bar, Interlaken Café, Charming Lake Chinese Restaurant, Akiba JAPANESE Restaurant & Sake Bar, Vista Lago Italian Restaurant, Lake Side Bar & Grill, Cigar Lounge & Library.

Our Viennese-styled Interlaken Grand Ballroom is the ideal place for your important engagements, weddings, both business and social functions. The private meeting rooms and secluded board rooms are the perfect setting for intimate social gatherings or small business meetings. The meeting rooms provide a range of audio visual features including digital wall display, conference call facilities and high speed, wireless Internet services. Snacks and light meals are also available to be served within meeting space. Interlaken Theater is a place which can hold various events such as performances, large banquets, business conferences and expositions. The 300-square-meter LED screen is the "No. 1 Screen in China". Its multimedia technology brings audiences an unprecedented visual spectacular.

1. 茵特拉根酒店大堂
   The Interlaken OCT Hotel lobby
2. 茵特拉根城堡酒店
   Castle Interlaken
3. 茵特拉根华侨城酒店
   The Interlaken OCT Hotel

1. 哥特吧
Gothic Bar
2. 酒店大堂
Hotel lobby
3. 日本秋叶餐厅及清酒吧
Akiba Japanese Restaurant & Sake Bar
4. Vista lago意大利花园餐厅
Vista lago Italian Restaurant
5. 湖逸轩中餐厅
Charming Lake Chinese Restaurant

1、2. 茵特拉根国际会议中心
   Interlaken International Conference Center
3、5. 茵特拉根宴会厅
   Interlaken Grand Ballroom
4. 行政会议室
   Meeting Room

1、2.茵特拉根温泉
The Interlaken SPA

1. 茵特拉根湖景家庭套房
   Interlaken Two Bed Room Loft
2. 豪华房
   Deluxe Room
3. 至尊湖景套房
   Premier Club Lake View Suite
4. 至尊湖景房
   Premier Club Lake View Room
5. 豪华湖景房
   Deluxe Lake View Room
6. 联排别墅豪华房
   Town House

OTIQUE AQUA HOTEL
深圳茵特拉根瀑布酒店

OCT 华侨城·东部　OCT 华侨城酒店管理

深圳茵特拉根瀑布酒店以"水"为元素，集合以"水"为主题的建筑艺术、影像艺术、室内装置艺术等作品。

酒店藏身于宽300米、高70米的巨岩之中，是当前国内落差最大的人工瀑布，瀑布由酒店楼体倾泻而下。客人要通过空中走廊穿越瀑布进入水晶宫般的酒店大堂，坐在大堂的任何区域，室外宏伟壮观的瀑布丽景尽收眼底。

酒店设有94间极具设计感的客房，均为人造大理石整体建造，墙壁、客床都呈现流水形态，灯光营造出海洋与太空的唯美效果。酒店除了给人以无限灵感的水为主题外，大胆的设计创新和无处不在的艺术渗透，更体现在每一个细节之中，从艺术品陈设到客房用品，到门牌，都以影像方式呈现，使茵特拉根瀑布酒店本身成为一件非凡的艺术精品。

简约、时尚的风格精心设计，可容纳70人的全日咖啡厅，拥有红酒储藏室和独立的音乐播放系统，在营造出令人叫绝的环境氛围同时，更将世界各国美食精致呈现。体现自酿啤酒屋风情，拥有原木紫铜装饰风格的啤酒工厂，共分为地面层与沙滩层两层，可分别容纳60和90个座位，而在沙滩层，露台式的空间让客人将优美的湖畔风光一览无余。集演艺、影像为一体的超现代宴会厅，占地近2,000平方米，拥有两个长

Using water as the main design element, the Otique Aqua Hotel is built hidden behind the biggest artificial waterfall (300 m in height) in Mainland China and behind a giant rock (70 m in height). The hotel fully utilized the concept of water to be the main interior and exterior design theme, making the whole hotel a massive contemporary art piece. Using artificial marble as the main construction material, and the vision of floating water, special lighting effects to create the effect of the ocean and Space, this Hotel shows its hip and chic elements perfectly. From art piece decorations to room consumption items, the hi-tech designs and the senses of visual, aroma and feel give visitors a brand new way to perceive the stunning boutique hotel, making it a unique art piece as a whole.

94 trendy guest rooms with unconventional design that will raise the benchmark of hip hotel design in China.

Simple and stylish, the Café Aqua is a place to fit 70 persons. With its red wine cellar and independent music system, the environment of Café Aqua will bring customers into a new world of enjoyment for international dining. To experience the sensation of a local brewery house, the Beer Factory has an interior design style full of wood and bronze elements. There are two separate floors that

方形主舞台和可升降圆形舞台,二层的独立包厢可将整个大厅景观一览无余,是举办表演、大型宴会、商务会议的绝佳场所。

1. 茵特拉根瀑布酒店
   Otique Aqua Hotel
2. 茵特拉根瀑布酒店大堂
   Otique Aqua Hotel Lobby

can fit in 60 and 90 seats respectively, along comes with the beach level, which its open area let customers to view the lake scene as much as they like.

Covering 2,000 m² with two rectangular main stages and one central arena stage, the Seafield Theater offers advanced equipment and audio visual facilities that can add value to your events.

1. 瀑布酒店大堂吧
   Liquid Point
2. 全日咖啡厅
   Café Aqua
3. 啤酒工厂
   Beer Factory

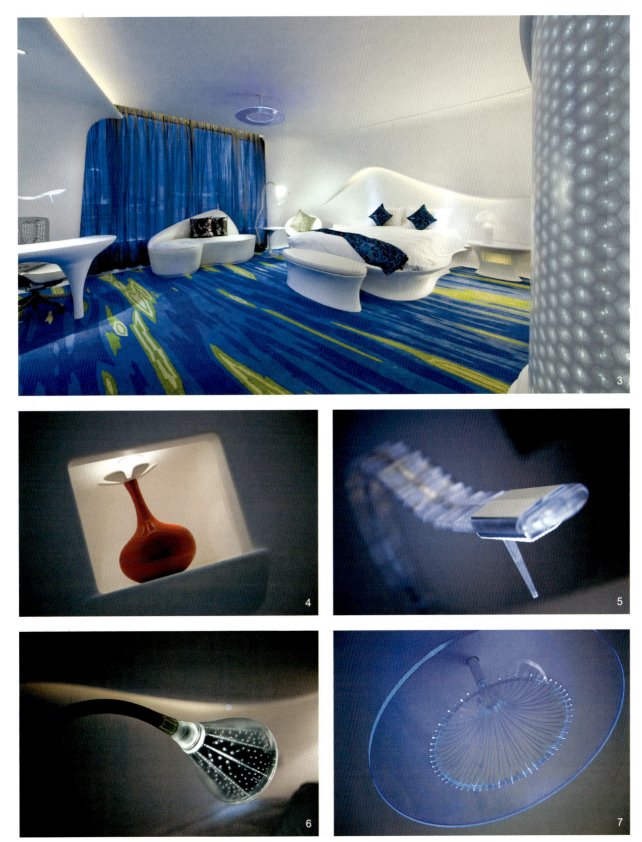

1、3.海洋主题客房
Ocean Theme Room
2.游艇主题套房
Yacht Theme Suite Room
4、5、6、7.客房装饰
Room Decoration

陽光酒店
SUNSHINE HOTEL

阳光酒店位于深圳市嘉宾路和东门南路交汇处，是一座具有国际水准的豪华商务型酒店。1993年9月18日被国家旅游局评定为五星级酒店。

酒店位于深圳市商业、文化繁华地段，商务、购物方便，交通便利。酒店紧邻国贸大厦、嘉里中心，距火车站仅数分钟车程，多线公共汽车经过并以"阳光酒店"命名设站，离地铁"国贸站"仅百米之距。酒店有巴士穿梭于各旅游景点；专车每日多班次送达香港九龙及香港赤腊角机场。酒店停车场可同时停泊车辆150部，领同行业之先。

酒店依据国际五星级标准精心营建。酒店主楼及"紫月楼"商务楼层共拥有精致装修的客房379间，其中豪华商务套房64间，高贵典雅，柔暖色调，衍映成趣，温馨袭人，洋溢心思。房内配以宽频互联网接入设备、电子保险箱、电子防盗系统、液晶电视、迷你吧、商务办公系统、套房配置CD音响、免费DVD影音设备、浴室干风设施、干湿洗衣、免费擦鞋及24小时随时送餐服务，体贴备至，至优完美，令您舒心惬意之至。

大型会议厅"阳光厅"，高雅亮丽，格调尊贵，设备先进完善，可满足400人会议、宴会、培训、展览、表演的不同需求。多功能宴会厅"紫月厅"组合分拆随意，可供各类中小型会议、培训、产品展示、会见等需要。

在五星级酒店优厚资源的支持下，更创立出"五星"中的五星会所"阳光会所"。阳光会所配以果岭推杆高尔夫球场及壁球室、

乒乓球室、桌球室、棋牌室、网球场、会所影院、全天候暖水泳池、桑拿浴、健身中心、会议室等，使酒店迈入更多功能、更高档次的行列。邀请国内外知名人士为会所名誉会员，吸纳商界精英为基本会员，更以阳光酒店的客人自动成为会所临时会员。务求会员置身其中，感受到超凡脱俗的尊贵享受。

食在阳光，有口皆碑。阳光食府设于酒店一至三层。"醉月轩酒吧"静卧大堂一隅，歌乐袭来，令人心醉；二层"东丽廊西餐厅"设200余自助餐位，集东南亚美肴于一身，汇欧美风范于一体，恰随君意，清爽怡人；"嘉宾路一号"中餐厅以江南小炒为主流，糅合经典与现代的装饰理念，在雅致环境与细腻服务中体现华夏饮馔食德；"潮江春酒楼"之岭南潮汕风味堪称一流，出品精致，烹调考究，可筵开50席。位于酒店三层的"海港大酒楼"，以粤菜海鲜系列为特色，装饰豪华。"禾田料理"为本市最大的正宗日本菜馆，全日式服务令客人风情尽享。居于酒店顶层的"聚贤阁酒廊"，享誉内外，以"红酒"、"雪茄"为特色，有国内建成最早的"雪茄房"、"红酒收藏室"。

酒店商务中心，以一流信息服务系统，为宾客提供Internet宽频接入、复印、传真、IDD、电子邮件(E-mail)收发及秘书、翻译、免费手机电池充电等服务。酒店在香港设有宾客服务处，并可在欧亚、北美及中东24国为宾客提供预订服务。

风华气度见于优美，温馨可人觅及娴雅。阳光酒店独有的优雅氛围与至微服务，关怀无尽，写意绝伦，是阁下商旅、休憩的最佳选择。

1994年深圳阳光酒店获得"深圳十佳酒店"称号；1995年获得"全国优秀星级饭店五十佳"称号；1996年深圳阳光酒店被国家旅游局评为"全国最佳星级饭店"；2005年深圳阳光酒店被广东省旅游局评为"绿色饭店"；1998～2003年连续多年被评为"全国外商投资先进饭店"。

1. 主楼外景
   Main Building Exterior
2. 大堂
   Lobby

Located at the juncture of the Jiabin road and Dongmen road of Shenzhen. Sunshine Hotel is a gorgeous hotel with international standards, which is managed by the Hong Kong Chinese International Team & Experts Management ltd. It is the first five-star hotel in the downtown of Shenzhen Special Economic Zone.

The Hotel is conveniently located near business and shopping areas and just a few minutes away from the railway station. In addition to daily shuttle buses to Hong Kong, the hotel can arrange tour bus for visits to scenic spots and historical and cultural sites in the city.

The Hotel has been built according to the international five-star hotel standards. Main building 379 spacious rooms with fully equipped facilities. Additional amenities includes: Adjustable air conditioning, In-house movies, Hong Kong TV, local TV, satellite TV, CNN International and NHK Channels for selection. Beside control panel, bathroom with fixed hair dryers and bathroom scales, refrigerators and mini-bars, 24-hours room service, broadband high speed internet access, IDD telephone system, telephone with bathroom extension, non-smoking floor.

Spacious ballrooms and meeting areas provide an array of elegant options for banquets and business meetings.

The Sunshine City Club offers the guests various recreation with the best club facilities in Shenzhen which include Luxury Sauna and Message, Indoor Nine Hole Putting Green, Snooker room, Gymnasium with the Computerized Equipment, Aerobic Classes tailored for Ladies and Warm Water Indoor Swimming Pool with Jacuzzi.

It is universally agreed that the best place to dine is the Sunshine Hotel. Seven restaurants for Chinese, Japanese, Western and special cuisine. The finest cigar and wine with the very pleasant atmosphere of the Connoisseur

1. 聚贤阁酒廊
   Juxiange Wine Corridor
2. 行政客房外景
   Executive Guest Room Exterior View

on the 16th Floor, the music in the Lobby Moonlight Lounge, the dainty dishes of the Melrose Grill, the all-day buffet in Oriental Delight and the flavor of the south of the Five Ridges in Chiu Chow Garden Restaurant may all entertain and fasciante guests with an everlasting memory.

The business center of the hotel provides the latest business facilities and equipment for today's discerning business traveler including Internet, Fax, Photocopying, Binding, Mobile telephone, Word-processing with computer system and laser printing service.

The perfect facilities, unique environment and excellent service make Sunshine Hotel the best choice for your travels.

1. 客房外景
   Guest Room Exterior View
2、3、4. 宴会厅
   Banquet Hall

1. 宴会厅
   Banquet
2. 聚贤阁会议室
   Juxiange Conference Room
3. 4. 聚贤阁红酒
   Juxiange Red Wine
5. 西餐厅
   Western Food Restaurant
6. 紫月楼
   Imperial Banquet Room

3

4

1. 西餐厅
   Western Food Restaurant
2. 游泳池
   Swimming Pool
3. 行政酒廊
   Executive Bar
4. 宴会厅
   Banquet
5. 客房
   Guest Room

5

1. 商务客房
   Business Guest Room
2. 复式客房
   Duplex Guest Room
3、4. 客房
   Guest Room

Kempinski Resort & Spa Sanya

HAINAN ISLAND · CHINA

三亚凯宾斯基度假酒店

三亚凯宾斯基度假酒店坐落于三亚湾17公里椰梦长廊的尽头——独一无二的私家海滩上，与300米延绵宽广的沙滩零距离连接，享受着碧海蓝天赐予的无限安详和宁静，堪称是"与世隔绝"。这里没有喧哗的声响、拥挤的人群、繁忙的交通、而是一个幽静的港湾，让您停下脚步放松身心、漫步休闲。酒店占地82,000平方米，拥有郁郁葱葱的热带花园和婉转于其中的大型露天游泳池。距离三亚凤凰国际机场和三亚市区商业中心仅15分钟车程。三亚年平均气温在25摄氏度左右，绝对是一个避寒消暑的好去处。

酒店拥有396间客房，面积为55～110平方米，包括2,600平方米的总统套房以及12套特色水疗套房、20套特色套房以及20间泳池房。酒店所有客房的设计都是为了追求更大的空间、更多的自然光线和更美的度假风情；每间客房都有超大的私人阳台和观景浴缸，您可以在沐浴的同时尽情欣赏秀丽的山景和壮丽的海湾美景。三亚凯宾斯基度假酒店独有的行政客房，配有单独的接待台办理入住手续，为入住的客人提供完全私人的室外泳池。在行政酒廊提供免费早餐、下午茶，全天供应饮料和小吃，另有免费的房间内上网接口等。除此之外，我们还设有专门的残障人士房间和非吸烟楼层，以方便不同顾客的需求。

多功能的商务中心设有私人会议室，并为您提供最贴心的秘书服务，包括翻

译、打印、复印、收发传真、装订以及上网等。

普拉那啤酒屋以其传统的德国香肠和巴伐利亚式菜肴、微型现酿的新鲜啤酒在全球享有盛誉,您可以在享用啤酒的同时欣赏啤酒的酿制过程。龙苑中餐厅舒适静谧的环境使您陶醉于美味、正宗的粤菜和海南传统菜肴。在此,您可品尝厨艺一流的邢涛大厨为您精心准备的粤式点心以及丰富多样的中国特色菜肴。客来思乐咖啡厅是一个融合了亚洲以及西方各国风味的国际化餐厅。沐浴着海风和阳光,悠闲地品尝着各式菜肴;让您的味蕾充分沉浸在醇美的葡萄酒和美食中。热带鸡尾酒、清凉饮品、各式美味汉堡套餐以及特色小吃,在您游历完我们的6个泳池后,花园泳池吧定会满足您的全部需求。让您休憩片刻,补充体力后重新征战。大堂吧是您放松身心,尽享无限热带风情的理想之地。在慵懒的午后或是深夜时分,沁人心脾的鸡尾酒、香醇的咖啡、中国茶,还有令人心醉的红葡萄酒和利口酒将让您深深沉醉。

三亚凯宾斯基度假酒店拥有户内、户外的多功能会议设施,是举行奖励旅游,公司年会等各类型会议的最佳选择。800米的无柱大宴会厅层高10米,装饰现代典雅,配以豪华的水晶吊灯,适合举办大型会议和奢华宴会。宽敞、通透的会议展览/休息区与户外露天的花园相连接,将整个会议及宴会区域融入了自然环境之中。

8个多功能厅总面积达1,400平方米,可举办15~1,000人的不同规模的会议及宴会。所有会议室全部集中在同一楼层,商务中心、会议服务中心近在咫尺,为与会客人提供最便捷周到的服务。户外草坪是展览、拍摄以及举办鸡尾酒会的最佳选择。在延绵柔软的沙滩上,我们乐意为您安排各种主题晚宴、现场乐队及特色风情表演,以满足您不同的需求。

三亚凯宾斯基度假酒店的悦椿水疗中心占地1,533平方米,与大自然完美地融合在一起,花园、亭台、水榭环绕其中。2个户外水疗亭可以让您在这个天然的大氧吧自由呼吸。还有10个户内水疗房可满足客人的不同喜好。全部配备蒸汽室和淋

1. 酒店全景
Hotel Panorama View
2. 酒店夜景
Hotel Night Shot

浴间。悦椿水疗的舒心疗法能有效的缓解疲劳，重塑一个神采奕奕的自我。

6个不同功能的户外游泳池能让您的假期更加难忘和刺激。其主泳池带有4个按摩泳池、涡流泳池；2个大型水上滑梯的儿童泳池。另外，极具特色的泳池客房与室外游泳池连接，从阳台即可跳入泳池。行政泳池以及总统别墅私人泳池能让您的海边假期更加多元化。

1. 日落沙滩吧
   Sunset Beach Bar
2. 大宴会厅
   Grand Ballroom

Kempinski Resort & Spa Sanya is located on the only private beach of Sanya, the Sanya Phoenix International Airport and Sanya city center can be reached in 15 minutes. Sanya enjoys more than three hundred days of sunshine each of the year and with the local temperature averaging at 25°C, Sanya has become the top choice for travellers both domestic and international.

The resort has a total of 396 spacious rooms which includes a 2,600 sq.m Presidential Villa, 12 Spa Villa rooms, 20 Suites, and 20 Cabana rooms which are luxuriously appointed and designed to provide the utmost in comfort and style. All guest rooms have the luxury of a private balcony fitted with a unique bath tub which offers spectacular views of Sanya hills or ocean. The room size varies from 55 sqm to 110 sqm. The resort also offers the luxury of an Executive Wing where guests can enjoy a much wider range of privileges such as an Exclusive outdoor pool, an Executive Lounge serving complimentary breakfast, afternoon tea, snacks and drinks throughout the day, a separate entrance and reception, free in-room internet access and much more. Specially fitted rooms are also available for the physically

1. 私家沙滩宴会
   Dining on Private Beach
2. 大堂
   Hotel Lobby
3. 普那纳啤酒屋
   Paulaner Brauhaus
4. 客来思乐西餐厅
   Kranzler's Restaurant
5. 泳池吧
   Shades & Waves Restaurant

challenged and we also offer non-smoking rooms.

The resort offers integrated business centre with secretarial and translation services.

Paulaner Brauhaus is a unique themed restaurant, famous for its traditional German food and freshly brewed Paulaner beer. A distinct feature of the restaurant would be that it offers guests a first hand glimpse of how beer is freshly brewed in-house. Dragon Palace-savor authentic Cantonese cuisine in a modern ambience. Traditional dim sum and a wide variety of Cantonese and Hainanese specialties are specially prepared by our very own Chef Xing Tao. A signature international restaurant of Kempinski, Kranzler's offers diners a wide range of Asian and Western cuisine for lunch and dinner. Sumptuous international breakfast buffet is also served at the Kranzler's. Diners also enjoy spectacular views of the landscaped tropical gardens and the pool.Tropical cocktails, frozen drinks, juicy burgers or a small snack after a long swim in one of our 6 outdoor swimming pools, whatever you choose, Shades and Waves has something for everyone! Rendezous Lounge is the perfect venue to relax in whilst enjoying spectacular views of the ocean and the resort's lush tropical garden. Let our tea experts introduce you to the large variety of revitalizing teas or sip our specially concocted cocktails or simply indulge in a lazy afternoon over your favorite bottle of wine.

The Kempinski Resort & Spa Sanya is the perfect venue for meetings, incentives, corporate events. The column-free, 800 sqm meter Grand Ballroom with 10 meter high ceiling, a spacious foyer, several break out rooms and an adjoining tropical garden to hold a full scale conference, a formal banquet or a high level meeting. The hotel offers 8 meeting rooms with a total of 1,400 sqm, that can accommodate 15 to 1,000 guests, and all meeting facilities are located on one level with a business centre and convention services centre and a separate entrance. The tropical Lawn area is ideal place for exhibitions, photo shoots or a cocktail party. Several outdoor venues in the tropical gardens or the exclusive beach, ideal locations for corporate events and theme parties.

Angsana Spa spreads over 1,533 square meters on two levels and features two beautifully appointed double deluxe outdoor Spa pavilions and ten indoor treatment rooms. Attached showers with Steam rooms in every treatment room ensure guests the convenience and privacy essential for a complete, relaxing experience. The treatment rooms on Level One boast additions of dip pools, Jaccuzzi and outdoor showers for a natural garden appeal. The Spa retreat includes a vitality pool, beauty salon and a dedicated area for pedicure and manicure with hair and nail services provided by the Spa.

Have fun with your friends and family in one of the six pools or relax in the Jacuzzi, or the two water slides. Enjoy a variety of water sports from diving to jet ski or just relax on the 300 meter private beach or build your own sand castle.

1. 龙苑中餐厅
   Dragon Palace Chinese Restaurant
2. 红酒雪茄吧
   Wine & Cigar Bar

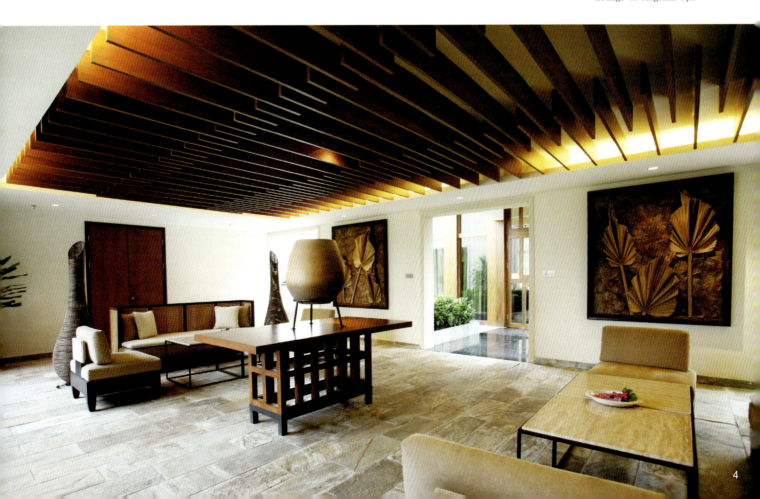

3. 普那纳牌酒尾二楼
Upper Level of Paulaner Brauhaus
4. 悦椿水疗休息厅
Lounge of Angsana Spa

1. 泳池吧
   Shades & Waves Restaurant
2. 悦椿水疗
   Angsana Spa
3. 现酿普拉那啤酒
   Freshly Brewed Paulaner Beer
4. 沙滩日落
   Beach Sunset
5. 花园泳池房
   Cabana Room
6. 悦椿水疗活力池
   Angsana Spa Vitality Pool

38) offer business travellers the highest levels of comfort and convenience.

From lively cocktail gatherings to sumptuous banquets, the hotel caters for every event with only the finest facilities, modern equipment and first class service. The magnificent Grand Ballroom is matched with the quality of its catering and state-of-the-art audiovisual equipment. Banquet choices range from Western-style to traditional Chinese cuisines, while meetings and conferences enjoy full audiovisual facilities, including advanced multi-media presentation and video conferencing facilities. All banquets and meeting facilities will be revolutionary in the market place, which include wired/wireless broadband, built-in LCD screens in meeting rooms, built-in projection screen and projectors in the ballroom. The Grand Ballroom also incorporates a spacious pre-function area. In addition, the hotel offers thirteen function rooms and high-tech Boardroom. At the InterContinental Chongqing we believe that incentives, meetings and conferences should be unique experiences. This is why we take great care to add a special touch of creativity to every aspect of the event. We can create special themes for delegate arrivals, for coffee breaks and of course, for meals. We can tailor the theme to suit your purposes or we can offer a choice of stylish, pre-planned themed events, with either an Eastern or Western cultural flavour. Our professional Meeting Sales Team will attend to your every detail and provide you with the most efficient service for your meetings and functions.

As the city's premier hotel, the InterContinental Chongqing exemplifies the excellent service and attention to detail for which the InterContinental name is globally renowned.

1. 西餐厅
   Gingers Restaurant
2. 雅轩中餐厅
   Emerald Sea
3. 宴会厅
   Ballroom
4. 亚洲风情餐厅
   Asia Live

1. 会议室
   Meeting Room
2. 宴会厅
   Ballroom
3. 行政高级客房
   Club King
4. 大堂吧
   Lobby Lounge
5. 西餐厅红酒包房
   Red Wine Private Dining Room (Gingers Restaurant)

1. 商务套房
   Business Suite
2. 大堂吧
   Lobby Lounge
3. 健身中心
   Gym
4. 游泳池
   Swimming Pool
5. 水疗中心
   SPA

1. 高级套房
   Studio Suite
2. 亚洲风情餐厅
   Asia Live
3. 宴会厅
   Ballroom
4. 雅轩中餐厅
   Emerald Sea
5. 客房服务
   House Keeping
6. 礼宾服务
   Concierge
7. 行政套房
   Club Business Suite
8. 总统套房
   Presidential Suite

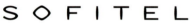

成都索菲特万达大饭店是成都唯一的知名法国高端品牌五星级饭店,将法兰西风情与中式格调完美巧妙地融于一体,演绎璀璨的人生,诠释奢华的真谛。位于市中心地段,坐拥锦江河畔,尽享蓉城美景。享誉蓉城的各式风味料理、一应俱全的完善娱乐休闲设施、全城专享的著名灵感会议服务、秉承索菲特优质奢华待客之生活艺术,为您演绎无限创意和惊喜。

轻松步行15分钟便可到达商业中心,20分钟的愉快车程可抵达成都双流国际机场。

酒店共有262间客房,其中包括162间豪华客房及100间各式套房。每间客房都配有缔造甜美睡眠的招牌索菲特"MyBed"概念卧具、独立控制空调、液晶电脑上网服务、超大屏幕液晶电视、卫星电视频道、国内国际直拨长途、迷你酒吧、客房保险箱以及独立浴室。

天府轩中餐厅:提供地道的川粤菜、精品燕鲍翅和鲜活海鲜,1个尊贵大厅和15个豪华包间满足您的不同需要,可同时接待230位客人。

巴赛丽西餐厅:优雅现代的就餐环境,让您尽享精美的零点西餐和国际自助餐。可同时接待160位客人。

富士日本餐厅:提供独特创意和配方的地道日式料理,可同时接待40

位客人。

聚贤廊大堂吧：提供精美点心和各类鸡尾酒以及晚间现场表演，可同时接待100位客人。

索菲特会所：专为入住套房的客人提供服务，免费提供欧陆式自助早餐、全天饮料及欢乐时光小吃。

提供礼宾服务、停车服务、24小时送餐服务、24小时洗衣服务、商务中心、豪华轿车服务、外币兑换、航空服务、旅游代理、保姆服务。

酒店配有室内恒温游泳池、棋牌室、健身房、桑拿按摩、水疗中心、美容美发、台球室。

您在构思活动的时候，敬请发挥天马行空的创作意念，结合索菲特灵感会议团队的专业和机智，让活动充满索菲特品牌独有的法式风采。无论是大型会议，还是私人派对、主题晚会、宴会、庆典等各类型活动，都令人难以忘怀。婚宴可以极尽奢华，也可以精致温馨，让人印象深刻。索菲特万达大饭店卓越超群的服务水准和独特创意的设计安排将为您的婚礼创造一个毕生难忘的美好回忆。

1. 饭店外观夜景
Hotel Exterior Night View
2. 饭店大堂
Hotel Lobby

Sofitel Wanda Chengdu is the only high-class French brand 5-star hotel in Chengdu, smartly integrating French flair with Chinese flavor, performing the life of brilliance and interpreting the truth of luxury. It's ideally located in city centre, embracing Jinjiang river and city sceneries. It boasts the highly-acclaimed dining, the complete recreational facilities and the exceptional Inspired Meetings service, making your life magnificent.

The Hotel is a 15-minute stroll to the commercial centre and a pleasant 20-minute ride to the Chengdu Shuangliu International Airport.

The Hotel has totally 262 rooms, 162 luxury rooms and 100 suites of any type. Each room and suite offers signature Sofitel "MyBed", individually controlled air-conditioning, computer with broadband internet access, LCD TV, satellite & domestic channels, IDD &DDD access, mini bar, personal safe and separate shower stall in bathroom.

The Palace Chinese Restaurant—level 3: Authentic Cantonese and Sichuan dishes, seating 230 guests in an elegant dining hall together with 15 private rooms of different sizes.

La Brasserie Western Restaurant—level 2: International buffets and a la carte menu, seating 160 guests in a graceful and stylish surrounding.

The Fuji Japanese Restaurant—level 2: Authentic Japanese cuisines with Sushi Bar and Teppanyaki Grill, seating 40 guests.

Le Rendezvous Lounge—level 1: Delightful refreshments and signature cocktails with nightly live entertainment, seating 100 guests.

Club Sofitel—level 23: Exclusively available only to our suite guests, providing complimentary continental breakfasts in the morning, beverages throughout the day and happy hours with snacks in the evening.

Concierge, parking, 24 hours room service, 24 hours laundry service, business centre, limousine rental, foreign exchange, airline ticket, tour and travel agency, baby sitting.

1. 饭店前台接待
   Hotel Front Desk
2. 饭店外景
   Hotel Outlook

Indoor swimming pool, game rooms, fitness centre, sauna & massage, SPA, beauty salon, snooker room.

You are encouraged to embrace your own creative vision in your event conceptualization combined with our savoir faire of the Sofitel Inspired Meetings team, to deliver exquisite and memorable events with the renowned French flair of Sofitel. Inspired Meetings team is prepared to stage any type of event from large scale conferences to intimate parties where you are welcome to experiment with even the most unconventional requests!

Wedding is once-in-a-lifetime special day. Here at Sofitel Wanda Chengdu, we have experts to assist you with all arrangements for your big day, bringing you a sweet memory with creative ideas and outstanding service.

1、3.凡尔赛宫
　Versailles
2、5.聚贤廊大堂吧
　Le Rendezvous Lounge
4.富士日本餐厅
　The Fuji Japanese Restaurant
6.巴赛丽西餐厅
　La Brasserie Western Restaurant

1、2、6.杜乐丽宫
　Tuileries
3.罗浮厅
　Le Louvre
4.凡尔赛宫
　Versailles
5.总统套房会议室
　Presidential Suite Meeting Room

1. 富士日本餐厅
   The Fuji Japanese Restaurant
2. 天府轩中餐
   The Palace Chinese Restaurant
3. 室内恒温游泳池
   Indoor Heated Swimming Pool
4、5. 水疗
   Touch SPA

1. 总统套房
   Presidential Suite
2. 豪华房
   Luxury Room
3. 标准套房洗浴间
   Prestige Suite Bathroom
4. 豪华房洗浴间
   Luxury Room Bathroom
5. 总统套房洗浴间
   Presidential Suite Bathroom
6. 总统套房夫人房洗浴间
   Presidential Suite Madam Bathroom
7. 索菲特套房洗浴间
   Sofitel Suite Bathroom
8. 总统套房客厅
   Presidential Suite Parlor Room
9. 豪华套房
   Opera Suite

中国首家藏文化主题博物馆式的超豪华酒店——雅鲁藏布大酒店及所属西藏岗日民俗艺术馆占地30,000平方米,建筑面积20,000平方米,坐落于圣地拉萨著名的阳城广场。独具藏民族文化特色的装饰艺术同现代建筑装饰风格的完美结合是酒店全新的策划设计理念。酒店所有设备设施均按五星级酒店设计配置,拥有以富丽堂皇的金色大厅为主体的各种风格独特的豪华房间185间,拥有豪华典雅的中西餐厅、酒吧,设备先进并同时具备博物馆展区功能的宴会厅、会议室及康体娱乐项目。雅鲁藏布大酒店地理位置优越,距市中心5分钟路程,距贡嘎机场仅40分钟车程。紧靠美丽的拉萨河畔和桑烟袅绕的贡巴日财神山旁,伫立在酒店窗旁可眺望雄伟的布达拉宫,观赏阳光灿烂的拉萨全景。

雅鲁藏布大酒店是世界上唯一能入住的博物馆式超豪华酒店,其深厚的文化底蕴和高贵典雅的品位,人性化和民族化的管理理念,严谨高效、宾至如归的真诚服务将把国内外宾客带进温馨神奇的雪域天堂。

西藏岗日民俗艺术馆是在以宏伟壮观的雅鲁藏布大酒店为载体的基础上建立起来的,是藏民族文化特色的装饰艺术同现代建筑装饰风格的完美结合。西藏岗日民俗艺术馆收藏、展示的近万件典型的文化遗物、艺术品,从西藏的艺术、宗教和民俗等方面展现出藏民族独具魅力的灿烂文化和悠久历史,令人叹为观止。

1. 酒店外观
   Appearances of Hotel

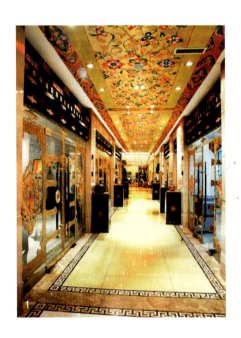

The Brahmaputra Grand Hotel is a luxury five star hotel, with the combination of traditional Tibetan architectural style and modern decorative technologies. The Hotel is located at Section B, Yangcheng Plaza, Gongbutang Road, Lhasa, Tibet, China, standing at north-eastern bank of Lhasa River. It is only take 5 to the down town and is within 40 minutes of Lhasa Gongga Airport. With this prime location, our guests will have very easy access to every travel spots of Lhasa city. Our hotel also provides well-equipped 185 rooms with different style, and each room has Internet access,use free of charge.

Brahmaputra Grand Hotel is the unique museum for accommodation in the world, owing to its deep cultural foundation, elegant tastes, human natural as well as ethnic managing idea, high efficiency with heart-warming service. Our hotel is right place for tourists home and abroad.

The Tibetan Folk Museum, one of the most important parts of Brahmaputra Grand Hotel, is a perfect combination of modern architecture technologies with Tibetan profound cultural concept. Many ancient cultural relics and delicate handicrafts are exhibited in the museum. One can get very quick understanding of Tibetan colorful ancient history as well as every unique cultural aspect after visiting Tibetan Folk Museum.

1. 商务中心
   B.C.
2. 西藏岗日民俗艺术馆
   The Tibetan Folk Museum

1. 雪域金色大厅
   Snowy Golden Hall
2. 大厅休息处
   Lobby Lounge

1、3. 雅隆会议室（转经筒展厅）
   Display Prayer Wheels (Prayer Wheel Boardroom)
2. 餐厅包间
   Private Cabin
4. 雪域金色大厅
   Snowy Golden Hall
5. 大堂吧
   Lobby Bar

1. 饰品展区
   Jewelry Showcase
2. 艺术馆主展厅一角
   Corner of Art Gallery
3. 大堂吧
   Lobby Bar
4. 昆仑会议室（唐卡展厅）
   Kunlun Boardroom
5. 艺术馆主展厅
   Art Gallery

1. 博古走廊
   Antique Gallery
2. 历史长廊
   The Long Porch of History
3. 观景单间
   Good View Single Room
4. 豪华标准间
   Deluxe Standard Room

甘肃阳光大酒店是中油阳光酒店集团所属标志性酒店之一,也是甘肃省首家五星级酒店。酒店地处兰州市政务、商务中心,居中而立,坐拥繁华。在2006年9月、2008年9月、2008年11月,甘肃阳光大酒店分别荣获"福布斯中国最优商务酒店50强"、"中国酒店百强十佳商务酒店"、"亚洲酒店业最佳商务品牌酒店"的荣誉称号,在国内外具有较好的知名度和美誉度,是高端会务、商务、政务活动接待的首选之地。

酒店拥有客房225间(套),设有行政楼层、无烟楼层以及专为女士准备的丽人名居;房间装饰高雅,设施完备,无论是郁郁葱葱的绿色植物,还是专为缓解北方干燥气候而配备的加湿器,点滴之处尽显无尽的人文关怀,用心用情为您营造一个温暖的家。

酒店中餐厅、西餐厅和法式铁板烧为国内外宾客提供独特的饮食文化、温情的细腻服务,倾情演绎美食精彩!

SPA水疗中心清新淡雅的天然精油,轻柔的丝竹古乐,技师娴熟的专业手法,让您感受清新的健康生活。同时游泳馆、健身中心、棋牌室等完备的康乐设施让您舒展身心,尽享清闲。

酒店拥有6个装饰高贵典雅、设备齐全的会议室,可分别为8~180人会议提供选择。专业的会场服务辅以先进的视听及会议设备,是您商务会议的理想选择。无线高

速的互联网接入，带给您置身国际商潮浪尖的体验。灵活有效的阳光会议计划更是充分尊重您的个性化需求。致臻完美的会议服务，让您的商务活动变得轻松惬意。

1. 大堂
   Lobby
2. 会议室
   Meeting Room

Grand Soluxe Hotel Gansu is one of landmark hotels of Soluxe Group, PetroChina and the first five-star hotel in Gansu Province. It is located in the busy political, business center of Lanzhou. It was honored the titles of "Forbes China Top 50 Best Business Hotel", "China Top 100 Hotel— Top 10 Best Business Hotel", "Best Business Hotel of Asian Hotels". With its wide popularity and good reputation, it is a preferred place for high-level meeting, business, and political affair activities.

The hotel has 225 guest rooms, and is established with executive floor, non-smoking floor, as well as rooms particularly for ladies. The rooms are decorated elegantly with complete equipment. The green vegetation and humidifiers equipped specially for relieving the dryness in the North. The hotel is creating a warm home for you whole heartedly in each detail.

Our Chinese Restaurant, Western Restaurant and French Teppanyaki in the hotel can provide both Chinese and foreign food, fully deducing the food delicacy through the unique catering culture with our considerate services!

SPA with fresh and natural essence oil, soft silk and bamboo music, skilled and professional techniques of the massage-girls will allow you to feel the fresh and healthy life; meanwhile, the swimming pool, gym center, card and chess room provided with complete recreational facilities will allow you to relax your body and mind, indulging in the leisure.

Grand Soluxe Hotel Gansu has 6 function rooms with noble and elegant decoration, and complete equipment, which can accommodate 8~180 persons to have a meeting. The Hotel offers you professional meeting service and advanced sound and video equipment necessary for meeting, making it the ideal choice for your business meeting. The high speed wireless internet access brings you international business information. The flexible and effective meeting plan fully respects your individual demand. Plus the perfect meeting service, your business activities will go just smoothly and easily.

1. 中餐厅
   Chinese Style Restaurant
2. 西餐厅
   Western Style Restaurant
3. 外景
   Exterior View

1. 健身房
   Gym Center
2. 游泳馆
   Swimming Hall
3. 水疗
   SPA
4. 套房
   Suite
5. 客房
   Guest Room

新疆海德酒店是新疆第一家中外合资的涉外五星级酒店，由海德国际（香港）有限公司管理。并通过ISO 9001/2000版国际标准质量认证。1997年开业至今，以国际酒店的标准、以先进的经营管理模式、不断创新，无论在服务、市场、管理都奠定并保持了酒店业的先锋地位，成为新疆酒店业的服务典范。作为新疆首府五星级酒店发展奠基人，为酒店业走向国际化，为新疆旅游业蓬勃发展作出了卓越的贡献。

酒店位于乌鲁木齐市中心繁华商业区，坐落于人民广场，与天山雪景遥相对应，无与伦比的优越位置没有其他酒店可与之媲美。置身结构优雅、设施一流的海德酒店，不仅可俯瞰乌鲁木齐全景，同时也是您商务活动和休闲的好去处。

酒店共拥有318间设施齐全的客房，从标准间、豪华间、豪华套、行政套到总统套，以满足客人的不同需求。客房内有可独立控制的空调、国际直拨电话、迷你酒吧、保险箱、有线电视、吹发器及互联网接口，并专门设立了无烟楼层及残疾人房。

口碑颇佳的六间餐厅为您提供不同风味的美食。装潢典雅，佳肴飘香。不论您来自何方，出席何种场合，新疆海德酒店的美食世界，总能让您流连忘返。

环境典雅温馨、风格高雅瑰丽的各

类宴会厅，为您提供热情、周到的贴心服务。可容纳250余人的宴会厅和3间具有独立设施的会议室，集合了现代化的设计和先进的视听技术，均可满足您的不同需求。

繁忙了一天后，您可以去享受涡流浴、桑拿或是蒸汽浴。如果您仍然感到精力充沛，您可以去充满艺术氛围的健身房或是室内游泳池轻松一下。夜幕来临之际，您若是在金银岛夜总会或其风格独特的某间卡拉OK包厢内，旋转几圈或高歌一曲，您绝对会倍感轻松。

历年的耕耘，获得了国内外宾客的认可与赞扬，对酒店作出了高度的评价，如连续几年被世界品牌实验室评估为"中国品牌价值500强"、被中国饭店业年会组委会授予"中国酒店金马奖"、被世界文化旅游论坛推介为新疆唯一一家"最佳商务酒店"、在中国社会科学院旅游研究中心发布的《中国饭店业百强品牌调研报告》中，荣获中国酒店百强金钻奖……

在这里，"您的感受，我们的关注"！

1. 外观（人民广场）
   Out View (People's Square)
2. 西餐餐台
   Western Food Table

1、2. 外观
Out View

The Hoi Tak Hotel Xinjiang is a Prestigious Hotel, rising 36 stories high from ground level, facing the People's Square and was the first official 5 star International hotel in Xinjiang, furthermore, was recently the first hotel in China to be approved by the China Quality Certification Center to achieve the ISO9001/2000 rating.

The total building area is 55,672 square meters at a 70 million US dollars investment, and the Hotel was opened on 28 August 1997. Hoi Tak International is the operator and Management Company of the Hotel.

The Hoi Tak Hotel offers 318 well-appointed guest rooms and suites, including Standard/Superior and Deluxe Twins, King Suites, Deluxe and Executive suites and 2 Duplex Presidential Suites all complimented with a Modern Bathroom, DDD, IDD Telephone, Internet access, in House Movies, Satellite TV. Air Conditioning, Hairdryer, Personal Bar and Private Safe.

Dining facilities include our Le Grand Cafe and Le Grand Restaurant, traditional Muslim Restaurant with 7 VIP rooms, Food Court, Village Inn, Chinese Restaurant with 15 VIP rooms, 24 hours Room Service, Lobby Lounge, Grand Ballroom with Multi-functional facilities, Cigar Bar and our Hoi Tak Club.

For your Entertainment needs, we have our Treasure Island Night Club with 10 theme KTV VIP rooms, 8 lane Bowling center and Bar with Snooker/Billiards and 7 Mahjong rooms, Lagoon Sauna has 5 VIP massage rooms with 13 private massage rooms, Sauna, Steam bath and Sauna Lounge area, our Health Center provides a sunlight Indoor Heated Swimming Pool, Gymnasium, Table Tennis and Beauty Salon, other facilities include IT lounge, Business Center with Secretarial services, Internet facilities, Kiosk and Safety deposit box.

"Meeting Our Guests Expectations" is the philosophy of Hoi Tak International. We assure you our best effort in attaining the highest guest satisfaction.

1. 大堂
   Lobby
2. 天下无双高级食府（内）
   The Palace Restaurant
3、4. 天下无双高级食府
   The Palace Restaurant

1. 天下无双高级食府外部
   The Palace Restaurant (Out View)
2. 农圃轩中餐厅
   Village Inn Chinese Restaurant
3、4. 穆斯林餐厅
   Restaurant
5. 美食街
   Food Court

1、2、3.宴会厅
   Grand Ballroom
4.健身房
   Health Club
5.咖啡厅
   Le Grand Restaurant
6.雪茄吧
   Giger Bar
7.居酒屋
   Izakaga
8.美容美发
   Hair Dressing and Beauty Salon
9.游泳池
   Swimming Pool

1. 总统复式套房 　 Presidential Duplex Suite	4. 海德复式套房 　 Hai Tok Duplex Suite	7. 商务间 　 Commercial Stand Room
2. 豪华套房 　 Deluxe Suite	5. 标准间 　 Standard Room	
3. 商务间 　 Commercial Standard Room	6. 豪华间 　 Deluxe Room	

《中国一流饭店（珍藏版）》
参编单位
（按笔画排序）

三亚凯宾斯基度假酒店
Kempinski Resort & Spa Sanya

上海大酒店
Grand Central Hotel Shanghai

上海四季酒店
Four Seasons Hotel Shanghai

上海龙之梦丽晶大酒店
The Longemont Shanghai

上海兴荣豪廷大酒店
Plaza Royale Oriental Shanghai

上海金茂君悦大酒店
Grand Hyatt Shanghai

上海柏悦酒店
Park Hyatt Shanghai

上海虹桥迎宾馆
Hong Qiao State Guest Hotel Shanghai

上海浦西洲际®酒店
InterContinental® Shanghai Puxi

上海斯格威铂尔曼大酒店
Pullman Hotels and Resorts, Shanghai Skyway

上海瑞吉红塔大酒店
St. Regis Shanghai

上海锦沧文华大酒店
Shanghai JC Mandarin, Managed by Meritus Hotels & Resorts

上海豫园万丽酒店
Renaissance® Shanghai Yuyuan Hotel

大连凯宾斯基饭店
Kempinski Hotel Dalian, China

广州天誉威斯汀酒店
The Westin Guangzhou

广州白云机场铂尔曼大酒店
Pullman Guangzhou Baiyun Airport

广州白云国际会议中心
Guangzhou Baiyun International Convention Center

广州香格里拉大酒店
Shangri-La Hotel, Guangzhou

广州富力丽思卡尔顿酒店
The Ritz-Carlton®, Guangzhou

中国大饭店（北京）
China World Hotel, Beijing

中国大酒店（广州）
China Hotel, A Marriott Hotel (Guangzhou)

天津喜来登大酒店
Sheraton Tianjin Hotel

日坛国际酒店（北京）
Ritan International Hotel (Beijing)

世贸君澜大饭店（浙江）
Zhejiang Narada Grand Hotel (Zhejiang)

东郊宾馆（上海）
Dongjiao State Guest Hotel Shanghai

北京万达索菲特大饭店
Sofitel Luxury Hotels, Wanda Beijing

北京友谊宾馆
Beijing Friendship Hotel

北京王府井希尔顿酒店
Hilton Beijing Wangfujing

北京丽晶酒店
The Regent Beijing

北京希尔顿酒店
Hilton Beijing

北京饭店
Beijing Hotel

北京国际俱乐部饭店
St. Regis Beijing

北京金融街丽思卡尔顿酒店
The Ritz-Carlton® Beijing, Financial Street

北京金融街威斯汀大酒店
The Westin Beijing Financial Street

北京金融街洲际酒店
InterContinental® Beijing Financial Street

北京贵宾楼饭店
Grand Hotel Beijing

北京香格里拉饭店
Shangri-La Hotel, Beijing

北京喜来登长城饭店
The Great Wall Sheraton Hotel Beijing

古象大酒店（上海）
Howard Johnson® Plaza Shanghai

甘肃阳光大酒店
Grand Soluxe Hotel Gansu

兴国宾馆（上海）
Radisson Plaza Xing Guo Hotel Shanghai

成都索菲特万达大饭店
Sofitel Luxury Hotels Wanda Chengdu

阳光酒店（深圳）
Sunshine Hotel (Shenzhen)

花园饭店（上海）
Okura Garden Hotel Shanghai

苏州金鸡湖凯宾斯基大酒店
Kempinski Hotel Suzhou, China

京瑞大厦（北京）
KingWing Hotel (Beijing)

凯宾斯基饭店（北京燕莎中心有限公司）
Kempinski Hotel Beijing Lufthansa Center, China

国宾酒店（北京）
The Presidential Beijing

宜兴宾馆
Yixing Hotel

昆仑饭店（北京）
Hotel Kunlun (Beijing)

武汉香格里拉大饭店
Shangri-La Hotel, Wuhan, China

罗星阁宾馆（浙江）
Luoxingge Hotel (Zhejiang)

郑州索菲特国际饭店
Sofitel Luxury Hotels, Zhengzhou International

金茂北京威斯汀大饭店
The Westin Beijing Chaoyang

南昌凯莱大饭店
Gloria Grand Hotel Nanchang

重庆洲际酒店
InterContinental® Chongqing

首都大酒店
Capital Hotel

香格里拉北京嘉里中心大酒店
Shangri-La's Kerry Centre Hotel, Beijing

浦东香格里拉大酒店（上海）
Pudong Shangri-La, Shanghai

深圳马哥孛罗好日子酒店
Marco Polo Shenzhen

深圳东部华侨城主题酒店群
Shenzhen OCT East Theme Hotel Cluster

深圳华侨城洲际大酒店
InterContinental® Shenzhen

深圳威尼斯皇冠假日酒店
Crowne Plaza® Shenzhen

厦门悦华酒店
Yeohwa Hotel Xiamen

富阳国际贸易中心大酒店（浙江）
Fuyang International Trade Center Hotel (Zhejiang)

彭年酒店（深圳）
The Panglin Hotel, Shenzhen

雅鲁藏布大酒店（拉萨）
Brahmaputra Grand Hotel (Lhasa)

新疆海德酒店
Hoi Tak Hotel, Xinjiang

锦江饭店（上海）
Jin Jiang Hotel (Shanghai)

中国一流饭店 珍藏版

China's First Class Hotels
Collection Edition

《中国一流饭店》编委会 编
Compiled by the Editorial Board of *China's First Class Hotels*

中国建筑工业出版社
China Architecture & Building Press

I

中国一流饭店（珍藏版）编委会

策 划

肖 青 Xiao Qing

左启华 Zuo Qihua

李东禧 Li Dongxi

参编人员
（按姓氏笔画排序）

尹迎萍 Yin Yingping

方莉苹 Fang Liping

毛轶群 Mao Yiqun

王 宁 Wang Ning

王 龙 Wang Long

王 振 Wang Zhen

王 磊 Wang Lei

冯济华 Feng Jihua

包秋萍 Bao Qiuping

卢 苇 Lu Wei

白茂国 Bai Maoguo

任 云 Ren Yun

刘国良 Liu Guoliang

刘 彬 Liu Bin

孙冠津 Sun Guanjin

朱 军 Zhu Jun

朱迪斯 Judith Los Banos

朱冠峰 Zhu Guanfeng

朱 虹 Zhu Hong

阮 樱 Ruan Ying

齐 曦 Qi Xi

何可人 He Keren

何 颖 He Ying

余彭年 Yu Pengnain

吴若乔 Wu Ruoqiao

吴 娟 Wu Juan

吴 朔 Wu Shuo

吴 绫 Wu Ling

吴翠明 Wu Cuiming

宋念博 Song Nianbo

张旭辉 Zhang Xuhui

张行峰 Zhang Xingfeng

张轶敏 Zhang Yimin

张 涛 Zhang Tao

张 崑 Zhang Kun

张 聪 Zhang Cong

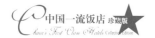

张黎琳 Zhang Lilin	陈小力 Chen Xiaoli	洪 嬑 Hong Yi	梁 思 Liang Si
李 卉 Li Hui	陈苗凤 Chen Miaofeng	胡 军 Hu Jun	盛 莉 Sheng Li
李 刚 Li Gang	陈菊梅 Chen Jumei	胡志跃 Hu Zhiyue	阎 旭 Yan Xu
李 明 Li Ming	陈超峰 Chen Chaofeng	赵前鹏 Zhao Qianpeng	黄伟文 Huang Weiwen
李 林 Li Lin	卓 越 Zhuo Yue	唐红琳 Tang Honglin	黄佩丽 Huang Peili
李 菁 Li Jing	卓 雯 Zhuo Wen	夏慧华 Xia Huihua	彭光芹 Peng Guangqin
李 婷 Li Ting	周贤澄 Zhou Xiancheng	徐 岚 Xu Lan	温秦晴 Wen Qinqing
李 晶 Li Jing	易 术 Yi Shu	徐 蔚 Xu Wei	童玲玲 Tong Lingling
杨 艺 Yang Yi	林 妍 Lin Yan	涂唐杰 Tu Tang Jie	窦双玲 Dou Shuangling
杨泽虎 Yang Zehu	林筱珊 Lin Xiaoshan	钱春蕾 Qian Chunlei	蔡 菁 Cai Jing
杨海鸥 Yang Haiou	范盈盈 Fan Yingying	高文征 Gao Wenzheng	潘 瑾 Pan Jin
沈文庆 Shen Wenqing	郑白成 Zheng Baicheng	曹 杰 Cao Jie	魏锁群 Wei Suoqun
沈 静 Shen Jing	俞立欣 Yu Lixin	曹 慧 Cao Hui	
苏 凌 Su Ling	柏 桦 Bai Hua	梁玉洁 Liang Yujie	

目录 Content

6 中国饭店三十年（1979-2009）：
见证、融合与引领
Witness, Integrate and Lead:
Chinese Hotels（1979-2009）

16 酒店的看与读
Looking and Reading the Hotels

26 北京饭店
Beijing Hotel

38 北京贵宾楼饭店
Grand Hotel Beijing

50 北京国际俱乐部饭店
St. Regis Beijing

62 北京金融街丽思卡尔顿酒店
The Ritz-Carlton® Beijing,
Financial Street

74 北京金融街威斯汀大酒店
The Westin Beijing Financial Street

86 北京金融街洲际酒店
Inter Continental® Beijing
Financial Street

98 北京丽晶酒店
The Regent Beijing

110 北京万达索菲特大饭店
Sofitel Luxury Hotels,
Wanda Beijing

122 北京王府井希尔顿酒店
Hilton Beijing Wangfujing

136 北京希尔顿酒店
Hilton Beijing

148 北京喜来登长城饭店
The Great Wall Sheraton
Hotel Beijing

158 北京香格里拉饭店
Shangri-La Hotel, Beijing

170 北京友谊宾馆
Beijing Friendship Hotel

182 国宾酒店
The Presidential Beijing

194 金茂北京威斯汀大饭店
The Westin Beijing Chaoyang

中国饭店三十年（1979－2009）：见证、融合与引领

中国旅游研究院副院长
中瑞酒店管理学院院长
戴斌　教授

尽管中国饭店产业的发展历史可以上溯到商朝时期，但是现代意义上的饭店产业则源于20世纪70年代末期的改革开放。在入境旅游市场需求累积释放效应的影响下，一方面包括北京友谊宾馆在内的国宾接待机构开始进入市场，形成了面向高端市场的初始供给主体；另一方面则是以建国饭店为代表的城市高端饭店，以接近国际主流运营模式的姿态进入商业接待市场。前者实质上是在转型的进程中去学习市场经济与商业知识，历经变革、重组、管理、竞争和创新，边学习、边成长、边竞争，基本上实现了从内部接待到面向市场的完美转身。可以说，它们在自身的艰难成长中，也实时见证了中国的社会演化进程。后者对于中国饭店产业而言，则是一种外生的变量。它们的进入，不仅仅给中国饭店业带来了建筑与空间意义上的亮丽，而且完全以欧美主流商业模式和管理范式为导向的运营体制，更是让中国的同行近在身边地感受了市场经济和商业模式双重推动下，制度创新意义上的震撼与冲击。在30年的历史进程中，越来越多的国际饭店品牌进入了中国市场，在导入新的理念、服务标准和管理制度的同时，也在潜移默化地接受中国市场和中国文化的影响。从这个意义上说，国际高端饭店品牌在中国的发展，既是一个导入的过程，也是一个融入的过程。放长历史的视野，来自于传统国宾接待机构转型而来的内生性饭店存量和国际高端品牌推动的外生性饭店增量，分别在见证和融入中国饭店产业，特别是高端饭店产业变迁的同时，还在更大范围内引领了中国经济社会很多方面的发展步伐。

一、中国住宿接待产业转型、变革与重组的历史见证者

中国一流饭店的历史至少可以上溯到商周时期。自那时开始，服务于国宾的"诸侯馆"、"迎宾馆"，服务于某一区域以工商人士以及各领域精英人士为主要目标的"会馆"，一直以来，都是构成我国一流饭店发展历史的供给主体。这些机构的存在与发展都是为特定人群，以非商业化的方式提供服务的。尽管在个性化服务方面积淀了大量的经验，但是在消费主体还需要依靠社会阶层进行身份识别，而不是依靠货币选票进行自由交易的情形下，这些接待场所只可能是现代饭店产业生长的基础，却不是现代饭店产业本身。

20世纪80年代以来，两个方面的原因导致了这批饭店开始了市场化和产业化进程。一方面，市场化取向的改革开放基本国策的确定与实施，使得包括政府接待型饭店在内的各级各类机构很快萌发了市场意识；另一方面，大量国际旅游者到访中国，导致高端饭店短期内严重供不应求。在政府主管部门的推动下，大批

原来用于内部接待的高端饭店被要求按商业规则去接待国际旅游者。事实上，当进入旅游市场的饭店获得了相应商业利益的同时，源于政府主导的强制型变迁就自然而然转化为利益导向的诱致型变迁。在相当长的历史时期内，源于市场演化的企业化变革已经成为一个不可逆转的过程。

随着早期进入旅游市场的饭店示范作用下，更多隶属于地方政府和国有企事业单位的饭店纷纷进入商业领域。1993年，为应对市场疲软，刺激国内需求，加上入境旅游消费的引导，国民旅游进入一个政府有意识引导的新时期。1999年以后，随着中央政府主导的节假日制度的调整，特别是"黄金周"的出现，中国旅游经济逐渐进入了一个大众旅游主导的新阶段。市场范围的扩大带来的需求同质化，必然导致供给方式的批量化和服务流程的标准化。正是在大众旅游住宿需求的深刻影响下，更多的中高端饭店开始改变自己过去面向小众市场的组织与管理方式，自觉不自觉地采用了工业化大生产的方式向客人提供服务。

由于员工与客人直接接触的服务可控性远比物化商品要难得多，所以完成了市场化和企业化改造后的传统饭店为了获得更多的规模经济优势，走向技术理性就是一种必然。表现在现实中就是20世纪90年代中后期的饭店装修改造更加倾向于使用一些标准化的技术和品牌化的设施设备。这些技术标准和设施品牌在为中国饭店经营管理带来更多便利的同时，也悄然失去了基于小众服务的精益求精的传统和员工直面客人需求的温情。好在市场经济内在的竞争规律对大规模的工业化生产方式也有着纠正机制，当饭店经营者认识到同质化的弊端以后，业界就开始在差异化方面寻求突破。近年来，度假饭店、温泉SPA饭店、会议饭店、主题饭店、机场饭店等不断涌现的新业态，商务楼层、数字客房、管家式服务等新型服务项目，以及不同程度地导入环境保护、社会责任、社区和谐等企业公民理念，都可以看作饭店产业在历经多年的市场经济洗礼以后，走上非竞争的蓝海领域的努力，也是当代饭店产业群体向传统服务理念和管理方式的致敬。

在这一大转折的历史时期，我们还需要关注饭店运营体系的深层次变化：在从政务接待到商务转型的过程中，饭店员工的服务理念和行为方式也在发生着剧烈的变革，并面临着精神支撑或者说价值取向层面的重大考验。市场化之前的饭店员工，可能以工资为主的物质报酬并不丰富，但是自我认同感还是比较高的。因为由于服务对象的特殊性，他们觉得是为政治或者事业服务，而且稳定的就业预期和相对统一的单位福利让员工对所在单位和所从事的工作都容易产生归属感。市场化以后，员工的薪酬固然在一定程度上得到了提高，但是服务的对象越来越泛化，只要拥有足够的货币选票，消费者就不再需要国籍、身份和地位的识别了。另外，在市场经济条件下，有限的薪酬增量同时还伴随着高度的不稳定性。在我们这样一个商业服务传统一直没有稳定的国度里，员工的职业认同感和服务意识的缺位确是一个极需重视的大问题。正是在深层次传统文化与现实中商业价值观的互动与耦合的过程中，那些有先觉意识的饭店企业家和经理人员开始重视饭店文化的建设。金陵饭店集团甚至把文化建设提升到了公司软实力的战略高度，锦江酒店集团新版的LOGO则试图回到传统文化的深层意味中去寻找商业的灵感。无论如何，这些领袖级的本土饭店在文化建设上的努力，都意味着一个基于价值观和文化底蕴的产业升级的新时代正在到来。

从更为宽广的视野而言，发生在住宿接待领域的这些变革与发展，也是30年来共和国改革开放的缩影。由此出发，我们也可以说，类似北京友谊宾馆这样的国宾接待机构，在30年的变迁进程中，不仅仅见证了旅游住宿产业的市场化改革和企业化发展的历史进程，而且也承载了整个国家制度变迁和社会发展的样本与要素。

二、国际化导向与本土化取向的双向融合

始建于1982年的北京建国饭店在中国现代饭店发展史上无疑具有举足轻重的地位。作为第一家中外合资饭店，也是第一家引进境外饭店管理集团管理的饭店，开启了本土饭店学习国际饭店服务标准和管理体系的先河。由于植入了西方商业饭店的运营模式，建国饭店在很短的时间里就积累了很高的商业声誉。1984年，由中央政府旅游行政主管部门主导的"学建国"运动，即号召全国旅游住宿接待机构全面学习由香港半岛酒店管理集团管理的北京建国饭店，可以视为国际饭店业界向中国输入现代饭店服务标准、管理模式和商业文化的战略转折点。自那时起，不管业主是哪级政府，或者是何种类型的商业机构，是否贴上了某一跨国公司的品牌，往往成为衡量饭店等级和品质的标准。加上早期由这些机构培养出来的职业经理人员，还有政府部门和深入欧美模式影响的学术群体的共同推动，客观上把市场上的饭店品牌区分为国际品牌和国内品牌。再加上跨国管理集团的商业化运作，直到目前为止，人们还是把国际饭店管理集团所拥有的品牌与一流、豪华、高端、品质等同起来。

从20世纪80年代中期开始，国际饭店管理集团从一线城市的高端商务饭店，到二、三线城市的中端和经济型饭店，展开了全国范围内的多品牌布局。从产业运营的效果而言，由于国际饭店运营商广泛拥有品牌、研究与开发、人力资源、营销网络及文化软实力等多方面的竞争优势，国内的饭店运营商除了近年来在经济型饭店领域有所突破以外，绝大多数的市场空间都显得日渐逼仄。撇开商业竞争层面不谈，我们不得不承认这些进入中国市场的国际品牌在商业规则的确立、市场体系的构建、企业文化的建设和国际视野的拓展方面确实对中国旅游住宿产业的国际化起到了积极的促进作用。正是这些近在眼前的标杆的存在，到访中国的国际旅游者，以及国内游客才能够在广泛的选择中持续提升自己的消费福利，我们的服务理念和管理水平才有可能在阵痛中完成转型与升级的战略目标。

随着国内市场基础的扩大和消费能力的提高，单向的输入和学习逐渐演化为双向的融合与交流。从国际饭店品牌运营商的角度而言，无论是人力资源、产品设计，还是企业文化建设都在逐渐适应中国市场的特殊性，同时也在从中国传统的历史文化资源和当代日渐变化的消费市场上积极主动地获取可持续发展的运营资源。从产品和服务的创新，到管理模式的变革，甚至发展战略体系的演化，国际饭店品牌都在不同程度地显示了本土化的色彩。可以预期的是，随着中国公民出境旅游市场的持续繁荣和本土饭店运营商的成熟，在不远的将来，会有一些源于国内的饭店资本和管理要素走出国门，在更大的范围内与国际品牌运营商一起，为饭店产业的繁荣与发展，为世界人民的旅行福利和社会发展贡献自己的力量。

三、在见证与融合的进程中传承文明，并引领社会发展

1988年，在充分借鉴国际经验的基础上，旅游行政主管部门制订并颁布实施了《旅游涉外饭店星级划分与评定标准》（以下简称《星评标准》）。可以说，这套标准也是影响中国饭店业最有力量的标准。正是由于《星评标准》实施过程所累积的广泛的社会影响力，更多的旅游接待设施，例如内河游船、旅游厕所、旅游景区、旅行社都采用了星级或者类似的等级方式进行分等定级。事实上，不仅在旅游业内部，而且在民用航空服务、高速公路服务、铁路服务，甚至包括农村居民户的社会管理都在借鉴和引用《星评标准》的概念和体系。在推动产业发展标准化进程的同时，饭店企业，特别是一流饭店的服务标准和管理模式在相当长的时间里成为服务品质的象征。

在很长一段时间内，国内对一流饭店的形象认知都是神秘的，至少是高高在

上的。早期进入市场的五星级饭店在开业时曾经吸引了大量的客人来到大堂,只是为了感知那里的非日常生活场景。偶尔有人到四、五星级饭店消费一次,往往会成为炫耀的资本或者难忘的回忆。30年时间过去了,高端饭店已经走入了社会的日常生活。"旧时王谢堂前燕,飞入寻常百姓家"。今天,人们外出旅行、餐饮消费、商务会议,甚至节假日聚会、结婚典礼和年轻人的约会选择在高端甚至豪华饭店作为消费场所正在变成日常的生活场景。源于饭店的礼仪与文化也是自然而然地向社会大众渗透,在消费和交往的过程中一点一滴地提升国民的生活品质。正如英国的福特爵士所说的那样:"一座好的饭店和餐馆能够改善所在国家和地区的人民生活水准"。

在自身发展的同时,饭店还对就业、教育和文化等社会事业作出了自己的贡献。今天,数以百万计的人口在星级饭店和旅游住宿机构中就业,数以十万计的大学生在一千余所高等院校中接受饭店管理的专业教育。受市场竞争、技术进步、可持续发展和产品创新等多重因素的影响,一批有着长期发展历史的高端饭店对积淀下来的历史文化价值进行了挖掘和开发。天津利顺德、北京饭店、东方饭店、上海老锦江等一批见证了百年社会变迁,承载了历史足迹的饭店开始有意识地保护和整合自身的文化资源,以期延续中国饭店接待的渊源,找回自己应有的自信。2008年的北京奥运会、2010年的上海世博会和广州亚运会,以及整个社会日新月异的发展都为当代饭店业的演化带来了难得的历史机遇。正是在与整个社会的互动中,中国饭店业呈现出旺盛的活力和勃勃的生机。

中国饭店业的发展进程与整个国家的发展和社会的进步息息相关,国家兴,则饭店兴。正如温家宝总理在英国剑桥大学演讲中所指出的那样:"我们的国家古老而又年轻,历经磨难而坚强不息,珍视传统而又开放兼容"。在这样一个伟大的国度里,在中华民族伟大复兴的历史进程中,中国饭店人已经见证了30年的改革与发展,已经学习了30年的开放与融合,已经引领了30年的品质与生活,我们同样有理由相信:一个更加繁荣、更加开放、更加融合,也更加自信的30年正在等待着我们。

业界内外的同志们团结起来,为建设一流的中国饭店而努力奋斗!

2009年7月31日

到二、三线城市的中端和经济型饭店，展开了全国范围内的多品牌布局。从产业运营的效果而言，由于国际饭店运营商广泛拥有品牌、研究与开发、人力资源、营销网络及文化软实力等多方面的竞争优势，国内的饭店运营商除了近年来在经济型饭店领域有所突破以外，绝大多数的市场空间都显得日渐逼仄。撇开商业竞争层面不谈，我们不得不承认这些进入中国市场的国际品牌在商业规则的确立、市场体系的构建、企业文化的建设和国际视野的拓展方面确实对中国旅游住宿产业的国际化起到了积极的促进作用。正是这些近在眼前的标杆的存在，到访中国的国际旅游者，以及国内游客才能够在广泛的选择中持续提升自己的消费福利，我们的服务理念和管理水平才有可能在阵痛中完成转型与升级的战略目标。

随着国内市场基础的扩大和消费能力的提高，单向的输入和学习逐渐演化为双向的融合与交流。从国际饭店品牌运营商的角度而言，无论是人力资源、产品设计，还是企业文化建设都在逐渐适应中国市场的特殊性，同时也在从中国传统的历史文化资源和当代日渐变化的消费市场上积极主动地获取可持续发展的运营资源。从产品和服务的创新，到管理模式的变革，甚至发展战略体系的演化，国际饭店品牌都在不同程度地显示了本土化的色彩。可以预期的是，随着中国公民出境旅游市场的持续繁荣和本土饭店运营商的成熟，在不远的将来，会有一些源于国内的饭店资本和管理要素走出国门，在更大的范围内与国际品牌运营商一起，为饭店产业的繁荣与发展，为世界人民的旅行福利和社会发展贡献自己的力量。

三、在见证与融合的进程中传承文明，并引领社会发展

1988年，在充分借鉴国际经验的基础上，旅游行政主管部门制订并颁布实施了《旅游涉外饭店星级划分与评定标准》（以下简称《星评标准》）。可以说，这套标准也是影响中国饭店业最有力量的标准。正是由于《星评标准》实施过程所累积的广泛的社会影响力，更多的旅游接待设施，例如内河游船、旅游厕所、旅游景区、旅行社都采用了星级或者类似的等级方式进行分等定级。事实上，不仅在旅游业内部，而且在民用航空服务、高速公路服务、铁路服务，甚至包括农村居民户的社会管理都在借鉴和引用《星评标准》的概念和体系。在推动产业发展标准化进程的同时，饭店企业，特别是一流饭店的服务标准和管理模式在相当长的时间里成为服务品质的象征。

在很长一段时间内，国内对一流饭店的形象认知都是神秘的，至少是高高在

上的。早期进入市场的五星级饭店在开业时曾经吸引了大量的客人来到大堂，只是为了感知那里的非日常生活场景。偶尔有人到四、五星级饭店消费一次，往往会成为炫耀的资本或者难忘的回忆。30年时间过去了，高端饭店已经走入了社会的日常生活。"旧时王谢堂前燕，飞入寻常百姓家"。今天，人们外出旅行、餐饮消费、商务会议，甚至节假日聚会、结婚典礼和年轻人的约会选择在高端甚至豪华饭店作为消费场所正在变成日常的生活场景。源于饭店的礼仪与文化也是自然而然地向社会大众渗透，在消费和交往的过程中一点一滴地提升国民的生活品质。正如英国的福特爵士所说的那样："一座好的饭店和餐馆能够改善所在国家和地区的人民生活水准"。

在自身发展的同时，饭店还对就业、教育和文化等社会事业作出了自己的贡献。今天，数以百万计的人口在星级饭店和旅游住宿机构中就业，数以十万计的大学生在一千余所高等院校中接受饭店管理的专业教育。受市场竞争、技术进步、可持续发展和产品创新等多重因素的影响，一批有着长期发展历史的高端饭店对积淀下来的历史文化价值进行了挖掘和开发。天津利顺德、北京饭店、东方饭店、上海老锦江等一批见证了百年社会变迁，承载了历史足迹的饭店开始有意识地保护和整合自身的文化资源，以期延续中国饭店接待的渊源，找回自己应有的自信。2008年的北京奥运会、2010年的上海世博会和广州亚运会，以及整个社会日新月异的发展都为当代饭店业的演化带来了难得的历史机遇。正是在与整个社会的互动中，中国饭店业呈现出旺盛的活力和勃勃的生机。

中国饭店业的发展进程与整个国家的发展和社会的进步息息相关，国家兴，则饭店兴。正如温家宝总理在英国剑桥大学演讲中所指出的那样："我们的国家古老而又年轻，历经磨难而坚强不息，珍视传统而又开放兼容"。在这样一个伟大的国度里，在中华民族伟大复兴的历史进程中，中国饭店人已经见证了30年的改革与发展，已经学习了30年的开放与融合，已经引领了30年的品质与生活，我们同样有理由相信：一个更加繁荣、更加开放、更加融合，也更加自信的30年正在等待着我们。

业界内外的同志们团结起来，为建设一流的中国饭店而努力奋斗！

2009年7月31日

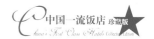

Witness, Integrate and Lead: Chinese Hotels (1979–2009)

By Prof. Dai Bin,
Vice President of China Tourism Academy,
President of Beijing Hospitality Institute
Translated by: He Keren

Although Chinese Hotels can be dated back to Shang Dynasty, modern hotel industry is actually originated from the reform and opening-up in the late 1970s. With the influence of cumulative request of incoming travelers, State reception institutions including Beijing Friendship Hotel have entered the tourism market, accommodating the high-end customers. On the other hand, city hotels like Jianguo Hotel, adjusting them to international mainstream business, step into commercial accommodation market. The former is essentially to study the market economy and business knowledge during the process of transformation. It has endured changing, restructuring, management, competition and innovation while learning and growing, which basically realizes the perfect transition from internal accommodation to facing the market. It can be said that the difficulties of their own growth have also real-time witnessed the process of China's social evolution. In terms of Chinese hotel industry, the latter is an exogenous variable. Their entry has not only brought the sparkling architecture space to the Chinese hotel industry, their operation system fully oriented by European and American's mainstream paradigm of business models and management also make the other Chinese competitors feel vividly the institutional innovation impact and shock driven by the market economy and business model. In three decades of the historical process, an increasing number of international hotel brands have entered the Chinese market. It introduces the new concepts, service standards and management system, and correspondently, is also influenced subtly by the Chinese market and Chinese culture. In this sense, the development of international high-end hotel brand in China is a process of importation, in the mean time a process of integration. Viewed from a historical perspective, the domestic hotel stock transited from the traditional state reception institutions and increase of foreign hotels driven by international high-end brand have witnessed and integrated into the Chinese hotel industry, and especially when high-end hotel industry changes, leaded China's economic development in the wider scope.

1. The historical witness of Chinese accommodation industry's transition, transformation and restructuring

First-class hotels in Chinese history can be traced back at least to the Shang and Zhou dynasties. Since then, "Lords House" ("Zhu Hou Guan") and "Guest House" serving state guests, as well as "Assembly Hall" serving the merchants of a particular region and elite in various fields, has long been the main characters in Chinese first-class hotel development history. The existence and development of these institutions are supposed to provide service to specific groups, in a non-commercial way. Despite they might have accumulated of a lot of experience in personalized service, the reception institutions still need to rely on the social class identification instead of free currency trade. That explains why these institutions are maybe only the foundation of modern hotel industry growth, but not the modern hotel industry itself.

Since the 1980s, two reasons led to the marketization and industrialization process of these hotels. On the one hand, the settlement and implementation of market-oriented reform and opening-up policy stimulate the market awareness of various types of institutions including the state reception-type hotel. On the other hand, a large number of international tourists visiting China leads to a serious shortage of high-end hotels. Under the impetus of government authorities, a lot of high-end hotels used to serve domestically were required to accommodate international tourists by business rules. In fact, when the hotels entering the tourism market have obtained the corresponding commercial benefits, they naturally transit from the mandatory government-led change to the profit-oriented induced change. In a fairly long historical period, the evolution of enterprises originated from the market reform has become an irreversible process.

With the demonstration effect of the hotels entering tourism market earlier, more and more hotels subordinate to local governments and state-owned enterprises have entered the business. In 1993, in response to the weak market and to stimulate domestic demand, coupled with the guidance of incoming tourism consumption, the national tourism enters into a government-led new era. After 1999, with adjustment of national holidays determined by the central government, especially the birth of "Golden Weeks", Chinese tourism economy has stepped into a mass-led new stage. The expansion of market area brings demand homogenization, which is bound to lead to the batch supply ways and standardization of service process. It is under the deep influence of the public demand for tourist accommodation, that a growing number of high-end hotels have changed their former organization and management methods facing the minority markets, consciously or unconsciously adopted the commercial process way to serve the guests.

Since it's much more difficult to control the service quality of direct contact between staff and guests than the objective goods, in order to obtain more scale economic advantages for the traditional hotels which have accomplished the marketization and transform, it is inevitable to head toward technical ration. What is shown in reality is in the late 1990s the renovation of the hotels are more inclined to use some standardized technique and famous-brand facilities. Technical standards and brand of those facilities have brought convenience to the hotel operation and management, but lost the tradition of perfection based on minority service and the warmth of staff facing the guests directly. Fortunately, the inherent competition rules of market economy somehow rectify the large-scale industrialization. When the hotel operators recognized the drawbacks of homogenization, the industry began to seek breakthrough in differentiation. In recent years, the Resort Hotel, SPA Hotel, conference hotels, theme hotels, airport hotels, and other new formats emerging; business floors, digital rooms, butler service and other new types of services; and concept of corporate citizenship such as environmental protection, social responsibility, community harmony etc. being introduced; those can all be seen as the hotel industry striking for the uncompetitive area of Blue Ocean after many years of market economy baptism. Meanwhile, they are contemporary hotel industry's tribute to the traditional service concepts and management methods.

At the turning point in this historical period, we also need to pay attention to the deep-rooted changes of the hotel operating system: dramatic changes of the hotel staff's service concept and behavior patterns taking place during the transition process from political reception to business accommodation, and them facing the significant test of beliefs or spiritual values. Hotel staff before marketization may not get a high pay, but their self-identity is still relatively high. Because of the specialty of the customers, they think they're

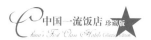

serving for political or career. And, the stable employment and relatively same welfare make the staff feel belonged to the hotel and their work. After marketization, the employee got paid more to a certain extent, but the service target is more and more generalized. As long as the customer has enough money, he or she no longer needs to be labeled with the nationality, identity or social status. In addition, under the conditions of market economy, limited salary increment is also accompanied by a high degree of instability. In such a country of no stable business service tradition, the staff's professional identity and the lack of service awareness are quite noticeable problems. It is during the interaction and coupling process of deep-rooted traditional culture and actual business values when the prerequisite hotel entrepreneurs and managers started to pay attention to corporate culture construction. Jinling Hotel Group even raises the culture construction to part of the soft power criterion. Jin Jiang Hotels Group's new LOGO is trying to find the inspiration from the traditional culture. Anyway, these leading local hotels' efforts in cultural construction indicate a new updating era based on values and cultural meanings is approaching.

Talking of a broader perspective, the reformation and development taking place in reception business are also a microcosm of three decades of Chinese reform and opening-up. Based on this, we can also say that in three decades of reformation, state reception institutions like Beijing Friendship Hotel have not only witnessed the tourist accommodation industry's market-oriented reform and enterprise development in the historical process, but also born samples and elements of the entire country's system reform and social development.

2. The two-way integration of international orientation and localization

Founded in 1982, Jianguo Hotel Beijing in China's modern history of hotel development plays an undoubted decisive role. As the first Sino-foreign joint venture hotel and the first hotel managed by foreign hotel group, it sets up an example of a local hotel implanting international service standards and management system. Following the Western hotels' operation mode, Jianguo Hotel has accumulated high reputation in the business within a very short period of time. In 1984, the central government administrative departments of tourism started the "Learning from Jianguo Hotel" campaign, which was to call on the national tourism accommodation institutions to study the successful mode of Jianguo Hotel managed by the Hong Kong Peninsula Hotel Management Group. This can be regarded as the strategic turning point of international hotel industry importing modern hotel service standards, management modes and the commercial culture. Since then, no matter which level of government property owners are, or what type of commercial entity is, whether or not to affix a certain brand of transnational corporation, is often seen as a measuring criterion of hotel grading and quality. With the promotion of professional managers trained by these institutions, as well as the government and academic groups deeply influenced by European and American paradigm, the hotel brands in the market are divided into two categories: international brands and domestic brands. So far, together with the business operation of transnational management group, people are more intended to think of the brand owned by international hotel management group as first-class, luxurious, high-end and high quality.

Since the mid-1980s, international hotel management group has launched a nationwide multi-brand distribution, from the high-end business hotels of first-line city to the mid-end and economic hotels of second and third line cities. Talking of the effects of industrial operations, international hotel operators usually have many competitive advantages such as famous brand, research and development, human resources, marketing network and cultural soft power, while domestic hotel operators only have made progress in the field of economic-type hotels, so most of the market seems to appear increasingly cramped. Leaving aside the level of business competitions, we must admit that these international brands having entered the Chinese market do have played a positive role for the establishment of business rules, the construction of market system, the building of corporate culture and the development of a global vision, all aspects of the internationalization of China's tourism accommodation industry. It is for the existence of those examples that the international tourists visiting China as well as domestic visitors are able to continuously upgrade their benefits within a wide range of options. Therefore, our service concepts and management level can reach the goal of transition and upgrading.

With the expansion of domestic market foundation and increase of consumer-based capability, one-way input and learning have gradually evolved into a two-way integration and exchange. International hotel operators are learning to adapt to the specificity of the Chinese market, e.g. human resources, product design, or construction of corporate culture. Meanwhile, they have also actively obtained sustainable operation resource from Chinese traditional history and culture, as well as contemporary evolving consumption market. From innovation of products and services, to the transformation of management modes, and even the evolution of development strategy system, the international hotel brands are in varying degrees painted with local colors. What can be expected is, with the continuous prosperous market of Chinese citizens traveling abroad and the growth of local hotel operators, in the near future, some of the domestic elements of hotel capital and management are to go out of the country. In a larger scope, along with international hotel operators, they are capable to contribute to the prosperity and development of hotel industry, the welfare and social development for the tourists around the world.

3. Inheriting civilization in the process of witness and integration, and lead the social development

In 1988, on the basis of international experience, the administrative departments of tourism promulgated and implemented the "Star rating and assessment standards of foreign-related tourism hotels" (hereinafter referred to as "Star rating standards"). It can be said that this set of standards are most powerful hotel industry standards of China. Star rating standards' implementation process leads to the result of a wide range of cumulative social influence. Following that, more and more tourism facilities such as river cruise, tourism toilets, tourism attractions and travel agencies have adopted the star rating standards or similar approaches to classification. In fact, not only in the tourism industry itself, but also in the civil aviation service, highway service, railway service, even social management of rural households are learning from the concept and system of Star rating standards. In the promoting process of industrial development standardization, the service standards and management modes of hotel business especially first-class hotel are the symbol of quality service for quite a long time.

The first-class hotels' image seems quite mysterious for a long period of time, or at least superior. When earlier the five-star hotel first entered Chinese market, the opening ceremony has attracted a lot of market to the lobby, only to sense the unusual life scene. Occasionally, when some people have consumed at a four-star or five-star hotel, they would often like to boast about the experience. Three decades have passed, and high-end hotels have entered people's daily life. "Swallow which used to stay in front of emir's house, now flew into the homes of ordinary people". Nowadays, when people plan to travel, have dinner, date, attend business meetings, hold holiday gathering and wedding ceremony, they prefer to choose high-end or even luxury hotels. The etiquette and culture originated from the hotel have also penetrated into the public naturally, and gradually enhance the life quality of citizens through consumption and communication. As Sir Ford of the United Kingdom said, a good hotel and restaurant can improve the living standard of its country and region.

While developing themselves, the hotels also make contributions to employment, education, culture and other social careers. Today, millions of people are working in star-rated hotels and tourism accommodation institutions; hundreds of thousands of students are taking professional education of hotel management in over a thousand universities and colleges. Influenced by market competition, technological improvement, sustainable development and product innovation and other factors, a group of high-end restaurants with a long history have excavated and developed the accumulative historical and cultural value. Tianjin Lishunde Hotel, Beijing Hotel, Oriental Hotel, Shanghai old Jin Jiang Hotel have witnessed the social transition of a century. Those hotels carrying the historical footprints began to intentionally reserve and integrate their cultural resources, in order to inherit and renew the reception tradition and find back their self-confidence. 2008'Beijing Olympic Games, World Expo 2010 Shanghai China and Guangzhou Asian Games, and the rapid social development as a whole, have brought precious historical opportunity for the evolution of contemporary hotel industry. It is for the interaction with society that Chinese hotel industry has shown strong vigor and exuberant vitality.

The development process of Chinese hotel industry is closely related with development and improvement of the entire nation and society. The nation is prosperous, thus is the hotel industry. As Premier Wen Jiabao's speech at the University of Cambridge said: "My beloved motherland is a country both old and young… China is a country that stood numerous vicissitudes but never gave up… China is a country that values her traditions while opening her arms to the outside world." In such a great country where the great rejuvenation of Chinese nation is taking place, Chinese hotel professionals have witnessed three decades of reform and development, have studied three decades of opening up and integration, have led three decades of quality and life. We also have reasons to believe that a more prosperous, open, integrated and confident 30 years are expecting us in the future.

I'm here to call on people who care about the industry—let's get together, strive for the first-class hotels in China!

31st July, 2009

酒店的看与读

清华大学美术学院
苏丹　教授

现代的酒店作为一种普遍生活设施，丰富着我们生活的内容，同时也改善着都市或者郊野环境的空间品质。这个对于中国内地不过30年发展历史的建筑类型，由于受民族习性以及中国多元而丰富的地域文化影响，在未来的时间和空间内依然保持着旺盛的发展态势。而在已经建立的相对丰实的物质积累的基础之上，回顾并思考我们过去对待酒店态度的变化，将有益于未来的设计和建造。

改革开放伊始，酒店作为一种和现代化社会相接轨的必要设施，对当时的中国城市提出了新的要求。这种有现代化特征的"新生事物"，在管理、卫生、设施配置和形象上都建立了一种新的范式。同时作为一种先进模式，现代化酒店对中国人民生活的居住品质提升也起到了促进作用。然而对于中国设计界而言，对其认识是一个充满艰辛和愉悦的复杂过程。眼睛的观赏、注视、浏览、窥视是表现于不同阶段的特征。依据这多种多样"看"的方式，设计界完成了对现代酒店学习的第一个阶段。

"看酒店"贯穿在自20世纪80年代至21世纪初长达20多年的时间里，从国营的大型甲级设计院到个体的初出茅庐的小设计师都依靠这种方法，笨拙地踏上了现代酒店设计之路。20世纪80年代初建立于北京、上海、广州几个中心或者口岸性城市的酒店是庞大的，它们如同城市中的城市。酒店的内容组成丰富多样、全面到位，从各种规格的餐饮，到满足商务需求的各种设施，还有娱乐和康体空间，它们的完整度和都市化程度俨然成为承载它的那些都市的榜样。其客房中的设备、设施也是人们热议的焦点。精致、整洁、自动化程度，都使得正处于半工业半农业社会转型之中的都市人羡慕不已。然而那个时期的酒店几乎无一例外都是封闭式的。门口站着时而威严、时而殷勤的门童。大堂中的服务人员或经理会察言观色，一旦发现有异样的情况立刻会像传统机关大院中的门卫一般盘问那些闯入的不速之客。

那时的不速之客基本上没有真正意义上的坏人，更没有当代一些地区频频袭击五星级酒店的恐怖分子。他们中的绝大多数只是对这个封闭之中的世界充满好奇而已，他们想跻身于此，感受不抽象的现代化。设计师也是这些被阻挡和防卫的对象之一，原因之一在于那时候的室内设计师境遇不佳，混迹于都市的平民之中难以辨识；原因之二在于酒店经营机构对抄袭的防范。然而，对酒店这个堡垒最有求知欲望的也正是这些设计师。那时中国的设计教育之中几乎没有完整的室内设计教育的体系，也没有成熟的现代酒店样本，因而能身临其境地"看"，既是唯一的，也是最佳的学习方式。然而威严的门童阻隔了大多数人便捷的感受现代化的途径。于是中国特色的介绍信就成为一种有效的媒介，这种始于红军苏维埃根据地时建立起来的凭证和信息传达方法，在中国现代化酒店和保守的公共社会之间搭建了一些类似浮桥式的临时性途径。因为那时的现代化酒店业都是中外合资的产物，红色的介绍信所代表的权威性在此依然有效。一些国有设计机构或者院校的人员在介绍信的指引下较为全面地对酒店外在的一些规矩、模式、形式进行了初步的参观学习。

在介绍信发挥积极作用的10年左右的时间里，我本人亦是受益者之一。20世纪80年代中期，大学三年级的我在暑假实习时期登上了北京西苑饭店的顶层旋转餐厅。在装修一新的那个会微微转动的空间中环顾四周时心旷神怡的心境，情境至今记忆清晰。在那张小纸片的护佑之下，"看"变得肆无忌惮，可以大胆地提出各种要求，从材料性能到设备配置，这种看的方式如饥似渴，不愿遗漏任何细节。但参观的时间往往是有限的，因此那时的参观多停留在对空间格局、设备体系配置的了解上。比如，酒店垂直和水平方向的功能安排、流线设计、电梯厅的位置、设备层位置、防火分区等，这些都属于建筑中的技术问题。而对于建筑中的室内设计专业问题，在那个时代尚不十分清晰。更为普遍的认识是建筑设计涵盖一切，室内设计工作只是建筑设计的工作延伸而没有其独立的意义。但那时一些酒店中的细节元素还是极大地刺激了我们空白的大脑。北京长城饭店大堂中的那些尺度巨大、以镜面不锈钢装饰的柱子，为我们创造出生动的视觉感受，在那种迷乱的镜像复合的视景中，我们无穷地想象着现代化的中国未来。西苑饭店的顶棚呈现出的几何形体富于韵律感的变化，其柔和多变的色彩组合令人从传统欧几里得几何学的立场透视宇宙奥妙的变相背后的真理。其实，酒店对学习者真正的诱惑正在其内部。这些有逻辑性或没有逻辑性的细节组合，完成了对商务和旅游活动的全部功能，风格和设施相互融合，最大限度地挖掘着客人们的消费潜力。它是一个既复杂又由多样的行为模式、多样的景观、多样的细节组合而成的世界。酒店设计的学习初级阶段，每一个学习者就如同潜入体内的内窥镜头，瞪大的眼睛即是学习的全部。

当没有任何有力的凭证能令门童们开恩时，学习者就聚集在酒店附近梭巡以寻找适当的机会。那时许多渴望学习的年青学子如同围绕在餐馆周围乞食的丐帮，顽强、坚韧，有时也闪现智慧的灵光。比如有衣着整齐、相貌姣好的女同学可以趁外宾团队到来时，以翻译的身份、扮相从容地从门童面前走过，也听说过有个别相貌奇特的学生，扮作外宾进入宾馆大门。这些奇人异事一时在参观学习者中广泛流传。

20世纪90年代初期，中国涉外的宾馆开始逐步向社会开放。这时期酒店的数量已达到了一定规模。风格多样化也开始呈现爆发的状态。国际化的酒店风格模式经过上一个阶段的普及，已经产生了一点单调感，这个时期的酒店设计开始表达地域文化，表现更加多元化的组成内容。这种设计思想和酒店之间的竞争也不无关系。经营者借助差异性来满足客人们多样性体验的要求，酒店设计中的创造性被提到一个新的高度的要求上来。社会上的酒店既为改革开放中的国家提供了一种设施上的保证，它们彼此之间组织又形成了城市的新景观，并且这种景观内向性的特点极为符合中国传统的审美习惯，即人们常常对内藏锦绣的营造方式赞叹不已。客观上，这些设计精彩的酒店的公共化还使它充当扮演了推动和普及设计文化的角色。

酒店的公共区域向社会开放，进一步掀起了"看"中学习的高潮。但此时在公共空间中摄影是被禁止的。因为摄影的快速、便捷、准确的特点使"看"的实质已经发生了质变。它记录的准确性，为"读"埋下了伏笔，同时也把剽窃的技术提高到了一个完全新兴的时期。每一个酒店出于自我的保护，严格地控制外来者使用照相机。20世纪90年代初期，我曾协助导师编辑一本有关室内设计风格精选的资料集，其中相当一部分内容涉及中国正在兴盛和发展中的酒店。于是我带着摄影师，揣着红色字印的介绍信前往那些酒店发达的城市收集资料。这是一个极为艰巨的任务，因为酒店这个堡垒此时的开放依然是个表态，它和现实社会巨大的反差，使它时刻保持着一种骄傲，也和陌生的闯入者依然保持着一种距离。和我同行的摄影师是摄影界的大腕，随身携带的专业行头庞大、复杂、扎眼。每当他拉开架式在酒店的厅堂内组装三脚架时，总会有酒店管理者来询问、阻止。于是我羞涩地拿出昔日威风八面的介绍信来搪塞。但在新的时期，不知是因为介绍信泛滥还是因为酒店管理的成分发生变化的缘故，这种证明的方式显然已不再有效，我们屡屡被禁止拍摄，甚至被驱赶。其实出版这类摄影集乃是一种把"看"酒店的行为扩大化、普及化的过程，每一个学习者都可以通过较为节俭的方式去在纸面上分享酒店设计师们的作品，同时在分享之中亦可适度提高个人的设计水平。但这种分享还是损害了、稀释了酒店现实的权威性，更为客观的一个可能就是它加速了酒店更新的频率，加大了其营运的成本。因此，我们这些拍摄和传播者理所当然成为酒店管理者所痛恨的人。那次拍摄经历在我的记忆中留下的尽是不良的映象，它像阴影一样挥之不去，和记忆中对酒店的敬仰混合在一起形成一种复杂的感情经历。若干年后在设计过程中遇到一些酒店的经营者竟多是喜欢阅读那些介绍酒店专业杂志的人士，他们一致认为翻阅这种彩色的、摄影讲究的杂志是一种享受，并且这种阅读的确在丰富着他们管理酒店的经验。在图片的引导下，一方面，翻阅者可以走入一个虚拟的世界，在令人痴迷的各种风格、各种场所、各种细节中游走；另一方面，一些精彩的细节往往以特写的方式被摄影者捕捉，然后呈现于阅读者的眼前，这是一种对学习者、感受者的提示，它告诉这些人酒店的品质和细节之间的密切关联。

无疑在众多的建筑类型之中，酒店的娱乐性、复杂性、静止性都是突出的，它对设计师的创造力、观察力和生活阅历都有较为苛刻的要求，因此，从事酒店设计的人一生都要不断地"看"酒店。"读"酒店是"看"酒店的升级，它暗示着在一种专业化的语境之中"看"，也暗示着观看酒店的方式和时间感发生的变化。专业类的酒店杂志或有关酒店题材的作品集是"读"酒店的一种良好素材，在这类出版物之中，编辑者按照一定的价值取向将之归类整理，为阅读者的搜寻指明了方向。同时，任何一本品质良好的此类书刊在对每一个案例的介绍方面都是科学和艺术性完美结合的。它表现为对案例高度的概括力和深入的表达力，重要的空间、重要的细节都在影像中得以充分表达，有时这种表达甚至超越了现场感。因为许多完美的画面也并非酒店中的常态，它是对一瞬间的等待与捕捉，当这种成功的捕捉成为永久的画面时，空间中隐藏的那种迷离的、恍惚的特质就得到了放大。人类的学习就是在这种不断地把对象放大的基础之上进行的，它既包括模仿，也包括超越。

"看"酒店侧重的是对信息的浏览和搜集，而"读"酒店侧重的是对信息的筛选与分析。"看"和"读"互为前提、互为条件，有时还会相互补充。生活中常常有按图索骥的模式，当在阅读中发现令人激动的案例时，我们会努力在现实中到达现场，去感受画面、验证画面，更有价值的是去挖掘画面中无法传递的质感与气息，还有煽情的声音等，这时后置的"看"就是对"读"的补充。20世纪90年代末进口的画册中频频介绍南非的酒店——失落的宫殿，这个以生动和复杂的写实手法堆砌的既残败又辉煌的酒店屹立于非洲荒漠之上，伪造的文明史和人类文明的印证和当代人高度消费方式、欲望相混搭、纠葛，无休无止地炫耀着传统艺术的表现魅力。模仿、变形将非洲土地上万类霜天竞自由之生生不息的景象或以立体又或以平面的方式镌刻于那个古怪的城堡之内、之外……这个酒店如同细密画一般的景象是阅读后留给读者的印象，那个年代的许多设计师就是一边翻阅画册一边忘情地想象，又一边复制它在中国的摹本。至2004年夏，我终于有机会去南非旅游，而驱动力之一就是身临其境去感受那个废墟。现场的观看能有力地看穿变戏法背后的玄机，从而也使那神秘和那份悬念荡然无存。我用手轻轻敲击那由一束植物树干组合而成的石材模样的柱式，它发出哐哐的声响。这仿佛一个拆穿骗局的孩童真实的表白，回荡在"废墟"早已复苏的场地，宣告着一场华丽之梦的结局。然而当我们对故事的真实性产生绝望之时，趣味就会转移至故事本身。酒店中非结构性的细节是真实生动无比的，尤其那客房中的细节会给人的现实生活一个真实的场景以抚慰一颗动荡又失落的苦心。

　　缺乏现场验证的"读"也会有其特有的价值。那就是所谓的"误读"。因为没真正居留的经验，简单的参观和纸面阅读会对形式的理解产生歧义，而这其中也包含着巨大的创造力。使用经验缺席造成认识过程中的局部真空状态，此时个人的经验和思维惯性就会悄然介入，从而改变了判断的轨迹。无数的误读会把具体事物背后所隐藏的价值激发出来。我想这是出版物的另一种作用。有时候我们不妨这样试想，出版就是一种真空状态的表现。它出于建筑纯粹性表现的目的，鲜活的生命迹象被从建筑这个容器之中抽掉了。同时表象的摄取是对三维物体或者空间的折叠或压缩。而这种折叠或压缩一方面把动态转化成为静态，使局部放大为整体，具有一种使事物的物理形式变得清晰的功效，而另一方面则掩盖了许多非物质性因素而使得原本清楚的状态变得模糊，因此也为文本多样解读留出了空间。在我们个人早期学习经历之中，常常是先读后看，目的是用亲临现场的经历来检验知识，希望能和作者在同一作品、同一现场和同一视角之中、之下取得共鸣，以这种方式建立一种机制结构。但随着专业学习的深入，学习方式渐渐又开始向先看后读转化，因此作为一名专业设计工作者，或特定类型空间的研究者，更多的时间耗散于广阔空间领域的观摩、体验之中。酒店类型的空间因其特殊性格亦使得这种"看"极富物质和精神的双重诱惑，但此时的"读"依然必不可少，并且在"读"的深度上有所升级，这是对"看"的归纳与升华。因此，我们的学习过程中"读本"不可或缺，即使是图形为主的读本，它是信息的线索，也是设计工作的范本，等待我们临摹与超越。

Looking and Reading the Hotels

By Prof Su Dan
Translated by: He Keren

Modern hotel as the basic facility for our time enriches our life style, and at the same time improves the urban or the suburban spatial qualities. This particular building type has only been developed in the Mainland China not more than 30 years ago. Its development potential will still be on the optimistic side in the future both in time and space because of the influence of national customs and the diversified regional cultures of China. Based on what we already physically established, we should retrospect and reflect our attitudes towards the hotel development in the past; hopefully it will benefit the design and construction in the future.

When the great reform started in the 1980s, hotel as a necessity to meet the modern social criteria placed a new request to the Chinese cities. This type of "new stuff" with the characteristic of modernization, established a series of new paradigms in term of hotel management, hygiene requirement, facility equipments and the appearances. As a more advanced prototype in general, modern hotel became an accelerator to improve the living qualities of Chinese people. While to us designers, it has been a process full of complication and hard working. We have experienced different phases of observing, speculating, browsing and peeking. By the various means of "Looking", the designers have accomplished the first phase of studying.

For more than 20 years from the 1980s to the 21st century, we have been simply "looking at hotels". Either mature architects from the first-class, government-run design institutions or the young designers freshly out of the school have all been stumbled to start their designs using this preliminary method. There are grand hotels constructed at that time in Beijing, Shanghai, Guangzhou and other coast cities in China. These hotels were the cities within the cities—the richness of their contents, the intensity of their functions, the variety of their dining, business, entertaining and recreation facilities, all of which became the representation of the modern cities with their integrity and urbanization. Living in those large cities, people whom are just experiencing the transition period from the half-agricultural, half-industrial society to the modern globalization became very appreciate to the clean, detail designed, and smartly controlled hotel room facilities. However, the hotels at that time were all closed to the public. They had porters standing at the entrance with the attitude either awesome or politeness. The managers in the lobby could also act as detectives to chase down the "un-welcomed people", just as those security guards at the traditional Chinese institutions.

While those "un-welcomed people" at that time usually were not even close to the bad people, like those terrorists attacking 5-stars hotels in the South Asia and Mid-east these days. Most of them were those who were simply curious of these new "forbidden cities". They wanted to get in and experience the modernization physically. Among them there were designers who looked just alike. Another reason for the hotel's defensive strategy was to prevent copying from other competitive institutions. The designers were the most curious group of all, for they were not able to obtain the systematic interior design education during that time in China, as well as lacking of well-developed examples of hotel design. As the matter of fact, "Looking and observing" became the only and the best method for most of the designers to learn. Because the awesome porters prevented most causal visitors from experiencing the modernization, a type of recommendation form became an effective way to penetrate these fortresses. This type of recommendation form originated from the Civil War period and was used as a type of certificate and information transit. It then was used again as a temporary medium between the Chinese modern hotels and the conservative public relation system. During the 1980s most of the hotels were funded by a combination of government and private investors, therefore the recommendation form with the governmental red seal still held certain authority over the hotel management. With the power of this recommendation form, a lot of designers from national institutions or colleges have visited and studied hotels in a more comprehensive way in terms of their appearance, scales and forms.

I was also among one of those who benefited from the recommendation forms during that decade. In the mid of 1980s when I was still a junior college student, I was able to get into the revolving restaurant on the top of Xi Yuan Hotel in Beijing. I still remember vividly the feeling of looking around the newly decorated restaurant slightly moving with the panorama views. "Looking" became daring and hungry at that time accompanying with numerous questions regarding everything including the building material and equipment used. The hunger of knowledge and the limited visiting time has caused us only get to know the spatial organization and mechanical and electric systems, such as the horizontal and vertical layouts of different functions, user's movement, the location of elevators, mechanic rooms and fire protection zones, etc. These all belong to the technical problems for architecture. When it happened to be the interior design concept, nobody was quite clear at that time. During that period, architectural design was for all and interior decoration was only an extension of it without its independent meanings. But the detail designs at some hotels did influentially initiate sparkers in our blank minds at that time—the huge, reflective stainless steel columns in the lobby of the Great Wall Hotel in Beijing created such a visual illusion in front of our eyes which made us dreamt about the infinitive globalization in the future; The variety of patterns and colors of the ceiling design with rhyme and smooth changes at Xi Yuan Hotel represented the infinite possibilities of the universe instead of the inspiration from the classical Euclid geometry. Indeed, the seduction of the hotels really lies within. The logical or non-logical combination of details accomplishes the function, style and accommodation for business and tourism, and at the same time explores the ultimate potential for consuming. It is a world full of complication, with a variety of details, scenarios and activities. As the designers, the preliminary study process and means depends on our eyes, which made us similar to the internal lens for the surgery.

When most of the students did not have the powerful recommendation to get to visit the interiors, they just wandered around the buildings looking for chances. They looked much like those homeless people except for their smart, endure and wisdom eyes. Sometimes a few good-looking female students pretended to be the interpreters walking along a foreign tourist group to get into the hotels; there were also some rumors heard as some strange looking students were mistakenly regarded as foreign guests and welcomed into the building. There were quite a few stories circling around at that time during my college years.

When it comes to the 1990s, the hotels in China started to gradually open to the public. In this era, the number of hotels has been increased and has popularized to a certain period time that people started to get a bit bored of their global appearance. The hotel design began to explore the regional cultures and represent the diversified combination. The design concepts were also related to the competition among the hotels. When the client intended to fulfill the diversity experiences initiated by the consumers, the creative concepts of the interior design were also brought out to a new level. The newly designed hotels not only provided accommodations for the developing China, but also created new urban landscape by their spatial relationship. They created the landscape with the internal characteristics that suited Chinese traditional aesthetics. This kind of internal beauty in the hotel design and management were deeply appreciated by the consumers, and at the same time it helped to promote and popularize the culture of interior design.

As the hotels opened their public spaces, "looking and learning" became a popular way for the designers. However, photography was prohibited in those public areas. The faster, convenient and accurate photography would change the essence of "looking" and prepare for the "reading" process. Since the technique would greatly help as well the plagiarism, to protect itself, each hotel strongly prohibited outsiders taking photographs. In the early 1990s, I used to assist my advisor to edit a book on interior design styles, part of which included the new developed hotels in China. I carried a recommendation form with the red seal, and took a professional photographer with me to collect information in the grand hotels. This was a tough task since hotels just started to open to public at that time with an attitude of arrogance and distance from the general public. The photographer accompanying me was a professional who carried a set of huge, complicated equipments that was unique enough to draw everyone's attention. Whenever he set up the equipment and got ready to shoot, there were always hotel managers came over to question us. The recommendation form that had been quite powerful has lost its authority for unknown reasons. Maybe there were just too many of the type of recommendations by then or it was because of changing of the hotel management system. Anyhow, we were often stopped and even expelled. Actually this kind of published picture collection is a new way to extend the study process of "looking", everyone could share the designers' work on the paper by a much less expansive way, and improve their own design at the same time. However, this kind of "sharing" also deteriorates or dilutes the authority of the hotel management, and eventually it might speed up the hotel renovation. As a result, we became the people whom are not welcomed. I had the unfortunate memory during that experience of photo shooting which always feels like a shadow in my heart, together with the complex feeling of appreciating the shining quality of the hotel design. During a few years design process I met a number of hotel managers who indeed are fond of reading these hotel magazines. They all think it is a pleasure to glance through these colorful, high-quality photographs, and it could enrich them management experience at the same time. The readers can walk into a virtual world through the images, gliding through the fascinating styles, scenarios and details; on the other hand, some excellent details presented to the readers are only caught through the photographers' eyes, which serve as a reminder to the readers of the important relationship between the design details and the quality of the hotels.

Among all the architectural types, hotel has its distinctive features in terms of entertaining, complication and serenity. Rigorous requirement has place upon the designers who need creativity, observation and experience. As a result, "looking at" the hotel becomes a continuous exercise for the designers. "Reading" hotels, somehow is the upgraded level, which implies a type of "looking" in a more professional circumstance, and as well as the changes of time and means to observe the hotels. A good resource of "reading" is the published professional hotel magazines or books, in which the editor analyzes and categorizes according to different values, and points out guidance for the readers. Meanwhile, for each case in any of this type of high-quality publication, scientific and artistic features are bound together. It is presented as a highly summarized and intensified case through a group of images showing important spaces and details. Sometimes this type of representation is even beyond the reality since some of the images are not static status but are captures of certain moments, which becomes permanent images that amplify the mysteriousness and vagueness of the hidden spaces. It is this kind of amplification that allows human being to learn, to imitate and to surpass.

The aim of observation of hotels is to browse and search, while reading hotels involves selecting and analyzing the information collected. "Looking" and "Reading" is reciprocal and complementary. When we discover some exciting spaces through reading, we always intend to be present in the real places to experience and confirm the images we find in the book, moreover, to discover more quality, feeling and sound that the images cannot convey. This accounts for the complementary to the reading. Among the imported publications during 1990s, there were often seen the introduction of a hotel in South Africa—the Lost Palace. This ruined and splendid hotel stands upon the African desert piles up with vivid, complex and surrealistic techniques. The man-made history, evidence of human civilization entangles with high-end consumption style and desire of modern people, flaunt with endless charms of traditional art. The technique of imitation and variation of the hotel design represents the circle of life of Africa by sculpting the 3-D or 2-D images on the surfaces of the unique castle. The impression that this hotel looks like miniature is what most people felt after reading the magazine. Many Chinese designers at that time have to imagine what it looks like when reading the magazine, and follow its magnificent power through imitating its design techniques. It was not until the summer of 2004 that I got the chance to travel to South Africa. One of my motives was to go to see that "ruin". I believed my on site experience would reveal the secret behind the magic and remove the mystery and suspension of this place. When I slightly knocked surface of the false stone, plant-like columns, the sound of the echo that assimilated the realness behind a child's trick prevailed the revived site of the "ruin", which declared the completion of my splendid dream that has last decades. On the other hand, when we finish our dreams and face the reality, the interest of the story itself would emerge. The false, but vividly designed details of the public spaces and the details of the hotel rooms all provided a real scenario to me that serve as a consolation for my feeling of disappointment and lost.

Reading without seeing on site actually does have some values, which is often called "misread". Because of the lack of the real accommodation experience, there would be misunderstanding by a quick visit or reading on paper, however, there could be potential creativity inherited in it. During the acknowledge process, because we are lack of utilitarian experience, personal experiences and our conventional thinking would take place instead, which would alter the direction of our judgment. Numerous "misread" could initiates the potential values behind the physical essence, which I consider another function of publication. Sometimes we might compare the publication as the vacuum status—scenarios of real life are extracted from the vessels (architecture) in order to present the pureness of architecture. The images captured are means of folding or compressing towards the three dimensional objects, which transform the dynamics into static, amplify the parts to the whole. It clears up something physically on one hand, and conceals many nonphysical factors that create ambiguousness among the conventional objects. It is this variety of "misread" leaves spaces for my essay. Early on when we began our learning, we always looked and then read with the purpose of using the experience on site to testify the knowledge. We wished to be consonant with the author under the same work, same site and same perspectives, thus to created a systematic design process. When we are deep into this professional field, the learning technique transforms to read and to observe later. As for a professional designer, or a researcher for certain types of space, more time would be consumed in the observation and experiencing in the wide space. Spaces created in a hotel structure have their unique characteristics that seduce us to look both in physical and metaphysical ways. But we should acknowledge the inevitable "reading" process, and to improve it to a high level of summary and sublime. As a matter of fact, during the learning process the "reading" materials are necessary. The images in the reading materials serve as the trend of information, and the guidance for the professional work, which await us to imitate and to transcend.

北京饭店始建于1900年,历经一个世纪的洗礼,依然焕发着蓬勃生机。饭店东侧与驰名中外的王府井商业街举步之遥,西侧与雄伟的天安门、威严的皇宫紫禁城相邻,尽享独特的地理优势。楼体建筑气宇轩昂、中西合璧,古典建筑与现代风格相得益彰。A、B、C、D、E5座不同时代的建筑错落有致,异彩纷呈。富有传奇历史色彩的北京饭店,以其自身的优势和国际上良好的口碑已连续多年获得了国际酒店业服务业的最高荣誉——"五星钻石奖"。

饭店拥有风格各异的客房700余间。皇帝套房雍容典雅、气度非凡;名人下榻房的幽幽意境令人思绪万千;行政套房方便快捷,在故宫观景房可纵览古都风貌,视角独一无二;豪华标准间整洁宽敞、舒适温馨;每间客房均配置了高速的宽带接口,缩短了宾客们与世界沟通的距离。舒适豪华的客房、独具特色的佳肴、先进完备的商务设施以及宾至如归的服务,使北京饭店成为高档商务、旅游休闲宾客的极佳选择。

北京饭店是中外顶尖厨师的汇集之地,厨师们精湛超群的厨艺,使北京饭店享有"中国烹饪大本营"的美誉。饭店所经营的谭家菜、淮扬菜、四川菜、广东菜、西餐及日餐品种繁多。各式菜系在北京饭店独领风骚,珍馐美馔与优雅舒适的就餐环境可谓相得益彰。其

中，历经百多年历史的官府菜——谭家菜更是北京饭店一枝长盛不衰的奇葩。

饭店拥有几十个规格各异并配备先进通信系统的会议厅堂，为举办从几人至千人的高档国际会议、宴会、大型演出、新闻发布会、时装表演及会展提供了理想的场所。大宴会厅具有12个声道的同声传译功能，各种投影及音、视频设备，使商务会议在这里轻松举办。

先进时尚的康乐健身中心设有健身房、室内及室外网球场、壁球、保龄球、乒乓球、台球及阳光游泳池等设施。舒适的健身环境将运动的乐趣提升到极致。

2008年北京饭店作为奥林匹克大家庭总部饭店，成功地接待了国际奥委会主席罗格、国际奥委会荣誉主席萨马兰奇、国际奥委会委员和204个国家和地区的奥委会主席。北京饭店周到热情的服务赢得了下榻贵宾们的高度赞扬。

今天，这座伫立在新世纪潮头的百年老店，正以开放的姿态和勃勃的生机向世人展示着它集历史、人文、审美、现代科技于一身的五星级饭店独具的风采。

1. 北京饭店夜景
   Beijing Hotel Night View
2. 1954年北京饭店全貌
   A View of Beijing Hotel during the 1954's
3. C座大堂
   Hotel Lobby

1. 20世纪20年代的北京饭店全貌
   The Beijing Hotel in the Early 1920s
2. 北京饭店外景
   Beijing Hotel Outside View

An ambiance inspired by an illustrious past and a dynamic modernity in the heart of Beijing. Situated at the crossroads of Wangfujing Street and Chang An Avenue, Beijing Hotel is adjacent to one of Beijing's major shopping areas and only a stroll away from the grandeur of the Forbidden City, Tian'anmen Square, National Grand Theater and other cultural and historical sites.
Spacious bedrooms, Asian and western dining venues, a wide variety of function rooms and recreation facilities, make it a perfect place, whether to stay for business or leisure. Beijing Hotel has been presented with the Five Star Diamond Award for consecutive years and has made history once again as Olympic Family Hotel and headquarters of the International Olympic Committee during the 2008 Summer Olympic Games.

1. 金色宴会厅
   Grand Ballroom
2. 阳光咖啡厅包间
   Private Room in Sunshine Café
3. 阳光咖啡厅
   Sunshine Café
4. 中华礼仪厅包间
   Private Banquet Room

1. 观景豪华包间
   Top View Banquet Room
2. 金色宴会厅
   Grand Ballroom
3. 18楼宴会厅
   Banquet Hall
4. 18楼会见厅
   Conference Hall

1. 游泳池
   Swimming Pool
2. 皇帝套客厅
   Emperor Suite

1. 皇帝套客厅
   Emperor Suite
2. 大床房
   King Size Room
3. 故宫景房
   Forbidden City View Room
4. 中式高级标准房
   Classical Twin Room
5. 名人房
   VIP Deluxe Suite
6. 行政豪华房
   Executive Room

北京贵宾楼饭店是北京首都旅游集团有限责任公司和香港霍英东投资有限公司合资建造的豪华五星级饭店。地理位置独特，毗邻紫禁城和天安门广场，面向长安街，是皇城内唯一一家五星级酒店，登上顶楼平台，皇城全貌一览无余。饭店周围会聚了首都著名旅游景点，菖蒲河、中山公园、北海、国家博物馆等历史人文景观可信步而至。在这里可以同时感受北京古老的东方文化氛围和首都蓬勃发展的现代脉搏。

贵宾楼饭店于开业之初加入世界一流酒店组织，于1999年荣获美国优质服务行业协会颁发的五星钻石奖，并连续三届获得"首都旅游紫金杯"、"永久保存杯"的称号。自开业以来，贵宾楼以独特的中式风格、中国人自己的管理和细致入微的服务，创造出骄人的业绩。邓小平、江泽民等党和国家领导人；时任英国首相撒切尔夫人、德国总理科尔、国际奥委会主席萨马兰奇，及现任国际奥委会主席罗格等外国领导人和世界知名人士先后莅临或下榻饭店。2008年，贵宾楼饭店作为奥林匹克大家庭总部饭店，圆满完成了对北京奥运会贵宾的住宿接待工作，赢得了广泛认可与好评。

贵宾楼内所有的陈设充满了中国情调，饭店拥有217套客房，其中标准客房及故宫观景间160套，各式套房共57套，包括豪华套房、大使套房、皇帝套房等。

217套客房全部采用花梨木家具，配以古典字画和有典故的装饰。客房内设有免费宽带互联网接口、传真机、私人保险箱。各式餐厅5间，宴会厅、会议室10多间，以及酒吧、茶室等设施。室内游泳池、健身中心、桑拿浴、蒸汽浴免费为住店宾客提供服务。

贵宾楼饭店不仅环境幽雅，更兼美食荟萃。5间餐厅风格各异，融合各方菜系之长，受到各界宾朋的青睐。著名品牌"御福官府菜"以选料上乘考究、技法一丝不苟、口味醇香浓厚而享誉全国。堪称一绝的御福翅泡饭味道鲜美、香糯润滑、口感绝佳，以其独特的魅力与极佳的口碑，赢得了"京城新派官府名菜"之美誉。历经多年精心研制的名菜"御福坛老大"，以几十种珍贵原料经长时间熬炖而成，盛入紫砂坛，开盖香气四溢，汁浓味厚，丰富的营养和味觉享受也赢得大批拥趸。御福会餐厅便因"御福官府菜"而得名，餐厅内设立的精品雪茄屋和红酒屋，更为用餐增添无尽享受。红墙咖啡厅因紧靠皇城红墙而名，布局精心别致，将欧陆格调融汇于大都会风情中。咖啡厅自助餐汇集中餐、西餐、日餐、东南亚风味等各地精品菜肴，百余种特色美食可供选择，是店外宾客聚会用餐的常选之所。

1. 前台大厅
Lobby
2. 紫金厅
Zijin Hall

1. 红墙咖啡厅
   Red Wall Cafe
2. 花园大厅
   Atrium

Grand Hotel Beijing is a joint venture between Dr. Henry Y. T. Fok (Hong Kong) and Beijing Tourism Group. Grand Hotel Beijing is a five star hotel, situated neighboring the Forbidden City and Tian'anmen Square and facing to the Chang An Ave. It offers the perfect combination between tradition and modern comfort.

Grand Hotel Beijing ranks among the best as a member of the Leading Hotels of the World .It was also awarded the Five Star Diamond Award by the American Academy of the Hospitality Science in 1999, and granted the permanent honor "ZiJin Gold Cup" by Beijing Tourism Administration. Since opening, Kohl, Margaret Thatcher, Juan Antonio Samaranch, Rogge and other celebrities from home and aboard have stayed in Beijing Grand Hotel. In 2008, as an Olympic Family Hotel, the Grand Hotel Beijing's successful reception and accommodation of the respected guest of IOC, had wined widespread recognition and acclaim.

The Hotel is entirely furnished with a Chinese motif, all of the 217 guest rooms including 160 deluxe rooms and Palace View Rooms and 57 suites such as Deluxe Suites, Ambassador's Suites, Emperor's Suite etc. All the furniture in the guest rooms is made of pear rose against a background of works of Chinese calligraphy and painting, which bring forth the essence of oriental culture. While basking in nice surroundings, the Grand Hotel Beijing serves exquisite food of different styles. The hotel's catering service provides a wide spectrum of menus, which are update from time to time,

drawing favorable comments. The wireless and broadband access can be supplied for the business convenience. Health Club free offer private facilities with sauna, steam bath room, indoor swimming pool and gymnasium.

Grand Hotel Beijing is not only excel in elegant surroundings and decoration, but also famous in the food and beverage. There have five restaurants of different style, which offers the delicacies with the master of various regional cuisines. The hotel brand "YU FU ROYAL DISHES" especially represented by "Yu Fu Shark's Fin w/ Rice" and "Yu Fu Big Tan", has well known for its exquisite materials selection, meticulous skill, great taste and rich cultural context. Its rich in nutrients and taste have won a large number of fans to enjoy. The newly renovated restaurant "Mask of China" with exclusively designed wine house and cigar house meets the personalized needs of guest. The Red Wall Café named after the red wall of imperial city outside the window, features over a hundred kinds of western and Chinese food to choose from, is an ideal place of gathering or enjoying a meal for the guests.

1.御园商务平台　　2.花园大厅　　3.明华厅　　4.明园餐厅
Imperial Business Terrace　　Atrium　　Ming Hua　　Ming Yuan

1、2、3.御福会
Mask of China

4.紫金厅
Zijin Hall

5.喷泉酒吧
Fountain Bar

1. 游泳池
   Swimming Pool
2. 总统套间
   Presidential Suite
3. 皇帝套间
   Emperor's Suite

1. 中式套房
Chinese Style Suite
2、4. 贵宾楼套房
Grand Hotel Suite
3. 豪华套间
Deluxe Suite
5. 贵宾楼大使套间
Ambassador Suite

北京国际俱乐部饭店

北京国际俱乐部饭店坐落于北京建国门外大街，紧邻使馆区、中央商务区购物中心，距天安门广场、故宫、秀水街和日坛公园仅数街之隔。其前身是历史意义深刻的北京国际俱乐部，那里曾是政府官员、外交使节和商界巨贾著名的会晤之所。

2008年，喜达屋酒店与度假村国际管理集团（NYSE:HOT）宣布，北京国际俱乐部饭店在经过7个半月全面升级改造工程后，现已重张开业。此次耗资2700万美元的装修主要投入在258间饭店客房（含102间设计豪华优雅的套房）、公共区域和全日营业的景苑咖啡厅。同时，北京国际俱乐部饭店以其屡获殊荣的丹尼艾丽意大利餐厅、天然温泉、占地1,221平方米的会议活动设施和享誉全球的瑞吉专职管家服务，成为世界各地宾客来到北京的首选之地。

喜达屋集团亚太区总裁高启昆先生表示："北京国际俱乐部饭店无与伦比的奢华享受和量身定制的个性化服务完美诠释了瑞吉品牌的精髓。从北京、上海、新加坡到正处于筹备中的巴厘岛、曼谷、雅加达、拉萨、吉隆坡和大阪，瑞吉品牌在一个又一个世界最佳的地理位置上展示着其独具魅力的核心价值。"

位于美国纽约卓有声誉的Alexandra Champalimaud & Associates设计公司负责此次北京国际俱乐部饭店的装修设计。

欧式的设计风格中融入了传统的中国特色，给人以典雅与现代的感受。手工绘制的顶部，真丝刺绣及特别定制的高档木材家具，衬托出大堂独特雅致的氛围。遵循着东方理念，风水设计与水的元素在新改建的瑞吉花园中有着全新的阐释，同样的理念也在景苑咖啡厅和大堂酒吧的设计中得以充分体现。景苑咖啡厅的户外就餐平台与瑞吉花园融为一体，宾客在享用美食的同时，还可观赏喷泉与花园的美景。

除景苑咖啡厅和大堂酒吧之外，北京国际俱乐部饭店为尊贵的宾客提供了多种用餐选择，让您足不出户尽享美味珍馐。丹尼艾丽意大利餐厅被誉为"北京最好的意大利餐厅"；艾斯特扒房是北京鲜有的经典美式牛扒餐厅；葡萄酒廊环境幽静、氛围浪漫；大堂酒吧提供瑞吉品牌独创并颇具传奇色彩的"血红玛莉"鸡尾酒及悠闲下午茶，宾客休憩的同时亦可聆听曼妙的世界名曲；记者俱乐部酒吧具有私人会所般舒服闲适的环境，置身于此，令人回想起北京国际会所鼎盛时期的美好时光。

饭店增加了19间全新设计的瑞吉套房，使套房总数增加到102间，占客房总数的40%。客房的设计融合了中西方特色，配以用材考究、工艺精细的樱桃木家具、丝绸家居用品、欧式餐具和宽屏液晶电视，宽敞舒适的办公桌与高速上网服务更为商旅客人提供了便利。

北京国际俱乐部温泉及健身中心是北京市中心第一家在饭店内提供真正天然温泉理疗服务的场所，开业于2001年9月，占地2,000平方米，拥有10间中西式按摩的豪华理疗室，来自地下1,500米的天然温泉水为宾客提供了绝佳的体验，是闹市中享受宁静的温泉殿堂。经验丰富的理疗师可提供西式或传统的中式按摩理疗服务，在训练有素的理疗专家悉心呵护下，客人可摆脱忙碌与压力，重新体会身与心的和谐，焕发新的活力。

北京国际俱乐部饭店拥有占地超过1,221平方米的室内会议和宴会设施，是举办会议及宴会的最佳选择。

1. 大堂酒吧
Lounge
2. 饭店外观（夜晚）
Hotel Exterior (Night)

这里配有便利先进的技术设备,专业的宴会销售人员可根据会议和活动的规模灵活调整会议及宴会厅的空间。饭店独有的瑞吉花园如同一片充满魅力的绿洲,远离城市的喧嚣,其舒适惬意的环境是户外宴请活动的上乘之选。

延续着纽约第一家瑞吉酒店的服务理念,北京国际俱乐部饭店秉承传统,接受过传统英式管家训练的专职管家可依照客人的个人习惯及喜好提供完美而含蓄的个性化服务,把享誉全球的专职管家服务、量身定制的卓越体验和奢华惬意的居住环境提供给来自全球的每一位宾客。

迄今为止,北京国际俱乐部饭店已走过12年光阴,凭其完美出色的对客服务和奢华卓越的入住体验赢得了国际上许多主流媒体的关注与认可,其中包括美国专业旅游杂志 *Condé Nast Traveler*、*Travel&Leisure*、*Elite Traveler* 以及国际专业财经杂志 *Institutional Investor*。

The St. Regis Beijing is located on Jianguomenwai Dajie in the heart of the city's diplomatic district, near Beijing's center for upscale shopping and business. Ideally located near Tian'anmen Square and the Forbidden City, the hotel is within walking distance of the Silk Market, Ritan Park and the historic Beijing International Club, a well-known gathering spot for domestic and international government officials, foreign dignitaries, journalists and business executives.

July 2008, Starwood Hotels & Resorts Worldwide, Inc. (NYSE:HOT) proudly announces the debut of the newly renovated St. Regis Beijing, following the completion of a comprehensive, seven and a half-month, $27 million renovation and restoration of its 258 guest rooms, including 102 luxuriously appointed suites, signature restaurants and public spaces. The St. Regis Beijing also features Danieli's, one of Beijing's finest Italian restaurants, a luxurious natural spring water SPA, more than 13,114 square feet of meeting and event space and the iconic St.

1. 瑞吉花园
   St. Regis Garden
2. 饭店外观(白天)
   Hotel Exterior (Daylight)

Regis Butler Service. For more than a decade, the award-winning St. Regis Beijing has offered global travelers an unrivaled dimension of luxury, sophistication and bespoke service at the heart of China's bustling capital city.

"We are delighted with the newly renovated St. Regis Beijing. The Hotel's exceptional service, luxurious interiors and sheer beauty make it a perfect fit within the St. Regis brand, beautifully complementing a portfolio which includes The St. Regis Singapore and The St. Regis Shanghai, with several others under development in Bali, Bangkok, Jakarta, Lhasa, Kuala Lumpur and Osaka." said Mr. Miguel Ko, President for Starwood Hotels & Resorts, Asia Pacific.

Designed by New York-based Alexandra Champalimaud & Associates, the renovated property combines European style with distinct Chinese design influences to create a unique, luxurious and modern space. The lobby is both inviting and elegant, featuring hand-painted ceilings, pure silk embroidery and custom-made rosewood and lemonwood furnishings. Respecting the heritage of the orient, the water features of the Hotel's newly landscaped gardens are visually integrated into the design for the renovated Garden Lounge and Garden Court restaurant. One of the most compelling new features of the Hotel's redesign is the Garden Court's cantilevered natural stone patio, which extends out over a pool of water.

In addition to Garden Lounge and Garden Court, the Hotel's line-up of distinguished dining establishments includes Danieli's, voted "Beijing's Finest Italian Restaurant," Astor Grill, Wine Lounge and Celestial Court, offering authentic cuisine from Southern China. The legendary St. Regis Bloody Mary and an enticing array of teas and signature cocktails are served daily in Garden Lounge, where guests can enjoy live entertainment throughout the evening. The Press Club Bar offers a lively, private club-style ambience reminiscent of a bygone era.

As part of the renovation, The St. Regis Beijing features 19 additional lavishly appointed St. Regis suites, bringing the total number of suites to 102, or 40 percent of its total room count. Overlooking the property's tranquil gardens, the upgraded guest rooms and suites feature

1. 景苑咖啡厅
   Garden Court
2. 天宝阁中餐厅
   Celestial Court
3. 记者俱乐部酒吧
   Press Club Bar
4. 葡萄酒廊
   Wine Lounge

extraordinary furnishing including cherry wood armoires, Chinese silk upholstery, fine European tableware, flat-panel LCD televisions and spacious work desks. In addition, WiFi service is available to all guests, throughout the Hotel.

The St. Regis Beijing houses, The St. Regis Spa & Club, the first natural spring water Spa in the city of Beijing. Since it opened in September of 2001, this urban sanctuary has featured exceptional services in a calm and exclusive setting. Drawing natural hot spring water from nearly 1, 500 feet below the earth's surface, this 21,480 square-foot facility provides guests with the ultimate Spa experience. In its 10 revitalizing treatment rooms, professionally trained therapists deliver various styles of European, Western and Oriental massages, as well as traditional Spa therapy treatments.

More than 13,114 square feet of meeting and event facilities are available at The St. Regis Beijing, named as one of the best choices for meeting planners in the capital city. Accommodating virtually any type of meeting, conference or social event, the hotel offers a variety of meeting rooms equipped with the latest technology offerings. In addition, the Hotel's elaborate gardens provide a unique and seductive setting for private functions.

The St. Regis Beijing features the famed hallmarks of the St. Regis brand including bespoke guest experiences and the iconic St. Regis Butler Service at one of the world's best addresses. Trained in the English tradition, St. Regis butlers provide ever-present, yet unobtrusive service while anticipating guest needs and customizing each guest's stay according to his or her specific tastes and preferences.

As the brand's first hotel in Asia Pacific, The St. Regis Beijing has enjoyed a proud legacy of accommodating Beijing's most prominent guests ever since its debut in October of 1997. In its distinguished 12-year history, The St. Regis Beijing has received extraordinary and consistent recognition from a wide array of prominent global lifestyle and travel publications, including Condé Nast Traveler, Travel & Leisure, Elite Traveler and Institutional Investor.

1. 至尊厅
   Grand Hall Ballroom
2. 艾斯特扒房
   Astor Grill
3、4. 艾斯特扒房露天平台
   Astor Grill's Terrace
5. 雪茄吧
   Cigar Lounge
6. 景苑咖啡厅包间
   Garden Court (Private Room)

1. 丹尼艾丽意大利餐厅
   Danieli's
2. 景苑咖啡厅
   Garden Court
3. 游泳池
   Swimming Pool
4. 天然温泉中心
   St. Regis Spa

1. 总统套房
   Presidential Suite
2. 中国套房
   China Suite
3. 政要套房
   Statesman Suite

4. 大使套房
   Ambassador Suite
5. 瑞吉套房
   St. Regis Suite
6. 外交豪华间
   Diplomat Deluxe

屡获殊荣的北京金融街丽思卡尔顿酒店现在俨然已成为首都北京金融中心的地标式建筑,酒店的现代设计与轻钢玻璃及铬合金结构外观完美融合,内部高贵典雅极具东方风情。距离首都国际机场和天安门分别为35分钟和10分钟车程。地理位置方便商旅及休闲度假客人通往繁荣的长安街和故宫等众多著名的历史文化古迹。酒店拥有253间配置卓越的客房,环境舒适,高科技便利设施一应俱全。酒店拥有3间别具特色的餐厅及大堂酒廊和酒吧,提供中式、意大利及全日美食。1,500平方米设施完善的SPA及健身中心,为客人提供非凡卓越的服务。此外,多间宽敞的会议室及可灵活划分为3间宴会厅的大宴会厅造就与众不同的会务场所。

酒店浓郁的现代设计风格,从餐厅、公共区域到客房,在沿用奢华典雅的同时,更对中国博大精深的传统文化精神进行了完美的提炼和诠释,处处绽放出高雅而内敛的气度。地下游泳池巧妙置入大荧幕,全天播放经典黑白影片营造出独特而优雅的氛围。253间豪华客房均以50平方米起,堪称北京豪华酒店中客房面积之最,客房环境舒适且配置卓越,无线上网等便利的高科技设施应有尽有。客厅和浴室均配有超薄液晶电视,通体落地窗户达到了最佳室内采光效果,套房内别具特色的独立浴盆以及皮质印花衣帽间都为酒店客房融入了无限的巧妙心思。别具一格的细节设计还包括带有"舒适"文字的床上用品;放置于客

房入口处的琉璃雕塑——蝙蝠、骏马、鸳鸯,及富有神秘色彩的"辟邪",——蕴含着美好的寓意和对客人无限的吉祥祝福。

拥有100多年历史的知名奢华酒店品牌丽思卡尔顿,在北京金融街延续着其在奢华酒店服务领域的声望和传统,为宾客提供最完善的个人服务及设施。酒店开业三年来获奖无数,近期又获得了著名的美国《私家地理》杂志"2010世界最佳酒店"称号,连续两年中国地区排名第一,以及《康德纳斯旅行者》杂志"2010旅游金榜——最佳酒店"称号,连续两年在中国北京地区排名第一,其中2009年以酒店客房评比满分成绩被授予"最佳客房"称号,更是中国地区唯一一家获此殊荣的酒店。

The Ritz-Carlton Beijing, Financial Street is a focal point of the rapidly developing Financial Street located 35 minutes from the airport and 10 minutes from the Tian'an men Square. Business and leisure travelers have easy access to Chang'an Avenue as well as the renowned Forbidden City and various cultural landmarks. The Hotel's 253 guest rooms are well appointed with luxury amenities and technological conveniences. Dining facilities include a lounge and bar, three signature restaurants, serving Chinese, Italian and all-day cuisines. A 1,500 square-meter full-scale lifestyle SPA with an extensive health club are featured, alongside

1. 中庭
Porte Cochere
2. 金阁中餐厅
Qi Restaurant
3. 四季汇餐厅
Greenfish Restaurant
4. 热诚欢迎
Warm Welcome

spacious function rooms and a ballroom divisible into three salons. The Hotel is stylish and contemporary throughout paying close attention to architectural excellence with oriental and Chinese accents in its design in all restaurants, public areas and guest rooms-it even offers an indoor swimming pool with a large screen showing black and white movies. The guest rooms are luxuriously inviting featuring all the contemporary amenities you would expect such as wireless access, flat screen TVs (including in the bathrooms), floor-to-ceiling windows, and some features you might not expect such as a free-standing bathtub in every suite and leather-lined wardrobes styled as luggage trunks. Clever design touches abound: the Chinese character for "comfort" is embroidered on the crisp white duvets; and each room's entryway is decorated with Liu Li crafted glass animal sculptures—bats, horses, ducks, and the mythical Bixies—to ensure good Feng Shui for the occupant. Starting from 50 square meters in size, they are the most spacious rooms in Beijing's luxury hotel tier.

The Ritz-Carlton Beijing, Financial Street was awarded 2010 Gold List in *Condé Nast Traveler* (U.S.A.), ranked No. 1 in Beijing for consecutive 2 years. And the Hotel was awarded 2010 World's Best Awards named World's Best Hotels in *TRAVEL+LEISURE* (U.S.A), ranked No. 1 in China for consecutive 2 years.

1. 北京金融街丽思卡尔顿酒店夜景
   Exterior / Night
2. 北京金融街丽思卡尔顿酒店日景
   Exterior / Day

1. 意味轩 意大利餐厅
   Cepe Restaurant
2. 金阁中餐厅
   Qi Chinese Restaurant
3. 丽思卡尔顿俱乐部/行政酒廊
   The Ritz-Carlton Club
4. 大宴会厅
   The Ritz-Carlton Ballroom

1. 大堂局部
   Lobby Part
2、5. 天坛厅
   Temple of Heaven
3. 董事会议室
   Boardroom
4. 茶艺
   Tea Art
6. 长廊
   Chang Lang

1. 水疗中心——游泳池
   Swimming Pool
2. 卡尔顿套房
   The Ritz-Carlton Suite
3. 水晶吧
   Crystal Bar
4. 下午茶
   Afternoon Tea
5. 丽思卡尔顿套房——浴室
   The Ritz-Carlton Suite Bathroom
6. 丽思卡尔顿套房——卧室
   The Ritz-Carlton Suite Bedroom
7. 丽思卡尔顿俱乐部——阅读区
   The Ritz-Carlton Club Reading Area
8. 浴室
   Bathroom

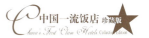

1. 行政套房卧室
   Executive Suite Bedroom
2. 行政套房
   Executive Suite
3. 豪华浴缸
   Executive Bath Tub
4、5. 豪华间
   Deluxe Room

THE WESTIN
BEIJING FINANCIAL STREET
北京金融街威斯汀大酒店

北京金融街威斯汀大酒店位于首都北京的中心地带，全新的酒店和公寓建筑，为入住这里的客人提供了宽敞的会议空间，花样繁多的世界级美食，威斯汀特有的待客礼仪带给人们焕发活力的感受。北京金融街威斯汀大酒店距离首都机场40分钟车程，从酒店出发可以直接抵达北京的商业、娱乐和购物区。离酒店不远就是北京的标志性建筑——故宫和天安门。整个酒店由两座26层的高楼组成：一座拥有486间客房，另外一座拥有205间不同规格的公寓。

为了向客人提供灵活的个性化服务，北京金融街威斯汀大酒店的大堂设计装饰采用了浅米色格调，大堂里光线明亮，并播放着轻松的背景音乐。来到威斯汀的每一位客人，都能享受到全新的服务和款待。这些项目包括威斯汀天梦之床、威斯汀健身计划、威斯汀儿童乐园和威斯汀感官欢迎礼仪。喜欢社交的客人可以参加"轻松时刻"活动：这是威斯汀推出的一个入夜仪式，客人们可以从视觉和听觉上尽情感受北京。

酒店荣幸地推出了中国第一家威斯汀天梦水疗，其融合了水疗和中国古代的养生治疗。这里是繁华都市中超凡脱俗的圣洁之地，为客人提供一系列的治疗和护理，帮助人们摆脱疲劳，重新找回身心的平衡、得到充分的休息，获得健康。

威斯汀公寓设施完备，有1～3间不同规格的卧室，适合长期居住。每间公寓都配备了最具时代气息的家具、功能完备的厨房、现代化的电器、家庭娱乐系统和LCD平板电视，客人还可以享受酒店免费提供的高速互联网服务。

北京金融街威斯汀大酒店拥有7家特色餐厅，提供丰富的国际化美食，金城阁供应备受喜爱的广东菜，意大利餐厅提供具有地方家乡风味的意式食物。喜欢餐后甜点的客人可以来美食甜品店，这里供应丰富多样的特色蛋糕、松饼、馅饼和手工制作的巧克力。

准备举行会议的朋友，酒店为他们提供了1,686平方米的会议和宴会空间，可以满足各种活动的需要。酒店在设计时保持了最大的灵活性，宴会厅可以分成3个区域。此外，酒店还有7个配备了现代化视听设备的会议室。会议和宴会层设有一个专业的会议组织方休息室和商务中心，客人可以在这里免费享受酒店提供的无线高速互联网接入服务。

Located in the heart of Beijing, The Westin Beijing Financial Street can offer ample meeting space, an array of world-class cuisine options and West0in's signature amenities designed to elicit personal renewal.

Just 40 minutes from the airport, The Westin Beijing, Financial Street provides direct access to Beijing's business, entertainment and shopping district and close proximity to cultural landmarks such as The Forbidden City and Tian'anmen Square. The hotel boasts two 26-floor towers: one housing 486 hotel rooms and suites and the other featuring 205 one, two

1. 酒店外景
   Area Surrounding of the Hotel
2. 酒店外景
   Day Facade
3. 酒店正门
   Entrance

and three-bedroom residences.

In addition to providing instinctive, personalized service, The Westin Beijing Financial Street enhances the guest experience with soothing touches, including a subtle earth tone decoration, mood music, and ambient lighting in the lobby. Available to both hotel guests and residents, Westin's renowned services and amenities include the Westin Heavenly Bed®, Westin WORKOUT® Powered by Westin, Westin Kids Club®, and Westin's signature sensory welcome. Guests seeking an opportunity to socialize will appreciate Unwind: a Westin evening ritual featuring the tastes, sights and sounds of Beijing.

The Hotel is proud to introduce China's first Westin Heavenly SPA®, fusing modern hydrotherapy with ancient Chinese-inspired treatments. This sophisticated urban sanctuary offers a series of therapies and treatments designed to cast off fatigue, while encouraging balance, repose and wellness.

The Westin Executive Residences are fully equipped apartments, offering a combination of one, two and three bedroom floor plans tailored for longer-term stays. Each apartment is outfitted with contemporary furnishings, fully equipped kitchens, state-of-the-art appliances, home entertainment system, LCD flat screen televisions and complimentary high speed Internet access.

The seven distinctive restaurants at The Westin Beijing Financial Street provide a rich array of international cuisine, including authentic Cantonese dishes at Jewel and regional home-style Italian fare at Prego. Those in search of a fulfilling dessert can visit Treats, which offers an extensive range of signature cakes, pastries, pies and handmade chocolates.

For meeting planners, the hotel offers more than 18,000 square feet of meeting and banquet space to suit every occasion. For greater flexibility, the ballroom can be divided into three areas and an additional seven meeting rooms are all equipped with state-of-the-art audio-visual facilities. This dedicated meeting and banquet floor includes a specialized meeting planners lounge and business center, and complimentary wireless high speed Internet access.

1. 酒店外观
   Exterior
2. 大堂酒廊
   Plush Lobby Lounge

1. 春厅
   Spring Room
2. 聚宝厅
   Treasury Ballroom
3. 味餐厅
   Senses
4、5. Prego意大利餐厅
   Prego
6. 金城阁中餐厅
   Jewel

1、5.会议厅
　　Meeting Room
2.聚宝厅
　　Treasury Ballroom-Classroom Set Up
3.酒店公寓——餐厅及厨房区域
　　Residences Kitchen and Dining
4.味餐厅贵宾厅
　　Senses Private Dining Room
6.味餐厅
　　Senses

1. 威斯汀儿童俱乐部
   Westin Kids Club
2. 威斯汀健身中心
   Westin Fitness Center
3. 美思悦兹
   Daily Treats
4. Zen露天花园
   Zen Garden
5. 按摩池
   Jacuzzi

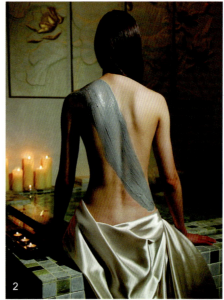

1. 天梦水疗大堂局部
   Part of Heavenly SPA Lounge
2. 天梦水疗——芳香去角质
   Heavenly SPA-Scrub
3. 威斯汀豪华套房
   Westin Deluxe Room
4. 总统套客厅
   Presidential Suite Living Room
5. 威斯汀行政套房
   Executive Suite
6. 威斯汀公寓起居室
   Residences Living Room
7. 威斯汀活力客房
   Renewal Room

85

屡获奖项的北京金融街洲际酒店以其高贵时尚的风格、宽大舒适的客房、优越的位置、名享京城的餐厅，以及卓越细致的服务著称，曾接待世界各国名人和政界要人，备受行家推崇。

酒店位于北京市中心，紧邻西二环，交通便利。周边金融机构、国家政务部门林立。距故宫、天安门广场、王府井商业街以及大型购物中心仅几分钟的车程，到达连卡佛和金融街四季购物中心只需步行几分钟，并方便到达颐和园、白塔寺、雍和宫等著名的历史文化古迹。

酒店拥有318套客房及套房，均配备无绳电话和高速无线上网设备。超大客房面积达45～50平方米，配合雅致的设计以及兼具当代和传统东方特色的装饰，时尚舒适，专为商旅客人设计，令您的居住体验心旷神怡。

酒店的就餐环境时尚优雅，为商旅客人及本地消费者带来国际化的就餐体验："巨扒房"餐厅及酒吧，专供澳洲200天谷物饲养的安格斯牛肉。"季候风"，气氛轻松友好，情调现代时尚。汇聚国际美食，满足不同需要。每周日的早午餐已闻名京城，各类海鲜及香槟令人大快朵颐；新派港式粤菜餐厅"采蝶轩"，拥有360度敞开式厨房，可以现场欣赏厨师的精湛厨艺。

专业的会议服务团队以及影音设备支持团队，专为高端会议而设计，精心

为您打造成功会议和创意宴会。大宴会厅——西安厅（面积384平方米，层高5.7米），可容纳200人的宴会、320人的鸡尾酒会，可分隔为两个独立空间，用于研讨等不同形式的会议，是理想的商务会议场所。5个多功能厅全部位于酒店的五层，面积为30~84平方米不等，所有会议室均可高速无线上网。位于酒店六层的露天平台，可以俯瞰金融街，是露天晚餐或是鸡尾酒会的理想场所。

客人可以随时到24小时开放的康体中心健身，独特的建筑构造会带给客人一份独特的舒适感受。健身中心位于屋顶18层透明空间，这是一个通透的中庭，可直接将自然阳光采集进来，犹如在户外呼吸清新空气，令心情豁然开朗；客人也可以畅游于室内的温水游泳池，或躺在池边沐浴阳光；还可以尝试一下特色的水疗按摩，缓解疲劳，放松神经，享受I·SPA带给您的神奇感受。

北京金融街洲际酒店荣获了如下奖项：

2008年度 Condé Nast 旅行者 世界最美好的居住地之一金榜。

《私家地理》杂志 2009年"中国百佳酒店"。

2008年度北京金融街洲际酒店被《品味生活》评为服务最佳酒店。

北京金融街洲际酒店被绿色环球授予2009年铜奖企业。

2008年度"巨"扒房和季候风西餐厅被《娱乐世界》餐饮指南评选为最佳餐厅。

2009年度巨扒房餐厅及酒吧被《玩家旅游》评为十佳餐厅。

2008年度季候风西餐厅周日早午餐被《城市周末》评为当地最佳早午餐。

2009年度季候风西餐厅自助餐被《城市周末》评为当地最佳自助餐。

1.酒店外景
  Hotel Exterior
2.酒店大堂
  Lobby

InterContinental Beijing Financial Street is situated at the gateway of Beijing's prestigious financial and business district. A magnificent 18-storey atrium, contemporary design and traditional Chinese art set it apart, as does the ideal location. Just minutes away are Tian'anmen Square, Wangfujing Shopping area; the Central Government Administration area and International shopping centres such as Lane Crawford and Seasons Place are just a short stroll away. It's also easy for leisure guests to reach famous historic heritage sites such as the Summer Place, the White Pagoda, the Forbidden City and Lama Temple etc.

The Hotel features 318 spacious guest rooms and suites, decorated in an elegant contemporary style with a touch of oriental accent. All of our guest rooms are quipped with cordless telephone and high-speed broadband Internet access, the dimension of superior room is from 45 to 50 square meters. All are designed with the needs of business and leisure travellers in mind.

The Hotel is proud to provide 5-star dining experiences for guest and international celebrities that frequent the vibrant dining venues. The Hotel's signature restaurant is the Steak Exchange Restaurant & Bar, renowned as a heaven for meat lovers. While ZEN is one of Hong Kong's most awarded culinary experience, a take on contemporary Cantonese cuisine. A view overlooking the bustling city makes Monsoon the ideal modern café for dining with friends and family over open show kitchen.

A prestigious hotel, the IntherContinental

1. 行政楼层
   Club Lounge
2. 中式婚宴
   Chinese Wedding
3. 大宴会厅——西安厅——西式宴会
   Grand Ballroom-Xi'an Hall-Western Style Banguet Setup

Beijing Financial Street provides professional convention service and a AV supporting team for hosting high-level meetings and upscale private events. Offering a Grand Ballroom – Xi'an Ballroom(384 sqm, height 5.7 m) for banquet of 200 persons or cocktail party of 320 persons. It can be divided into two separate sections for breakout meetings or other events. The Xi'an Ballroom and five additional meeting rooms from 30 sqm to 84 sqm on the 5th floor are all equipped with wireless internet access. An al fresco terrace on the 6th floor overlooking the bustling Financial Street is an ideal place for unique event too.

Designed to keep the modern business and leisure travellers in shape, the health centre offers a broad range of cardio-vascular and weight machines around the clock. Our indoor heated swimming pool is adjacent to the sun terrace — a great place to practice tai-chi or yoga. Discover what makes the I·SPA a unique, comforting urban SPA in Beijing, indulge in a wide range of refreshing pampering, and healing therapies from the professional treatments that we offer.

InterContinental Beijing Financial Street is awarded by the followings:

Condé Nast Traveler 2008 Gold List, one of world's best place to stay.

One of the China's Top Hotels 2008 awarded by *Travel+Leisure*.

The Hotel that best defines excellent services 2009 by *Lifestyle*.

Bronze 2009 Company certified by *Green Globe*.

Steak Exchange Restaurant & Bar , The best restaurant in 2008 by *Beijing Tattler*.

Steak Exchange Restaurant & Bar, The Top 10 best restaurant 2009 by *Gootrip*.

Monsoon , the best brunch in 2008 by *City Weekend*.

Monsoon, the best buffet in 2009 by *City Weekend*.

1. 时尚的中式婚宴装饰
   Stylish Decoration of Chinese Wedding
2. 季候风餐厅周末早午餐的香槟
   Brunch Champagne at Monsoon
3. 特色中餐
   Chinese Cuisine
4. 季候风餐厅现场手工制作的新鲜寿司
   Freshly Hand-made Sushi at Monsoon
5. 西式婚宴
   Western Style Wedding
6. 巨扒房餐厅及酒吧的厨师在开敞式厨房里用天然木炭扒制的安格斯牛肉
   Chef at Steak Exchange Restaurant & Bar Grill Angus Beef at the Open Kitchen
7. 采蝶轩中餐厅的360度开敞式厨房
   360 Degree Open Kitchen at ZEN
8. 婚礼蛋糕
   Traditional Wedding Cake
9. 澳洲200天谷饲安格斯牛肉
   Australian Angus Beef

1. 季候风餐厅的海鲜自助
   Unlimited Seafood Buffet at Monsoon
2. 巨扒房餐厅及酒吧的侍者殷勤有礼
   Courteous Service at Steak Exchange Restaurant & Bar
3. 中餐厅采蝶轩
   ZEN
4. 亲切的服务
   Friendly Service
5. 采蝶轩的私密包间
   Cosy Private Room at ZEN
6. 行政楼层酒廊的会议室
   Private Meeting Room of Club Lounge

1. 水晶厅——董事会议
   Crystal Room—Board Meeting
2. 大宴会厅——西安厅——教室型会议
   Grand Ballroom—Xi'an Hall—
   Classroom Setup
3. 室内游泳池
   Indoor Pool
4. 明亮宽敞的健身中心
   Gym

1

2

1. 洲际水疗
   I·SPA
2. 经典洲际香薰草本热石疗
   Signature InterContinental Aroma Herbal Hot Stone Treatment
3. 宽大舒适的客房
   Comfortable Room
4. 豪华双人间
   Deluxe Twin
5. 贴心的服务
   Tedious Services
6. 送餐服务
   Room Service

北京丽晶酒店将现代时尚与古典优雅风格完美结合，拥有500间豪华客房，由房地产开发公司——香港富华国际集团投资兴建，并委托全球知名酒店管理集团、卡尔森全球酒店集团亚太区管理。

豪华客房，几尽极致的现代舒适感，先进一流的设施，亲切的好客之道以及细致入微的服务共同缔造出北京丽晶酒店无与伦比的旅居体验。丽晶酒店位于繁华的王府井商业区，只需几分钟即可步行至商业中心区、购物区以及著名旅游景点。北京特色的"胡同"民居建筑交织其中，乘坐人工三轮车或信步于古代与现代建筑林立的北京街道，即使是短暂居停，也能深切感受当地的风土人情。

500间宽敞的客房集时尚与传统的设计风格为一体。所有房间均提供免费宽带高速上网，等离子电视及DVD播放机。套房玻璃窗安装新型安全防爆膜，使居住更加舒适安全。一些房间可以全景观看到紫禁城的壮丽雄姿。

5间不同风格的餐厅提供世界各地精品美食。酒吧和扒房——风格经典优雅，空间布局私密，错落有致。以众多的特色扒类美食以及琳琅满目的上乘法国香槟佳酿为特色。迪卡博——这间处处洋溢浪漫亚平宁风情的意大利餐厅是精品餐饮的首选。咖啡厅——简约而时尚的咖啡厅，全天候提供西式和亚洲美食

零点以及丰盛的自助餐。丽晶轩——萃聚粤菜精华的丽晶轩设有一个就餐大厅和10间贵宾包房，装饰以传统中式为主，手工雕刻的拱门、古色古香的家具，散发着紫檀的淡淡幽香，营造出儒雅别致的氛围。花园酒廊——格调气派的花园酒廊位于酒店的大堂，提供香醇咖啡、沁脾茗茶以及晚间鸡尾酒等饮品。

北京丽晶酒店的会议及宴会设施一应俱全，625平方米的无柱大宴会厅和8间不同规格的多功能厅适宜举办各种规模的宴会会议。在每个会议场所都装配了独特先进的新型照明控制系统，可以根据需求任意调节灯光。

北京丽晶酒店配备了各种娱乐项目为宾客提供增值服务。13间独立的水疗护理间，提供按摩和理疗服务。宾客在清幽芬芳的氛围中，化解所有的压力。设备精良的健身中心和室内泳池为您提供尽情畅游的极致空间。徜徉在酒店内的高档品牌精品店，也是不错的休闲购物体验。

1. 丽晶酒店大堂和花园酒廊
   Full View of Hotel Lobby & Crescent Lounge
2、3. 丽晶酒店夜景
   Night View of the Regent Beijing

The Regent Beijing Hotel is subordinate to Hong Kong Fu Wah International and is entrusted to Asia-Pacific Region of American Carlson Hotels which globally ranks among the top 10 hotel management groups. It has 500 luxurious guest rooms and suits. Top design and advanced facilities perfectly present the essence of elegance and luxury as well as the soul of classicality and modernism, which is the model of ideal integration of modern sumptuousness and Chinese traditional essence.

In the heart of China's dynamic metropolis, The Regent Beijing is an exclusive sanctuary that elegantly interweaves contemporary luxury with the exquisite charm of historic China. Luxurious accommodation, the ultimate in modern comforts, state of the art facilities, gracious hospitality and intuitive service seamlessly come together to create an inspired experience that is distinctly The Regent Beijing. Set comfortably between the sleek modernity of the business district and the ancient Hutongs of traditional China, The Regent Beijing is 45 minutes drive to the Beijing Capital Airport.

Designed in a classic yet contemporary style, the 500 luxurious guest rooms and suites are spacious and boast modern features and stylish amenities. Anti-rupture Glass installation for suites room make your stay more comfortable and safety. Some rooms enjoy panoramic views of the spectacular Forbidden City. The Regent Club Lounge encompasses three top floors with large floor to ceiling glass windows offering natural day lighting and overlooking the Forbidden City. The main floor measures a total area of 630 square meters. The Regent Club Lounge provides exclusive benefits, for the discerning traveler, 24 hour a day, guests staying in the suites enjoy complimentary access while a premium fee is required for guests staying in other room categories.

1. 丽晶花园酒廊
   The Crescent Lounge
2. 热情的迎接——丽晶体验
   Warm Welcome—The Regent Experience
3. 丽晶行政酒廊的美丽日落
   Regent Club Lounge with Beautiful Sunset

Five restaurants with different styles are presented, namely, The Bar & Grill, Daccapo, Café 99, Lijingxuan Chinese Restaurant and Crescent Lounge, which provides guests with worldwide delicate food.

A lavish function room with high ceiling and no pillars, the Ballroom is an excellent venue for meetings or banquets. Eight additional function rooms are available for small to medium sized events. A unique feature of the Ballroom is the state-of-the-art lighting equipment with motorized moving heads and remote-controlled spotlights that allow versatile focus while color changing cove lighting set a variety of moods. Adjoined to it is a balcony style pre-function area that overlooks the garden and water features of the Crescent Lounge.

Guests at the Regent Beijing are also provided with a range of on-site recreation options. For those who wish to pamper themselves, a SPA sanctuary offers 13 private rooms for massage and treatments. A fully-equipped fitness centre including in door swimming pools and a Jacuzzi are ideal for keeping in shape, cooling off and relaxing. A selection of luxury boutique shops, housed in the Hotel, make for excellent browsing. Local entertainment is also abundant. Minutes walk from top attractions such as the Forbidden City and Tian'anmen Square, The Regent Beijing promises easy access to the best diversions in Beijing. Shopping, dining, wining and exploring the curiosities of daily Chinese life are all activities that the Regent boasts excellent access to.

1. 宴会前厅
   The Ballroom Foyer
2. 宴会厅——会议风格
   The Ballroom—Classroom Style
3. 宴会厅——宴会风格
   The Ballroom—Banquet Style
4. 宴会厅——婚宴风格
   The Ballroom—Wedding Style

1. 99咖啡厅自助餐
   Café 99-Buffet
2. 迪卡博意大利餐厅
   Daccapo-Italian Restaurant
3. 热情周到
   Dao of the Regent
4. 酒吧和扒房
   Bar & Grill
5. 感官的满足——丽晶轩中餐厅
   Li Jing Xuan Chinese Restaurant

1. 会议专家确保您每次会议的成功
   Mice Specialist is Dedicated to Ensure the Success of Your Every Event
2. 关注于细节
   Details Speak to Volumns
3. 董事会议室
   Meeting Room—Boardroom
4. 丽晶健身俱乐部
   Health Club
5. 京臣水疗的幽雅走廊
   Corridor of Serenity SPA
6. 纵情享受
   Pamper Yourself
7. 沉浸在舒适的室内游泳池
   Indulge in an Indoor Swimming Pool
8. 瑜伽课程——愉悦身心
   Yoga Class—Refresh Your Mind

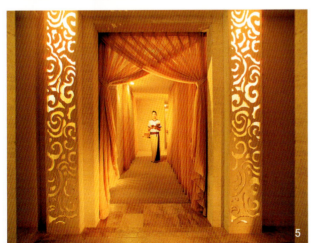

1. 金宝套房——起居室
   Jinbao Suite—Living Room
2. 忙碌一天后，在房间里也可以放松身心
   Relax Your Body in Room after Full Day Business
3. 丽晶豪华间
   Deluxe Room
4. 总统套——起居室
   Presidential Suite—Living Room
5. 丽晶行政间
   Executive Room
6. 丽晶行政套间
   Executive Suite
7. 总统套——餐厅
   Presidential Suite—Dining Room

SOFITEL
LUXURY HOTELS

北京万达索菲特大饭店
WANDA BEIJING

北京唯一的法式奢华白金五星级酒店——北京万达索菲特大饭店，楼高27层，内设417间客房与套房，其中包括63间行政房及一个索菲特会所。酒店潜心将法式奢华风姿与中国华丽韵致完美璧合，为那些在商务或度假旅途中探寻时尚、文化、艺术与舒适感的旅行者们提供至尊旅居体验。北京万达索菲特大饭店拥有6家餐厅和酒吧，包括：Le Pré Lenôtre法餐厅、VIC国际美食餐厅、老上海中餐厅、笼屋八兵卫日本餐厅、法国风情的M吧及Vous大堂吧。北京万达索菲特大饭店的10个会议厅集中在一层楼面上（七层），高贵宽敞的大宴会厅面积达1,368平方米，可以分隔成3个独立会议厅，每个房间都装配了顶尖高科技设备，可谓是北京最好的多功能场地之一。酒店五层整层楼面的休闲健身设施，包括28米恒温泳池、健康中心以及健身房。LeSpa水疗中心将传统地道的华韵美容之道与前卫时尚的法式护肤理念完美结合，启用中国草本植物为宾客提供美容疗程，使其领略身心的双重愉悦。北京万达索菲特大饭店地处交通便利的北京商业核心区，可轻松到达中国国际展览中心及故宫、天安门广场等主要名胜古迹。另外通过机场高速公路，只需30分钟即可抵达首都国际机场。

北京万达索菲特大饭店斥巨资全力打造符合中国市场需求的白金五星级酒

店，在其室内设计中加入了别具一格的设计元素，以颠覆传统与时尚的分界，力求在都市的喧嚣中完美呈现雍容的法兰西风情，使得奢华风格瑰丽上演、尊贵异彩与浪漫风情完美绽放。酒店内，巨幅大唐盛世图与法式摩登风格元素邂逅，营造出优雅高贵的独特情怀；而位于大堂的3朵精致典雅的施华洛世奇手工艺术牡丹花将中西文化共同演绎，怒放盛世之情。

北京万达索菲特大饭店的所有客房及浴室内都安装有内嵌式LCD电视，行政客房更是配备了独一无二的自动玻璃隔断，将浴室与客厅分隔开，宾客只需轻按电钮，采用了前沿科技的玻璃隔断就立即会由透明变为不透明，让宾客尽享属于自己的私密时光。

每间客房还配备免费的无线互联网、舒适的工作台及由下至上开启式保险箱，同时宾客们还能享受到全方位的商务服务。

北京万达索菲特大饭店的另一点睛之笔是与法国传奇式美食品牌Lenôtre合作创造而成的Le Pré Lenôtre法餐厅，在米其林三星级餐厅Le Pré Catelan的灵感冲击下，Le Pré Lenôtre将独特的巴黎餐饮格调带到了北京。餐厅充布法国时尚气息，纯正的法式葡萄酒更使客人们平添对餐厅的喜爱与眷恋；而当家主厨以其精湛的法式烹饪手法及个性的时尚烹饪理念，为客人奉上一道道佳肴美味。凭借着独特时尚的烹饪手法，加之对各色季节性美食元素的巧妙运用，Le Pré Lenôtre为宾客提供了无与伦比的法国美食体验。

北京万达索菲特大饭店将10个会议厅集中在一层楼面上，供各个会议团体选用。酒店沿用索菲特著名的"灵感会议"理念，为宾客量身策划不同会议方式，以满足每位宾客的不同需求，其高贵宽敞的大宴会厅面积1,368平方米，可以分隔成3个独立房间，每个房间都装配了顶尖高科技设备，可谓是北京最好的多功能场地之一。

1. 北京万达索菲特大饭店外景
   Exterior of Sofitel Wanda Beijing
2. 大堂
   Lobby

1、2. 大堂
Lobby

Sofitel Wanda Beijing brings French-style luxury to the heart of Beijing Accor launched a new era of luxury hotels in China on August 19, 2007 with the official opening of Sofitel Wanda Beijing. The 27-storey Sofitel Wanda Beijing has 417 guest rooms and suites, including 63 Luxury Room Club Sofitel and a dedicated Club lounge. The Sofitel Wanda Beijing boasts Le Pré Lenôtre French Gastronomic restaurant, VIC (Voyage of International Cuisine) interactive restaurant, Vous Lobby Lounge, Old Shang Hai (Chinese cuisine), Kagoya Hachibay (Japanese BBQ), and the M Bar cocktail lounge and night venue. Meetings, conference and incentive groups can choose from a total of 10 rooms all conveniently located on the same floor. A full floor of leisure facilities is available to guests, with a 28-metre swimming pool, health club, gym and LeSpa. The Hotel enjoys easy access to the China International Exhibition Centre, the city subway, major tourist attractions such as the Forbidden City and Tian'anmen Square, and shopping malls. It is only 30 minutes via airport expressway to Beijing Capital International Airport. All the luxury rooms within 38 – 46 sqm., offer Sofitel MyBed, motorized curtains, separate shower and bath, fine collection of luxury amenities, LCD TV of 20" in the bathroom and 37" in the bedroom, free WiFi & high speed Internet, safe, leather covered desk with an adjustable executive chair and mini-bar. The rooms are rich in colors with exquisite decoration and elegant ambiance of French touch. Located on the top four floors (23rd to 27th), 38 – 46 sqm. Club Lounge on 26th floor providing a sanctuary of unparalleled luxury and personalized service for the travelers. Luxury Room Club Sofitel offers Sofitel MyBed, DVD player, LCD TV of 20" in the bathroom and 37" in the bedroom, a radio clock with CD player, safe, glass top desk with an adjustable executive chair, mini-bar and luxury bathroom amenities. A special feature in our Luxury Room Club Sofitel, which separate the bathroom and bedroom and can change from clear to frosted instantly, providing a feeling of spaciousness while also offering privacy at

the flick of a switch.

Suites at Sofitel Wanda Beijing are separated into Junior Suite, Prestige Suite, Opera Suite and Imperial Suite, all with scenic view of the city skyline, are chic havens, combining the best of modern living with distinctive, traditional Chinese touches. Designer lighting and modern amenities fuse with elegant antique vases, enchanting paintings and literature to create a warm, yet stylish environment to relax and unwind. The ultra-modern bathrooms feature oversized vanity basins, a separate bathtub silhouetted by a LCD TV screen, a glass-encased shower, and floor-to-ceiling mirrors. State-of-the-art conveniences include high-speed Internet access LCD TV of 20" in the bathroom and 37" in the bedroom and Bose sound systems. Located on top level (27th floor), the 800 sqm. The Imperial Suite provides the ultimate luxury and glamour. The suite boasts a living room, a library, a dining room, a terrace, a master bedroom and second bedroom both of which feature the unique Sofitel Mybed and a complete kitchen for in-suite entertaining. Indulge in one of the spacious bathrooms with sauna, steam room, Jacuzzi and 20" LCD TVs along with a collection of luxury bathroom amenities. Comfort is pushed to excellence with walk-in closet and make-up table, 24-hour butler service and access to Club Lounge, mini-bar with complementary soft drinks. The lounge and bedrooms feature the latest technology in TVs and multimedia facilities along with free WiFi and Internet.

1. Le Pré Lenôtre 法餐厅
Le Pré Lenôtre French Restaurant
2. VIC 自助餐厅
VIC—Voyage International Cuisine
3. M吧（酒吧）
M Bar
4. Vous 大堂吧
Vous Lobby Lounge

1. 大堂吧"大堂盛世"
Vous Lobby Lounge
'TANG DYNASTY OPULENCE'
2. 索菲特行政会所
Club Lounge
3. 贵宾室
VIP Room
4. 大宴会厅
Grand Ballroom
5. 会议室
Meeting Room

1、2、3.LeSpa 水疗中心
　　LeSpa
4.游泳池
　Swimming Pool
5.健身房
　Gym

1. 剧艺房
   Opera Suite
2. 行政楼层豪华房
   Luxury Room Club Sofitel
3. 总统套起居室
   Imperial Suite Living Room
4. 索菲特总统套浴室
   Imperial Suite Bathroom
5. 施华洛世奇牡丹花
   Swarovski Peony Flowers
6. 总统套餐厅
   Imperial Suite Dining Room

北京王府井希尔顿酒店拥有255间客房，其中包括58间套房，是希尔顿酒店家族中一个独具风格的新增成员。酒店地处北京闻名遐迩的繁华闹市区王府井大街，占尽城市商业及文化中心的绝佳位置，整体设计风格时尚别致，为客人提供"贴心"的舒适服务体验。酒店由Wilson & Associates建筑事务所设计，该公司在国际上广受赞誉并屡获殊荣。

北京王府井希尔顿酒店内部设计时尚别致，其灵感源自毗邻的紫禁城古建筑群。酒店大堂和前台处处彰显"宾至如归"的主题，温馨的壁炉让客人顿生融融暖意，烘托出酒店热情欢迎四海宾朋的待客之道。

酒店内设有4家风格各异的餐厅和酒廊，并在细节处洋溢着浓厚的艺术气息。每一个餐厅都独具风格和特色，精美别致的风味、独一无二的美馔佳肴、品种丰富的菜单选择，皆体现酒店愿景，即提升美食体验，为京城的美食家增添更多乐趣。

北京王府井希尔顿酒店的餐厅包括万斯阁澳门餐厅和秦唐中餐厅。万斯阁澳门餐厅是北京唯一一家主打澳门菜系的餐厅，而秦唐中餐厅则是一家有着绚烂夺目的剧院式装潢的中餐美食馆，其菜单新颖别致，将中国各地菜系的精品美馔与现代烹饪技术完美地合二为一。秦唐中餐厅特邀一位驻店茶师为客人讲解茶道的历史和特色。

北京王府井希尔顿酒店的豪华标准间风格鲜明且功能齐全。舒适宽敞的客房采用开放式布局，客房面积则为京城之最，最小面积亦有50平方米。此外，其现代化设施堪与城中各豪华套房媲美。

另外，客房内均配备时尚且现代的固件设施和深色实木家具，融合了顶级通讯系统和高级娱乐设备，例如iPod®家庭迷你音乐站和42英寸液晶电视。北京王府井希尔顿酒店还是唯一一家在北京引入了希尔顿VGA插入式电缆的酒店，可将室内电视机连接至客人的笔记本电脑。客人只需将电缆插入自己的笔记本电脑，即可将电视屏幕分割，这样一来，在欣赏电视节目的同时，还能查收邮件或进行互联网冲浪、观看私人电影，甚至连接数码相机查看照片。

明亮宽敞的豪华套房面积最小的也有92平方米，是客人放松的全新理想住所。行政层客房配备有宽大的行政办公桌、符合人体工程学要求的座椅、配有语音信箱服务的双线电话机、数据接口，以及一条单独数据线，可供连接传真/打印/复印一体机，通信极其便利。行政层的客人可以享用行政酒廊的服务与设施，包括私人安全进入权限和专业礼宾团队提供的服务，协助客人登记入住和结账退房、打包和整理行李，以及其他各种旅行服务等。行政酒廊全天候免费提供食物和饮料。在此凭窗而望，更可一览紫禁城的瑰丽风景，美不胜收。

说到顶级舒适，宽达257平方米的楼顶套房堪称现代居室的典范。这里不是家却胜似家，宽敞的空间是工作和休闲的最佳场所；套房被合理地分为4个舒适的区域：宽敞的卧室和休息区、设计典雅的起居室、款待朋友和商务伙伴的厨房区，还有精心设置在起居室和厨房区之间的书房，客人可以在工作和休息之间轻松转换。房内高尖端技术、点播娱乐设施，以及迷人的北京城景，为客人营造奢华的极致享受和无限的自由空间。

北京王府井希尔顿酒店的SPA水疗中心共设9间私人疗养室，提供一系列令人神清气爽的疗法，这些理疗均依照中国传统的疗养秘方精心设计，并融合丰富的本土

1. 酒店正门外观
Exterior
2. 大堂
Lobby

天然物质精华。除了理疗服务,SPA水疗中心还建有一个豪华玻璃穹顶控温户外游泳池,一座休闲露台,以及一个静谧的花园,美轮美奂。

对于喜欢运动的客人,酒店设有24小时营业的健身中心,配备有综合Precor®健身器材,包括LifeStride脚踏车、Lifecycle健身器、Stairmasters台阶器、多功能有氧健身器和一系列自由重量器械等。

在北京王府井希尔顿酒店,每间会议室都安装了落地窗,自然光线充足,一览北京城的美丽风光。会议室配备有最尖端的技术,无线网络、有线电视、保证手机在使用高峰期也能正常使用的内置手机中继器天线,应有尽有。另外,酒店还有一支经过认证的专业会议服务团队,随时都可以协助会议策划者为与会各方筹备难忘的会议或活动。我们深知即便是所有的会议代表均已到场,酒店的服务也仍未结束,因此,酒店在会议室近旁设置了一个24小时开放的商务中心,提供最新的技术和秘书支持服务。

Hilton Beijing Wangfujing has 255 guest rooms, including 58 suites and is a unique addition to the Hilton Worldwide portfolio of brands in Asia. Located in the heart of Wangfujing, Beijing's prominent commercial and social district, the Hotel is designed to be a chic, intimate, lifestyle sanctuary designed by internationally acclaimed and award winning Singaporean based architectural firm Wilson & Associates. Hilton Beijing Wangfujing's chic interiors were inspired by the traditional architecture of the nearby Forbidden City. The lobby and reception areas communicate the intimate lifestyle theme incorporating cozy fireplaces that provide a warm and inviting backdrop to the Hotel. The artistic touches are also reflected in the Hotel's dining experience with four dramatically styled restaurants and lounges. Each restaurant concept delivers distinctive cuisine accentuating exceptional flavours, unique produce and varied menus, reflective of the Hotel's desire of raising local culinary standards and bringing a new level of excitement to the

1. 大堂吧
   Lobby Lounge
2. 酒店外观
   Exterior

1. 大堂吧
   Lobby Lounge
2. 书阁
   The Library
3、4. 万斯阁澳门餐厅
   Vasco's Restaurant
5. 秦唐中餐厅
   Chynna Restaurant

Beijing dining scene. The restaurants include Vasco's, one of the few Macanese restaurants in Beijing. Another of the restaurants is Chynna, offering regional Chinese classics combined with modern cooking techniques and will have a resident Tea Master, who will introduce diners to the history and natural wonders of tea.

The Hotel's deluxe guest rooms combine style and function and are amongst the largest in the city, starting at a comfortable 50 square metres and featuring sophisticated technology.

The guest rooms incorporate highly sophisticated in-room entertainment such as iPod® docking stations and 42 inch flat screen plasma televisions and DVD players. In addition the Hilton Beijing Wangfujing is pleased to be the only hotel in Beijing to offer Hilton's VGA plug-in cable that connects the in-room TV and the guest's laptop. By simply plugging — in their own laptop — the television screen can be split so that guests can watch TV while checking e-mail or researching on the Internet, watching their own movies or even pluging-in their digital cameras and previewing photos.

The bright and airy deluxe suites are sized from 92 square metres and offer a whole new way to recharge. The Executive Level rooms feature generously scaled executive desks, ergonomic desk chairs, two-line phones with voicemail, data ports and a separate line for a combination fax/printer/copier for ease of communication. Executive Level guests may enjoy the services and facilities of the executive lounge including private secured access, a dedicated concierge team that will assist with check-in and check-out, packing, unpacking and other travel services. The executive lounge also offers complimentary food and beverage throughout the day and sweeping views of the Forbidden City.

The penthouse suite, at a generous 257 square meters, is a testament of modern sophistication. This glamorous home away from home offers the ultimate spacious retreat for work and play and is conveniently divided into four comfort

zones including a spacious bedroom and relaxation area, a tastefully designed living room, a kitchen area for entertaining friends or business partners and a study nook that is strategically positioned between the living room and the dining room so guests can easily transition between work and play. Highly sophisticated in room technology, bespoke entertainment facilities and stunning views of the city add to the sense of indulgence and privacy.

The SPA at Hilton Beijing Wangfujing offers a wide range of inspiring treatments which have been carefully designed to honour local traditions in healing and incorporate indigenous natural elements are offered in 9 private treatment rooms. In addition to treatments, the SPA also offers a stunning glass-enclosed, temperature controlled swimming pool, relaxation deck and a serenity garden has been added to further enhance the wellness experience.

For active travelers the hotel offers a comprehensive 24 hour fitness centre by Precor featuring LifeStride, treadmills, Lifecycles, Stairmasters, Cross Aerobic Trainers and a selection of free weights.

At Hilton Beijing Wangfujing all the meeting rooms are enhanced by floor to ceiling windows offering generous natural lighting and inspiring views of the city. The meeting rooms feature the most sophisticated technology, from wireless Internet access to cable television in meeting rooms and an in-building cellular repeater antenna to ensure uninterrupted service in periods of high business usage.

A team of certified Conference Services professionals are on hand to work in partnership with meeting planners to create truly memorable events. Recognising that the world does not come to a halt while delegates are on site, a dedicated 24 hour business centre, fully equipped with the latest technology and secretarial support is located within close proximately of the meeting rooms.

1. 焰吧
   Flames
2. 万斯阁包房
   Vasco's Private Dining Room
3. 书阁
   The Library
4. 美酒河酒窖
   Vintage Bank
5. 秦唐包房
   Chynna Private Dining Room
6. 万斯阁早餐
   Vasco's Breakfast

1. 宴会厅
   Banquet Room
2. 四合多功能厅
   Courtyard Meeting Room
3. 行政酒廊
   Executive Lounge
4. 商务中心
   Business Center
5. 会议室
   Meeting Room

1. 游泳池
   Swimming Pool
2. 健身中心
   Fitness Center
3、4、5. 紫禁城总统套房
   Presidential Suite

1、2、3.豪华套房
Deluxe Suite

4.生活套房
Lifestyle Suite Twin

5.风格套房洗浴间
Lifestyle Suite Bathroom

6.豪华房
Deluxe Room

7.行政豪华房
Deluxe Room

　　北京希尔顿酒店地处东三环北路，周边环绕使馆及商务地区，距离首都机场只有20分钟车程，无论到主要旅游景点还是到奥运场馆都非常方便。酒店拥有503间精致的客房，更推出创意独特的多元餐饮娱乐设施，囊括风格餐厅、时尚酒吧、品味大堂，以及配备最先进、最具现代化会议服务设施的会议中心与宴会厅。无论是上班前的外带咖啡、下午的商务聚会、傍晚的闲聊小酌，还是周末的午夜狂欢，北京希尔顿都会给您带来全新完美的体验！

　　世界著名室内设计公司Hirsch Bedner & Associates以最大限度地利用空间为核心理念，为所有在此下榻的客人打造温馨舒适的感觉。暖色调木制墙板与石头及豪华的丝绒布料等充满自然情趣的材料交汇使用，使客人下榻北京希尔顿酒店可以感到"在外如在家"。而商务需求也是整体设计中不可或缺的一部分。房间内配有宽带连接，双线路电话、留言系统、硕大的办公写字台和设计科学的靠背椅，确保客人能够随时有效地处理商务事宜。酒店还设有非吸烟楼层及为行动不便的客人所单独设计的房间，处处体现了对客人的关心与体贴。

　　酒店二十层及以上楼层的房间为酒店的商务楼层客房。这里所有的房间均提供私人办公系统，备有传真机、复印机、扫描仪、打印机等设备，浴室内置

电视。此外,客人还可免费使用二十二层的商务酒廊,那里内设一个开放式的小型厨房,整日为客人免费提供精致的茶点。可变换的座位安排可以灵活应对各种场合和人数的需要,是商务楼层的客人们进行工作和休息的理想场所。

作为主楼的延伸,新行政楼为九层的圆形建筑,提供126间高档次的行政客房及套间。全新的行政客房及套房面积为41～165平方米不等,在九层更有精心打造的高级行政套房及一个总统套房。

所有行政楼的客人均可使用行政酒廊。独特剧场设计风格的行政酒廊内拥有现场烹饪台,客人可在周围环绕的座椅上随意享用正餐或小食。自然光线透过7层的天井洒满行政酒廊,把整座行政酒廊装饰得舒适、宁静。高靠背沙发和坐椅设计采用温暖的大地色,同时木质地板视觉上又营造了现代家居的气氛。除了行政酒廊之外,客人们还能够在行政楼与主楼相接大堂内的咖啡基诺里享受健康美味的咖啡及零点。

新北京希尔顿酒店的独特之处还体现在饮食"一处多品味"的理念上。依照这一新颖的创意,本地和世界美食、创新鸡尾酒以及现场表演在此融会贯通:元素阁提供亚洲美味佳肴,东方路一号提供现代全美食品,汤尼酒廊和咖啡基诺全天提供精致饮品及小吃,这里的闲适气氛令客人倍感放松。颐达吧,是北京最具时尚色彩的酒吧之一,位于酒店二层及三层环廊。在这里,您可以享受其中并感受到我们员工提供的贴心服务。

"希尔顿会议"能够满足各种中等规模的会议需要。此项服务旨在提供最先进的设计和最新模式的室内技术,以一支敬业且富有经验的专业团队队伍和一个具专业水准的商务中心作为后台支持。除4个名仕轩和1个空间充足的运筹室,我们还为高规格的会议以及特殊的社交活动倾心准备了里程宫。

行政楼内配有额外的5个多功能室,面积为30～120平方米不等,均提供灵活的空间及先进的会议设施。不得不提的

1. 大堂
   Lobby
2. 酒店外观
   Exterior

是，行政楼内拥有京城第一家圆形的宴会厅，称为天元宫，能够举办500人的鸡尾酒式活动。天元宫共计640平方米，设计优雅，其顶灯设计的灵感来自于牡丹花的形状，豪华的隔声墙壁更加增强了隔声效果。此外，行政楼的客人们还能够免费使用具有上网等商务功能的私人会议空间。

Strategically situated along the East Third Ring Road, a stroll away from the diplomatic and business districts, a 20 minutes drive from the Beijing Capital International Airport, and with easy access to major tourist attractions and Olympic sites, Hilton Beijing offers 503 superbly crafted guest rooms and suites, an innovative multi-outlet dining and entertainment experience, and the most high-powered meeting facilities in town.

Leading hotel interior specialist Hirsch Bedner & Associates maximized the use of space in the newly renovated rooms, crafting guest rooms and suites to convey a sense of blissful comfort. Natural elements of warm wood paneling, stone and plush fabrics in soft and earthy tones create a stylish, yet tranquil, home-away-from-home, fully equipped with the latest technology and amenities for comfort and convenience. High-speed Internet, two-line telephone set, voice-mail messaging system and work space with a large desk and an ergonomically-designed chair ensure that guests can efficiently conduct business at all times. Dedicated non-smoking floors and rooms specially equipped for movement-impaired guests cater to all requirements.

The upper floors of the main hotel building have

1. 行政楼内景
   Executive Tower Interior
2. 行政酒廊
   Executive Lounge

added amenities for more productive work and playful rest. These Business Floor rooms offer personal home office system that combines fax, copier, scanner and printer, along with Bose entertainment system and bathroom inset TV. For added comfort, guests have access to the Business Lounge on the 22nd floor. This contemporary lounge features a kitchenette for all day coffee, tea and soft drinks and an eclectic mix of seating suitable for meetings or simply lounging around.

Adjoining the main hotel building, the newly opened Executive Tower includes an additional 126 Executive rooms and suites spread over nine floors. Tasteful and refined, the new rooms and suites range in size from 41-square-meters to 165-square-meters, offering a number of specialty suites including deluxe 9th floor Executive Junior Suites, as well as the luxurious Chairman's Suite.

All Executive Tower guests have access to the stylish new Executive Lounge, with theatre-style steeped seating around an opulent Food Theatre designed with live cooking stations dishing up exquisite meals and snacks. Flooded with natural light thanks to a seven-story atrium and skylight, the Lounge is an oasis of comfort and serenity. Plush, high-backed sofas and armchairs feature warm, earthy colours and designs, whilst wooden floorboards create a modern, homey environment. Aside from the lounge, guests can also pick up light, healthy snacks in Caffé Cino–a contemporary cafe relocated to the Executive Tower lobby from the main hotel tower.

The unique character of the property is reflected in the Hotel's innovative all-in-one spot for the best in local and international food, creative cocktails, and live entertainment. It encompasses Elements, for authentic and tasty Asian dining fare, One East for sophisticated, modern all-American cuisine, Tonic Lounge and Caffè Cino for all-day quality drinks in a relaxed ambiance, one of Beijing's hippest night spots, Zeta Bar, and the Galleria for creative

1. 天元宫
   Infinity Ballroom
2. 里程宫
   Signature Ballroom
3. 元素阁
   Elements
4. 东方路一号
   One East

art exhibitions and informal events. Hilton Beijing provides all this and more, under one roof.

The Hotel can also accommodate virtually all types of medium-sized meetings with its dedicated "Hilton Meetings" floor. This service has been designed to provide the most up-to-date facilities and the latest in-room technology backed with a dedicated and experienced team and the support of a professional business center. In addition to four Vision Rooms and a spacious boardroom, the Strategy Room, the Signature Ballroom is a focal point for high-end meetings and conferences, as well as exclusive social events.

The new Executive Tower features an additional five multi-purpose function rooms, ranging in size from 30-square-metres to 120-square-metres, offering flexible space arrangements and state-of-the-art facilities. With space for a 500-person cocktail reception, the Tower is also home to Beijing's first round ballroom. The dramatic, 640-square-meter Infinity Ballroom boasts an elegant interior with a moveable stage, stunning peony-inspired ceiling chandeliers, mirrored pillars, and plush, padded walls to ensure exceptional acoustics. In addition, Executive Tower guests will have exclusive complimentary access to the Planning Room-a business lounge and private meeting room with Internet facilities.

Commenting on the newly renovated and fully refurbished Hilton Beijing, Michael Nagel, General Manager said, "Our hotel captures the new spirit of Beijing-vibrant, visionary, inspiring and on the move. It is setting new standards for innovative dining and entertainment, luxury accommodation, high-powered meetings and state-of-the-art amenities. At the same time, it enthralls with service that is attentive and from the heart to make the stay of each and every guest a moving and memorable experience".

1. 天元宫细部
   Infinity Ballroom Detail
2. 行政酒廊
   Executive Lounge Food Theater
3. 天元宫围廊
   Infinity Ballroom Foyer
4. 咖啡基诺
   Caffe Cino
5. 颐达吧
   Zeta Bar
6. 里程宫
   Signature Ballroom

1. 商务中心
   Business Centre
2. 名仕合轩
   Vision Room 2 & 3
3. 天元宫
   Infinity Ballroom
4. 会议室门厅
   Meeting Room Foyer
5. 名仕七轩
   Vision Room 7

1. 健身中心
   Health Club
2. 行政豪华间
   Executive Room
3. 汤尼酒廊
   Tonic Lounge
4. 皇家套房
   Imperial Suite
5. 总统套房——起居室
   Chairman's Suite—Living Room
6. 小套间
   Junior Suite
7. 高级豪华间
   Twin Deluxe Room
8. 行政小套间
   Executive Junior Suite
9. 超豪华套房
   Premier Suite

北京喜来登长城饭店，酒店地处中国的文化和商业中心，地理位置绝佳。酒店毗邻北京中央商务区和使馆区，国家农业展览馆和中国国际展览中心也近在咫尺。

入住我们的酒店，您即可方便地前往紫禁城、天安门和著名的丝绸市场购物和游览。酒店距离北京首都国际机场仅20分钟车程。

您可在宽敞的大堂随时享受到酒店员工热情的欢迎。当您在24小时开放的前台办理登记手续时，我们的行李员将为您提供行李帮助。酒店共有827间温馨舒适的客房，每个房间均配有舒适无比的"甜梦之床"（Sweet Sleeper(SM) bed），以及其他各种设施。若想感受进一步的舒适，请前往行政和尊贵楼层，该楼层设有精心布置的贵宾厅并可享用各种优惠套餐。

如果您是因公来北京出差，酒店设有总面积为1,700平方米的集体会议/多功能空间，其中包括1,131平方米的豪华宴会厅（无立柱），可灵活为您提供各项会议服务。无论您是计划举行5人的小型聚会、20人的董事会，还是多达1,000人的大型活动，这里都能够满足您的需求。

我们的酒店设有三间餐厅，每间餐厅的美食和环境均独一无二，它们都是北京最好的餐厅之一。我们的餐厅将为您提供地道的中式、法式和意式菜肴，并且还会全年举行各式各样的季节性促销活动。

敬请您光临北京喜来登长城饭店，并享受我们的热情欢迎和完全便利的入住体验。

我们的员工真诚而热情，并以慷慨的精神和关爱与关心之情对待您的各种需求。您可以感到自得其所。即使远离故乡，您也能够通过我们的招牌空间、设施和服务与对自己重要的各方保持联系。我们的各酒店为大家能够相聚在一起，共同分享各种体验提供了一个社交场所。无论在世界上的哪一个角落，只要是在喜来登，您都会有所归属。

在这里联系世界，这是您心之向往的归属。您心属此。

1. 东花园喷泉
   East Garden Fountain
2、3. 东花园
   East Garden

The Great Wall Sheraton Hotel Beijing, ideally located in the heart of the cultural and commercial center of China. Beijing's central business district and diplomatic district are nearby, as are the Agricultural Exhibition Center and the China International Exhibition Center. It is an ideal base for shopping and exploring the Forbidden City, Tian'anmen Square, and the famed Silk Market. Beijing Capital International Airport is just a 20-minute drive away.

The spacious lobby warmly welcomes you into our hotel. Let our bellmen handle your luggage as you check in at our 24-hour front desk. Warm and cozy, our 827 guest rooms each feature the ultra-comfortable Sheraton Sweet Sleeper Bed and a host of other features. For an additional level of comfort, our Executive and Elite floors include well-appointed lounges and benefit packages.

If business brings you to Beijing, our collective meeting/function space of over 1,700 square meters, including our 1,131-square meter pillar-less Grand Ballroom, provides great versatility. Whether you're planning a five-person gathering, board meeting for 20, or an extravaganza for 1,000, you'll find exactly what you're looking for.

Our hotel is home to three of Beijing's finest restaurants, each unique in flavor and setting. Our restaurants serve authentic Chinese, French, and Italian cuisine with a myriad of seasonal promotions offered continuously throughout the year.

Our well experienced associates are genuine and welcoming, offering a home-away-from home to you and your guests. You don't just stay here. You belong.

1. 甜品
   Dessert
2. 外观
   Hotel Exterior

1

2

1. 贵宾楼层酒廊
   Elite Floor Lounge
2. 丝绸之路意大利咖啡厅
   Silk Road Trattoria
   Italian Restaurant
3. 法餐厅
   French Bistro
4. 二十一层餐厅
   21st Floor Restaurant

1. 行政楼层酒廊
   Executive Floor Lounge
2. 二十一层餐厅厨师长田秋明
   Chef Tian 21st floor Restaurant
3. 意大利果木比萨
   Italian Pizza
4. 意大利面食
   Italian Pasta
5. 室内游泳池
   Indoor Pool
6. 健身房
   Gym

1. 大宴会厅
   Grand Ballroom
2. 豪华间
   Deluxe Room
3. 贵宾楼层套房
   Elite Suite
4. 贵宾楼层豪华间
   Elite Room

作为京城顶级酒店之一的北京香格里拉饭店于1987年8月开业后，以良好的声望，赢得了各方的赞誉，相继接待了众多国家元首及政府要人。

2007年3月，随着饭店新阁的开业，饭店客房与套房总数达670间，室内装饰高雅舒适。另设7家风格迥异的餐厅和酒吧。在大堂酒廊及春榭吧享用各种精美小点和饮料的同时，可以欣赏到拥有池塘和中式亭台的花园美景；在九霄云外酒吧，调酒师精心调制的特色鸡尾酒满足您各种心绪的需要，来自菲律宾的乐队的精彩歌曲演唱带来整晚的好心情；重新装饰后的西村日餐厅具有时尚的氛围，拥有别具特色的寿司台、铁板烧烤台和炉端烧，还有传统榻榻米单间可供选择。香宫中餐厅里来自香港的厨师们可烹制各种地方美食和金牌菜，每日还提供传统粤式午茶；广受欢迎的咖啡Cha，可容纳220人同时就餐，提供多种口味的自助餐，开放式的厨房和现场制作餐台为客人带来无与伦比的用餐体验，更可欣赏到迷人的花园美景；时尚高雅的蓝韵西餐厅，提供独具创新的西式佳肴以及室内首屈一指的波尔多葡萄酒珍藏。

所有客房均配有最现代化的豪华设施，并提供宽带无线上网服务。位于饭店十二层和二十一层的贵宾廊专为穿梭于世界各地的商旅人士提供私有化的个

1. 景阁大堂前台
   Garden Wing Reception
2. 花园长廊
   Garden Lounge Corridor
3. 景阁大堂花坛
   Parterre in Garden Wing Lobby

性服务以及免费早餐、饮料、国际国内报纸等。

私人司机、豪华车接送、专属的接待酒廊、12小时贴身管家使入住新阁的客人享受到无与伦比的尊崇待遇。您可以在堪称中国地区香格里拉饭店中最大的行政酒廊中享用免费早餐、点心和饮料，更可畅饮香槟、红酒。免费使用会议室和电脑及网络设备设施是这里为您提供的又一项优惠。

喜爱健身的客人可以来健身中心，这里有最先进的健身设施、室内游泳池以及桑拿和按摩服务。奢华的「气」水疗中心堪称经典，豪华精致的各式理疗项目精彩纷呈，华丽私密的理疗室化分成各种功能区域，满足不同需求。

优质迅捷的服务才可以满足商务人士的要求。商务中心每天24小时为客人提供秘书、翻译、国际互联网、图文传真和复印服务。

令人印象深刻的大宴会厅，堪称为经典之作，豪华、典雅且具有艺术性。在进入宴会厅的那一瞬间，就被天然大理石的金碧辉煌所包围。熠熠闪烁的枝形水晶吊灯将大宴会厅装饰得如同豪华的大舞台，镜子和大理石的完美搭配装饰，淡化了金色耀眼，显得格外的典雅别致，红葡萄酒色的地毯又增添了东方的色彩。两座大宴会厅都可以根据不同规模的会议灵活地分割为独立的小宴会厅，从小型、中型到大型。

与宴会厅同等豪华的是它的高科技设备，如最先进的音像及电子排版系统。场地外设有3台数码电视，可以播放宴会平面图、座位的安排以及会场内活动的现场直播。电子显示屏位于宴会大堂及多功能厅入口，方便客人展示活动名称、公司标志等。

20余所大小不等、功能齐全的多功能厅配备先进的会议设备设施，更有专业的会议工作人员提供细致入微的服务。

Opened in August 1987, Shangri-La Hotel, Beijing has earned a reputation as one of the finest hotels in Beijing and played host to numerous dignitaries from all over the world. With the opening of the Valley Wing in March 2007, the award-winning Shangri-La Hotel, Beijing has a total of 670 well-appointed guest rooms and 7 exceptional restaurants and bars. A variety of refreshing beverages are served in the Lobby Lounge, Garden Bar and Terrace, offering a stunning view of the landscaped garden, complete with a Koi pond and Chinese pavilions. At the Cloud Nine Bar, there are very distinct Signature Cocktails specially concocted by our bartenders to pamper to your every mood, and our live band will keep you entertained throughout the night with an exotic blend of popular Chinese/English songs. The newly-refurbished Nishimura Japanese restaurant, offers Japanese cuisine in a fun, modern and exciting environment with a sushi bar, teppanyaki, robatayaki and traditional Tatami Rooms. The Shang Palace is the ideal setting for savouring exquisite Cantonese cuisine, by our team of Hong Kong chefs, with signature dishes, regional specialties and daily dim sum lunch. Also, the 220-seat Café Cha offers a stimulating dining experience with a multi-cuisine buffet served at open kitchens and individual food stations, and an unrivalled garden setting. Last but not the least, led by the award-winning chef, Blue Lobster offers creative and inventive cuisine in a modern and chic décor with the most extensive selection of Bordeaux wines.

All guest rooms with modern facilities, luxurious amenities and upgraded with broadband and wireless Internet access. The exclusive Horizon Floors welcome executives to the top floors of the hotel, offering the privileges of complimentary breakfast and beverage at the Lounge, complimentary local and international newspapers and more.

With a chauffeur-driven limousine service, a private driveway and an exclusive check-in lounge, guests of the new Valley Wing enjoy an unparalleled level of service, including

1. 大堂
   Lobby
2. 酒店外景
   Hotel Exterior

1. 大堂酒廊
   Lobby Lounge
2. 酒店员工
   Service Staff
3. 新行政酒廊
   Valley Wing Lounge
4. 景阁豪华阁酒廊
   Horizon Lounge

24-hour butlers and concierge services. Complimentary breakfast, snacks and beverages, including free flowing champagne, wines and canapés, are available all day in the grand Valley Wing Lounge, the largest executive lounge in the Shangri-La Hotels and Resorts group worldwide in China. Guests also have complimentary access to meeting rooms and computers with broadband and wireless Internet connections For the health conscious and fitness-motivated, the hotel's health club offers the latest in exercise equipment, a 25-meter heated indoor swimming pool, relax in the whirlpool, sauna and steam room, or enjoy the convenience of a private outdoor running track. Meanwhile, Shangri-La's exclusive Spa, CHI, brings some of the largest and most luxurious private treatment suites to the city, offering guests their very own "Spa within a Spa." Each of the 11 CHI suites features a changing area and rain shower, in addition to heat treatments, bathing and relaxation spaces.

Business travelers require on the spot, quality service. The Hotel's 24-hour business centre meets the needs of every executive offering complete secretarial, translation, Internet access, facsimile and photocopying services. Impressive may not be enough to describe the Grand Ballrooms, modern, contemporary, artistic and elegant is the best description of the two grand ballrooms. Upon entering, one is immersed in the golden effects of the marble decoration. Glittering chandeliers stirs up the ambience of the Grand Arena. Mirroring the marble lightings and wood paneled walls is the soft golden and burgundy carpet with a touch of oriental. The two ballrooms are divisible into separate rooms to cater for any events up to 2100 guests in total.

For more intimate occasions, a selection of 20 elegant function rooms is available, each with state-of-the-art audio-visual technology, and serviced by an attentive and professional team.

1. 咖啡Cha自助餐厅
   Cafe Cha
2. 西村日餐厅
   Nishimura Japanese Restaurant
3. 香宫中餐厅
   Shang Palace Chinese Restaurant
4. 春榭吧
   Garden Bar & Terrace
5. 九霄云外吧
   Cloud Nine Bar
6. 蓝韵西餐厅
   Blue Lobster Western Cuisine Restaurant

5

6

1. 新阁大宴会厅
   Valley Wing Grand Ballroom
2. 景阁宴会厅
   Garden Wing Ballroom
3. 婚宴
   Wedding
4. 多功能厅
   Function Room
5. 景阁宴会厅前厅
   Garden Wing Ballroon Foyer

3

4

5

1. 游泳池
   Swimming Pool
2. 健身房
   Gym
3. 景阁豪华阁行政套房
   Garden Wing Horizon Club Executive Room
4. 新阁外交套房
   Valley Wing Diplomat Suite
5. 新阁超豪华客房
   Valley Wing Premier Room
6. 新阁总统套
   Valley Wing Presidential Suite

在北京中关村南大街与北三环交汇处，坐落着一组具有浓郁中国民族特色的建筑群——北京友谊宾馆。这个亚洲最大的园林式宾馆，是1954年在周恩来总理的指示和关怀下，为解决前苏联援华建设专家的生活而建的。北京友谊宾馆毗邻北京大学、清华大学等多所知名学府，与举世闻名的颐和园遥相辉映。这个由中国著名建筑设计大师张镈先生亲自设计的宾馆，1995年荣获国务院发展研究中心颁发的"亚洲最大花园式宾馆"证书，被编入《中华之最大典》。宾馆以其恢宏的规模和浓郁的民族特色被载入英国剑桥大学出版的《世界建筑史册》一书。

北京友谊宾馆是一组极具中国民族特色的大型建筑群，占地面积335,000平方米，建筑面积320,000平方米，其中绿地面积达6万平方米，整个建筑群以贵宾楼和友谊宫为中轴成对称的扇形分布。中轴线两侧有4座大楼，分别是敬宾楼、迎宾楼、怡宾楼及悦宾楼。宾馆四周还有公寓式单元楼50栋，被划分成4个独立的小区，根据其建筑风格，分别被冠名为苏园、乡园、颐园和雅园。

在喧闹的都市中建园造景，除塑造出风景供人欣赏之外，还要创造出舒适的生活环境。只有达到了两个境界和谐统一，艺术才算是完美的，宾馆的园林特色正是这种完美的体现。整个庭院繁花碧树，满植冬青绿草，院内树木和花卉的品种达百余种，

有9,000多棵树木，其中，22棵古树被北京市园林局定为保护树木，还有被称为植物活化石的水杉以及在北方罕见的广玉兰树。在此，春天可赏玉兰、迎春、海棠；秋天可品核桃、柿子、木瓜。

友谊宫前的中心广场是宾馆庭院建设中的点睛之笔。广场绿地面积达4,000多平方米，草坪、松树、假山、奇石、锦鸡、飞鸽构成了一幅优美的图画。中国园林艺术讲究有山、有水，山水融合，中心广场内有一个占地400多平方米的旱地喷泉，规模宏大，可喷出几十种不同的造型，在高达5米的水幕映衬下，由松树、奇石组成的假山显得幽静迷人。

4个公寓小区内的园林风格各具特色："苏园"为苏州园林的北京再造；"乡园"是中国北方农家院落的缩影；"雅园"是为居住在宾馆的儿童们修建的游艺乐园；"颐园"则是仿照颐和园的风格及特点建造的。这其中以苏园的建造最为精致，它的设计风格仿苏州著名的"网狮园"，占地约9,000平方米。园林四周以长廊环绕，220米的长廊内有58个漏窗和2个景窗，图案简洁、造型各异。整个园林分为4个景区，每个景区各有主题和特色。在设计上，苏园采用山池花木、雕梁画栋和楼台水榭的有机结合，形成"多方景胜，咫尺山林"的效果。

北京友谊宾馆有多种规格的标准间、中西式豪华套房、公寓式套房、写字间共1,757套。经历7个月的全面装修改造，贵宾楼于2007年9月通过了全国旅游星级饭店评定委员会专家组的验收，成为五星级饭店。贵宾楼为商旅人士而设计，现代、舒适、宽敞、典雅；拥有188套各式客房，分别是豪华标准间、豪华商务间、豪华行政套房、友谊套房以及总统套房；房间的设计风格简洁明快，处处留有民族风格的印记；每个房间都选用了中国当代中青年艺术家赋有视觉冲击力的原创油画作为装饰，为宾客提供精神层面的享受。新建的豪华酒店式公寓——嘉宾楼，一居室至五居室12种户型的公寓共60套，每套面积为62～547平方米不等，配有4部电梯。地下1层，地上8层，一层为大堂。公寓内装修设计意在"淡淡的华夏味，融于浓浓的时尚风"，既传统又现代。

北京友谊宾馆有大小餐厅、宴会厅28

1. 贵宾楼外观
Day Exterior of Building 1

2. 友谊宾馆全景
View of Beijing Friendship Hotel

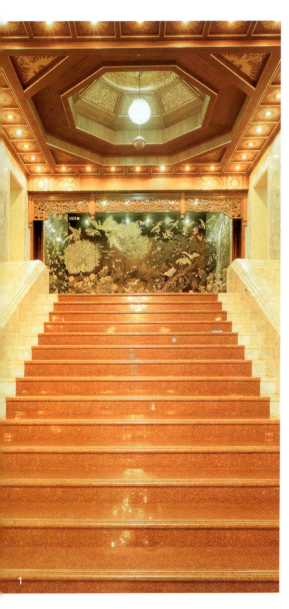

个。中餐菜系以淮扬菜、潮粤菜及川鲁菜为主；西餐以俄、法、英式为主。厨师力量雄厚，有30多名特级中、西餐技师，可同时容纳2,600人就餐，可举办1,000人的大型宴会。友谊宫内的15个宴会厅房，是厅房中的精品，其格调、灯饰、布局设计风格各不相同，厅房内摆放各种艺术品，在用餐的同时，突出文化品位和享受。厅房的装修突出以人为本的原则，在私密性、舒适性上别具特色；餐厅服务打破厨房界限的菜品互通点菜方式，使客人有更加多样化的选择。庭院餐饮是友谊宾馆一大特色，在春、夏、秋之季，在中心广场可举办1,000人的大型露天中西式自助餐；友谊啤酒花园为忙碌一天的现代都市人提供了放松身心、享受自然的场所。

北京友谊宾馆会议设施十分完备，有多种规格的会议室40个。其中有4个多功能厅，1个可容纳500人的阶梯式报告厅及各种会议配套设备。

康体中心拥有齐全的康乐设施，建有室内游泳馆、网球馆、乒乓球室、健身房、台球厅、跳操房。

经历了半个世纪涉外服务的北京友谊宾馆，是中国特色建筑风格与造园艺术完美结合的宾馆。这座拥有完备现代设施的宾馆，在常龙元总经理的带领下，秉承"诚信、务实、奉献、创新"的企业精神，为每一位宾客提供至尊至美的服务！

北京友谊宾馆——都市中的大自然。

With complete modern facilities, this well-equipped hotel has been offering quality service to its guests for more than half a century. The famous national institution sits at the intersection of Zhongguancun Nandajie and the North Third Ring Road. The largest garden-style hotel in Asia, Beijing Friendship Hotel was built for former Soviet Union experts who came to assist and instruct China in cooperation with late Premier Zhou Enlai in 1954. Adjoining China's top two universities of Peking and Tsinghua, the Beijing Friendship Hotel is also only a short distance from the radiant and beautiful Summer Palace. Designed by master architect Zhang Bo, the Hotel was honored by selection for *China's Book of the Biggest and certified* in 1995 as the biggest garden style hotel in Asia by the Development Research Center of the State Council. Recognizing its grand historic character, Cambridge University Press of the United Kingdom included the Hotel in its *History of World Architecture*.

The 335,000 square metres of Beijing Friendship Hotel buildings spans across 320,000 square metres of land that includes 60,000 square metres of green space. The whole complex is in a fan shape, with the Grand Building and Friendship Palace on opposite sides. On either side of the middle stand four large buildings: Building 2, Building 3, Building 4 and Building 5. Four separate compounds with four different styles Suyuan, Xiangyuan, Yiyuan and Yayuan-house

1、2. 贵宾楼大堂
Lobby of Building

1. 金玫瑰西餐厅
   Golden Rose Restaurant
2. 米兰咖啡厅
   Milano Coffee Shop
3. 雅仕厅
   Yashi Restaurant
4. 乔治酒吧
   George Bar
5. 贵宾楼翠竹轩
   Banquet Room in Building 1
6. 嘉宾楼
   Building 8

50 apartments (buildings).

The purpose of creating lavish gardens and gentle landscapes in the bustling city is not only for pure enjoyment but also for a comfortable living environment. Only when both are harmoniously integrated can perfect art be accomplished. The character of our garden is the embodiment of such balanced perfection. The compound is blanketed with flowers and lawns, with more than 9,000 shady trees, of which 22 are old enough to be protected by the Beijing Gardening Bureau. The dawn redwood, a "living plant fossil", and the seldom-seen magnolia can be found here. The magnolias especially attract guests in spring, crab apple and jasmine in winter and in autumn they can taste walnut, persimmon and papaya.

The 4,000-square-metre central garden in front of the Friendship Palace provides a triumphant finishing touch with its pine trees, artificial hills, exotic stones, lawns of golden pheasants and doves.

The four apartment complexes have different garden styles: Suyuan is influenced by Suzhou, the spiritual home of Chinese traditional gardening; Xiangyuan is in the style of a farmer's courtyard in the north; Yayuan is like a playground for children; Yiyuan is modeled after features of the Summer Palace. Of the four, Suyuan is the most exquisite. Covering an area of 13 hectare, its design is modeled after the famous Master of Nets Garden in Suzhou. Surrounded by a 220-metre long corridor, the garden is divided into four scenic sections each with its own special character and features. Suyuan is a perfect combination of hills with ponds, trees and flowers, rich ornamental buildings with waterside pavilions: a unique panorama of scenery and landscaping.

Beijing Friendship Hotel has 1,757 different types of rooms including standard rooms, Chinese and western style suites, apartments and offices. After undergoing seven months' renovation, the Grand Building was rated five stars by the National Evaluation Committee of Ratings for Tourist Hotels in September 2007.

The 188 modern, comfortable and spacious suites are exclusively designed for business people and travelers. There are standard rooms, deluxe executive rooms, deluxe executive suites, friendship suites and presidential suites. The architectural style is simple but lively. Traditional Chinese characteristics can be spotted

everywhere. Each room is decorated with striking oil paintings by young contemporary Chinese artists whose masterpieces provide spiritual sustenance.

Building 8 has newly-built deluxe apartments, 12 types ranging from 1 to 5 rooms, 60 rooms in total varying in size between 62 and 547 square metres. There are four elevators running from the first floor lobby to the eighth floor. The idea of merging Chinese tradition with the latest fashion can be felt immediately by its interior renovation.

The Beijing Friendship Hotel has 28 restaurants and banquet halls of different sizes. As many as 2,600 people can be served at one time. The banquet halls hold up to 1,000. Huaiyang, Cantonese, Sichuan and Shandong dishes are served. Russian, French and British menus are also available. The Hotel employs more than 30 Chinese and western food expert chefs. Each of the 15 private dining rooms of the Friendship Palace is unique in terms of style, lamp ornaments and layout. Different works of art have been placed in each so that guests can dine in a cultured ambience where service, privacy and comfort come first. Guests enjoy a wide range of choice by ordering their favorite food served in different restaurants. Dining in the open air is a unique feature of our service. A Chinese and western style buffet for 1,000 people can be arranged in the open air in spring, summer and autumn. The Friendship Beer Garden is an ideal place for people living in the metropolis to relax and enjoy nature.

There are 40 well-equipped meeting rooms of various sizes, including four multi-functional halls. The symposium hall has a seating capacity of up to 500. The Fitness Center includes an indoor swimming pool, a tennis hall, table-tennis room, fitness room, snooker and aerobics rooms. In short, the Beijing Friendship Hotel is a perfect combination of Chinese architectural flair and gardening artistry.

Headed by general manager Chang Longyuan, the soul of the hotel's management combines faith, dedication and innovation.

At the Beijing Friendship Hotel, relax and savor nature within the bustling metropolis.

1. 友谊宫咖啡厅
   Friendship Palace Coffee Shop
2. 行政层大厅
   Executive Floor
3. 贵宾楼多功能厅
   Ballroom in Building 1
4. 友谊宫聚英厅
   Ballroom in the Friendship Palace

1. 会议室
   Meeting Room
2. 园林
   Garden
3. 网球馆
   Tennis Court
4、5. 健身房
   Fitness Room
6. 游泳池
   Swimming Pool

1. 总统套
 Presidential Suite
2、3、4. 友谊啤酒花园
 Friendship Beer Garden
5、6. 苏园公寓
 Suyuan Apartment
7. 贵宾楼客房
 Guest Room in Building 1
8. 园林
 Garden

坐落于快速发展的北京西城，国宾酒店俨然已成为这一地区新型商务酒店的代表。走进金碧辉煌的酒店大堂，很难想象这里距离举世闻名的天安门广场和故宫仅10分钟之遥。毗邻金融街、国家政府机关、高科技开发区、钓鱼台国宾馆、北京展览馆、北京动物园及购物中心。置身于24K金铂镶嵌的华丽大堂令您享有帝王般的感受。

酒店高16层，拥有502间豪华客房，三层行政楼层及该楼层客人专用的休息室。

所有客房都配有写字台，两部IDD电话及数据插座，快速互联网接口，卫星国际电视频道。无论您下榻在豪华客房，还是富丽堂皇的总统套房，都会感受到真正国际标准的舒适和享受。

宴会及会议设施

国宾酒店高品质的服务还体现在其一流的宴会及会议设施上，多功能厅形式多样，可以承接20～1000人各种类型的会议、鸡尾酒会、大型晚宴、展览展示、主题派对等特别活动。大宴会厅585平方米，配备视频会议设施，多个光纤宽带高速上网接口、同声传译及国际直拨长途电话。

我们可以根据会议者的需求特别定制各类规格的菜单，满足不同客人的需要。

一流的会议设施、舒适的客房和真诚

的服务,都将是国宾带给您的真实体验。

餐饮

尽情享受各式美味,无论是在皇朝玉园品味粤菜,还是在花园咖啡厅体验具有异国口味的自助餐,抑或是在索菲亚餐厅挑选自己可口的意式菜肴,我们的厨师都会令您大快朵颐,满意而归。

休闲和健身

16米×11米的室内游泳池毗邻四层四季屋顶花园,是极佳的休息场所,同时提供完备的健身、康乐设施,如桑拿、漩流浴、蒸汽浴、先进的健身器材和体操房,是摆脱一天工作疲劳的理想去处,还配有游艺室及中医按摩室。

The Presidential Beijing

The Presidential Beijing represents a new breed of business hotel in the fast developing West side of Beijing. As you enter into the magnificent atrium lobby, it is hard to imagine you are situated just 10 minutes from the world famous Tian'anmen Square and the historic forbidden City.

With close and easy access to China's commercial banking institutions, government ministries, high-tech industrial basin, Diao Yu Tai State Guest House, Beijing Exhibition Hall, Beijing Zoo and shopping, this elegant lobby is lavishly decorated with 24 carat gold, and it makes you feel like an emperor yourself.

This 16-story hotel hosts over 502 rooms and suites including 3 Executive Floors with a private Executive Lounge exclusive to our Executive Floors guests.

All rooms in the hotel have an executive desk and are equipped with a 2 line IDD phone, data port, high speed Internet access and satellite international television channels. Whether you are staying in a deluxe room or one of the stately Presidential Suites, you will enjoy all the comforts of a true international hotel.

Banquet & Conference Facilities Setting new standards of service at The Presidential

1. 酒店大堂
   Lobby
2. 四季屋顶花园
   Four Seasons Roof Garden

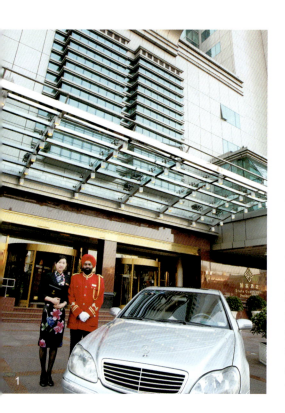

Beijing are our superbly designed conference and meeting facilities. Whether it is a conference for 20 or 1,000 delegates, we have the perfect venue for you. Function rooms are directly accessible from the front of the Hotel and can accommodate any event to suit your needs, meetings, cocktail party, conference, gala dinner or special occasion. There is a full range of state of the art audio visual equipment including simultaneous translation service, high-speed internet access, video conferencing and IDD telephones.

A la Carte menu selections, snacks and personal assistance are all available in packages tailor-made to suit the wishes of you and your delegates.

Conferences, accommodation, genuine service and hospitality, they are all part of The Presidential Beijing experience.

Dining

Eat until your heart is content. Whether it is the wonderful Cantonese cuisine in the Dynasty Jade Garden Restaurant, the great buffet in the Garden Cafe or choosing a magnificent Italian food in the Sophia's Restaurant, our chefs are bound to delight your taste buds.

Relax and Keep Fit

The beautiful 16 metre x 11 metre heated indoor pool is adjacent to the spectacular 4th floor Four Seasons Roof Garden. A wonderful area to relax and unwind, there is also a fully equipped health and recreation center with sauna, jacuzzi, and steam room. With all the latest Life Fitness equipment and exercise room, this is the perfect place to get rid of tension after a long day's hard work. Billiards and Games Room on site and special inhouse Chinese massage is available.

1. 国宾酒店正门
   Main Entrance
2. 阳光大堂
   Magnificent Atrium Lobby

1. 龙吧
   Long Bar
2. 皇帝晚宴
   The Emperor Dinner
3. 豪华宴会
   Luxury Banquet
4. 大宴会厅前门
   Grand Ballroom Foyer

1. 花园咖啡厅
   Garden Café
2. 皇朝玉园中餐厅
   Dynasty Jade Garden
3. 索菲亚意大利餐厅
   Sophia's—For the Italian Moments in Your Life
4. 艺术装饰
   Art Decoration
5. 黄河黄埔厅
   Huang He and Huang Pu River Room

1. 大宴会厅
   Grand Ballroom
2. 多功能厅
   Function Room
3. 游泳池
   Swimming Pool
4. 健身中心
   Health Club

1. 高级豪华间
   Premier Room
2. 商务中心
   Business Center
3. 旋流浴
   Jacuzzi
4. 总统套房
   Presidential Suite
5. 行政酒廊
   Executive Lounge

THE WESTIN
BEIJING CHAOYANG
金茂北京威斯汀大饭店

金茂北京威斯汀大饭店坐落于京城中心商务区，为商务客人和休闲度假客人提供了便利的周边环境。酒店距离北京首都国际机场仅25分钟车程，15分钟步行可达主要商场和酒吧，毗邻北京国际外交和商务社区。作为亮马河地区自20世纪90年代中期发展以来首家新建的五星级国际酒店，金茂北京威斯汀大饭店拥有非常理想、便利的地理位置。

酒店的550间客房拥有朝阳区最宽敞的房间，从最小40平方米的豪华客房至320平方米的套间均提供多项舒缓、休憩的便捷设施，使每位客人都能找到自己喜欢的放松方式。当您离开酒店时，会感到从未有过的活力焕发。金茂北京威斯汀大饭店的所有客房均拥有四项特色设施：天梦之床、热带雨林淋浴、高科技设备和室内休闲中心。

酒店最高的四层是威斯汀行政楼层，所有入住行政楼层的客人均可以使用位于酒店顶层的威斯汀行政俱乐部，享受每日不同的自助餐以及在晚6点至8点间完全免费的软饮和含酒精饮品。这里同时也坐落着320平方米的金茂总统套房。

与酒店为每位客人创造独特的休闲体验的目标一致，金茂北京威斯汀大饭店的8间餐厅和酒吧分别侧重于不同的风味和设计，带给客人焕彩、健康的生活方式。

金茂北京威斯汀大饭店作为京城最便捷、明智的会议场所之选，拥有720平方米的金茂大宴会厅，可招待多至600位宾客，并提供全套婚宴服务。如需较小的活动场地，其他包括朝阳宴会厅在内的小型会议室提供了多样的选择。专业的会议策划专家会全程协调客人的会议，并解决关于技术、餐饮或服务上的所有问题。超出标准的专业创新餐饮理念将为您的活动增色不少，从活力休闲主题茶歇到纯氧呼吸以及巧克力主题茶歇，全面配合您的会议主题量体打造各种活动项目。

金茂北京威斯汀大饭店整个5层楼面积超过2,000平方米，其设计完全体现了"滋养肌体、愉悦精神"的核心理念。整个楼层分为3个部分：威斯汀健身中心、天梦水疗中心和拥有自然光照的25米室内游泳池，另有按摩冲浪池和独立桑拿室。免费毛巾和饮用水服务等细节之处让客人的焕彩体验更加轻松便捷。

1. 酒店外观夜景
   Night View of Hotel Exterior
2. 大堂吧
   Lobby Lounge

1. 外景
   Day View of Hotel Exterior
2. 大堂
   Lobby

The Westin Beijing Chaoyang is located in the very heart of Beijing's Central Business District. This central location offers a convenient retreat for business people and leisure travelers alike. It is a 25-minute drive from Beijing Capital International Airport and a convenient 15-minute walk to the major malls and bar district. Adjacent to the international diplomatic and business community of Beijing, this makes the central presence of the Westin Beijing Chaoyang ideal, appropriate and exciting. The Westin is the latest upper upscale hotel to open in booming Liang Ma He area since the mid-1990s.

The 550-room hotel offers some of the largest guest room size in the Chaoyang District with a minimum guest room size of 40 sqm and up to 320 sqm for suites, all offering reprieve and renewal catered for guests' needs. The rooms are designed with sensitivity to each person's unique path to unwind, to ensure that everyone leaves feeling better than they felt upon arrival. All The Westin Beijing Chaoyang rooms come with four signature features Heavenly Bed®, Rainforest Shower, Technology Support and Refreshment Center. The top four floors of the Hotel are reserved for the Westin Executive Club rooms. These rooms come with full access to the Westin Executive Club located on the top floor of the Hotel. The Westin Executive Club has daily changing buffet and free premium spirits and alcoholic drinks from 6:00—8:00 with an open bar. It also houses the 320 sqm Jinmao Presidential Suite. In keeping with the hotel's goal of ensuring each guest's experience is unique,

1. 金茂大宴会厅晚宴摆台
   Jinmao Ballroom Banquet Setup
2. 金茂大宴会厅剧院式会议摆台
   Jinmao Ballroom Theater Meeting Setup
3. 中国元素餐厅用餐包间
   Zen5es Restaurant Private Dining Room
4. 迷酒廊
   Mix Lounge

revitalizing and relaxing, the Westin Beijing Chaoyang offers eight different restaurants and bars all celebrating different aspects of the philosophy of renewal and wellness lifestyles.

With the easy yet intimate accessibility of its meeting space, The Westin Beijing Chaoyang is positioned to become the city's first choice for meetings and events. The magnificent Jinmao Ballroom, 720 sqm in size, has a capacity of up to 600 seats. There are smaller meeting rooms available too, including the Chaoyang Ballroom. A dedicated Star Meeting Concierge is on hand to assist with any technology or catering support as one-point contact for event organizers. Creative mix of innovative food and beverage concepts make every event stand out from the norm. Off-site catering service is also available.

The entire 5th floor of the Westin Beijing Chaoyang spreads over 2,000 sqm and is devoted for renewing the body and nourishing the soul. The floor has three main zones: Westin Workout, the Heavenly SPA and 25-meter swimming pool with natural daylight, a Jacuzzi and separate saunas. Subtle touches such as complimentary towels and water service make fitness renewal experience hassle free.

1. 朝阳宴会厅中式婚宴
   Chaoyang Ballroom Chinese Wedding
2. 金茂大宴会厅西式婚宴
   Jinmao Ballroom Western Wedding
3. 朝阳宴会厅局部
   Chaoyang Ballroom Wedding Setup
4. 中国元素餐厅
   Zen5es Restaurant
5. 威斯汀行政俱乐部
   Westin Executive Club
6. 威斯汀扒房
   Grange Restaurant

1. 知味自助餐厅
   Seasonal Tastes Restaurant
2. 金茂大宴会厅休息厅
   Jinmao Ballroom Foyer
3. 天梦水疗中心理疗套房
   Heavenly Spa Treatment Room
4. 室内游泳池夜景
   Indoor Swimming Pool
5. 威斯汀健身中心
   Westin WorkOut Center

1. 总统套房客厅
   Presidential Suite Living Room
2. 天梦水疗中心接待台
   Heavenly SPA Reception
3. 行政外交套房
   Diplomatic Suite
4. 豪华客房
   Deluxe Room
5. 焕彩套房
   Renewal Suite
6. 焕彩客房
   Renewal Room
7. 行政外交套房浴室
   Diplomatic Suite Bathroom
8. 董事会议室
   Meeting Boardroom
9. 总统套房卧室
   Presidential Suite Bedroom

图书在版编目（CIP）数据

中国一流饭店（珍藏版）/《中国一流饭店》编委会编．—北京：中国建筑工业出版社，2009
ISBN 978-7-112-11498-6

I．中… II．中… III．饭店－简介－中国－汉、英 IV．F719.2

中国版本图书馆 CIP 数据核字（2009）第 188257 号

策　　划：肖　青　　左启华　　李东禧
整体设计：冯彝诤
责任编辑：陈小力　　吴　绫　　李东禧
责任校对：陈晶晶

中国一流饭店（珍藏版）
《中国一流饭店》编委会 编
*
中国建筑工业出版社出版、发行（北京西郊百万庄）
各地新华书店、建筑书店经销
北京圣彩虹制版印刷技术有限公司
北京方嘉彩色印刷有限责任公司印刷
*
开本：880×1230毫米　1/16　印张：53½　字数：1712 千字
2010年6月第一版　　2010年6月第一次印刷
定价：598.00元（共四册）
ISBN 978-7-112-11498-6
　　　（18736）

版权所有　翻印必究
如有印装质量问题，可寄本社退换
（邮政编码 100037）

中国一流饭店 珍藏版

China's First Class Hotels
Collection Edition

《中国一流饭店》编委会 编
Compiled by the Editorial Board of *China's First Class Hotels*

中国建筑工业出版社
China Architecture & Building Press

II

目录
Content

4 京瑞大厦
KingWing Hotel

16 凯宾斯基饭店
（北京燕莎中心有限公司）
Kempinski Hotel Beijing
Lufthansa Center, China

28 昆仑饭店
Hotel Kunlun, Beijing

40 日坛国际酒店
Ritan International Hotel

52 首都大酒店
Capital Hotel

64 香格里拉北京嘉里中心大酒店
Shangri-La's Kerry Centre
Hotel, Beijing

76 中国大饭店
China World Hotel, Beijing

88 天津喜来登大酒店
Sheraton Tianjin Hotel

100 大连凯宾斯基饭店
Kempinski Hotel Dalian, China

112 东郊宾馆
Dongjiao State Guest Hotel Shanghai

124 古象大酒店
Howard Johnson® Plaza Shanghai

136 花园饭店（上海）
Okura Garden Hotel Shanghai

148 锦江饭店
Jin Jiang Hotel Shanghai

160 浦东香格里拉大酒店
Pudong Shangri-La, Shanghai

168 上海柏悦酒店
Park Hyatt Shanghai

180 上海大酒店
Grand Central Hotel Shanghai

192 上海虹桥迎宾馆
Hong Qiao State Guest Hotel Shanghai

204 上海金茂君悦大酒店
Grand Hyatt Shanghai

京瑞大厦，位于CBD商圈内，紧邻北京东三环路，距国贸中心仅5分钟车程，距北京首都机场30分钟车程；北邻著名的北京古玩城，南接京津塘高速路入口，可方便到达北京经济技术开发区，地理位置优越，交通便利。

酒店拥有标准客房、套房和总统套房等各种房型共341间套，并设有行政楼层和商务酒廊。酒店B座为商住两用公寓，采用国际标准智能化管理，并进行了时尚装修，是您家居、办公的理想选择。

酒店还有总面积为550平方米的阳光大厅，气派辉煌，现代会议设施和场地应有尽有。酒店的餐饮项目有尊贵复古的"瑞府中餐厅"，和恬淡的上海豫园"绿波廊"，还有环境幽雅，品味纯正的"瑞苑咖啡厅"。

绿波廊餐厅以经典上海菜为主，名厨主理，为宾客奉献原汁原味的上海菜肴，京瑞绿波廊餐厅7间装饰豪华的贵宾厅房，配以江南淑女的油画，更显环境幽雅、安静。绿波廊的菜式融合了中、西餐饮食文化，把传统的上海菜衍变为适合现代都市人口味的极品上海菜。"闻香留步名酒楼，知味停车绿波廊"。绿波廊以一流的菜点、一流的服务、良好的企业形象欢迎中外宾客光临。

瑞府中餐厅由二层宽敞舒适的航空

厅、典雅华丽的宴会厅及酒店四层装修新颖的华清宫、文君庭、娥桃苑等豪华经典、各具浓郁中国古典特色的8间厅房组成。可同时容纳400余人就餐！既有红烧海参、鱼翅等名贵出品，又有正宗鲁式海鲜小炒，您可携好友小酌，让您在亲朋聚会时丰俭由人！

位于大厦十六层的行政楼层和商务酒廊，阳光透过别致的木格窗框，照在屋内经典的家具之上，让您在金色余晖中感受温暖悠长的美好时光。

京瑞大厦一层的瑞苑咖啡厅24小时全天候经营中西自助及零点商务套餐。

京瑞大厦三层的京瑞国都温泉会馆环境清净悦目，舒适惬意，让您体验独特的芳香味道，沐浴在来自1,600米下的地下矿物温泉中，聆听天籁的音乐，远离城市的喧嚣，纵情享受温泉的乐趣，让您流连忘返。

Situated in the Central Business District, KingWing Hotel is only 5 minutes from the International Trade Center, 30 minutes away from the Beijing Capital International Airport. Neighboring the most famous Beijing Antique City and the Jingjintang Expressway. It is convenient to the Beijing Economic Development Zone.

Building A owns 341 rooms with various type. It also has the business floor and the executive lounge. With an international standard system, apartment Building B is the ideal choice for your business choice.

On the third floor, the 550 m^2 Sun Shine Hall with modern facilities and equipments

1. 前台接待处
   Reception
2. 金碧辉煌KTV
   Gold & Jade Green KTV

satisfy all different confreres or exhibitions. There is "Raffle Chinese Restaurant" and "Lvbolang Restaurant" which specialized in Shanghai cuisine. Moreover, in Regent Restaurant, the guests can enjoy the most convenient western food style.

Lvbolang is a shanghai tasty restaurant. There are 7 well-decorated VIP rooms, offering first class food and serivce.

Raffle Chinese Restaurant is composed by the comfortable Aviation Hall, elegant Banquet Room and other independent halls on the fourth floor each with unique characteristic. It accommodates 400 people having meal simultaneously. Providing nutritious Chinese famous food and orthodox Shandong dish.

The Business floor and the executive lounge are located on the 16th floor. Over the unique wooden frame, the sunlight is spilling on the classic furniture, you would be pleased by the warm atmosphere.

Harvest cafe is located on the first floor of KingWing Hotel. It offers western food and French style buffet 24 hours all day long.

JingRui Guodu Hotspring Resort is in the quiet and comfortable environment, it is mineral water from 1, 600 meters underground. Experiencing that sounds of nature, you may feel away from the clamor and enjoy yourself so much without any thought of leaving.

1. 大堂
Lobby
2. 酒店外景
Hotel Exterior

1、3.瑞府中餐厅包间
　 Raffle Chinese Restaurant
2、4.阳光大厅
　 Sunshine Hall

1. 行政酒廊
   Executive Lounge
2、3、6、7、8.瑞府中餐厅
   Raffle Chinese Restaurant
4. 绿波廊
   Lvbolang
5. 瑞苑咖啡厅
   Harvest Café

1、2.会议大厅
　Conference Centre
3、4.金碧辉煌KTV
　Gold & Jade Green KTV
5.游泳池
　Swimming Pool

1

2

1、6. 行政酒廊
　　Executive Lounge
2、3、4. 总统套房
　　Presidential Suite
5. 商务套房
　　Commercial Suite
7. 标准间
　　Standard Room
8. 豪华间
　　Luxurious Room

北京凯宾斯基饭店位于使馆商务区内，距离首都机场20分钟车程，拥有526间客房及套房，各种会议、宴会厅设施完备，多种风味国际美食餐厅，包括普拉那啤酒坊。北京燕莎中心是京城设施最齐全的综合性建筑，包括顶级办公楼、全方位服务的公寓、展厅、燕莎友谊商城，以及银行、主要的航空公司办事处、24小时医疗中心、健身俱乐部、幼儿园等。凯宾斯基饭店是燕莎中心的核心组成部分。

Kempinski Hotel Beijing is located in the city's diplomatic/business district. It is a mere 20-minute drive from the Capital Airport. The Hotel, with 526 well-appointed guest rooms and suites, is offering full banqueting/conference facilities and international dining options including the Paulaner Bräuhaus, and is part of the Beijing Lufthansa Center. The Center incorporates offices, apartments, showrooms, YouYi Shopping City, banks, airlines, 24-hour medical centre, health club and kindergarten.

1. 外观 Exterior
2. 花园 Garden

1. 普拉那啤酒坊
   Paulaner Prauhaus
2. 花园
   Garden

1、2. 客来思乐餐厅酒吧
   Kranzler's Restaurant & Bar
3. 意大利威尼斯餐厅
   Trattoria La Gondola
4. 龙苑中餐厅
   Dragon Palace
5. 聚合酒吧
   Rendez-vous Bar & Lounge
6. 凯宾美食廊
   Kempi Deli
7. 意大利威尼斯餐厅
   Trattoria La Gondola

1. 莫扎特厅
   Symphony Room
2. 客来思乐餐厅酒吧
   Kranzler's Restaurant & Bar
3. 龙苑中餐厅
   Dragon Palace
4. 开封厅
   Kaifeng Room

1. 顶层游泳池
   Swimming Pool
2. 都市脉搏健身俱乐部
   Pulse Club
3. 饭店大堂
   Lobby
4. 书报亭
   News Stand

1、3、4.公寓
　　Apartment
2.总统套房
　　Presidential Suite
5.聚合酒吧
　　Rendez-vous Bar & Lounge
6、7.行政楼层酒廊
　　Executive Lounge
8.公共区域
　　Foyer

北京昆仑饭店坐落于风景秀丽的亮马河畔，位于北京CBD中心区，周边有中国国际展览中心毗邻使馆区，据北京首都机场仅20分钟车程。

北京昆仑饭店是由锦江国际酒店管理有限公司管理的五星级豪华饭店，也是首个被授予五星级饭店称号的华人管理的酒店。昆仑饭店被国家旅游局评为"全国50佳星级饭店"，2009年，昆仑饭店荣获《时尚旅游》中文版"读者票选旅游金榜"的北京首选商务酒店，在全国"首选商务酒店"中，昆仑饭店是唯一一家由中国人自己管理的星级饭店。

北京昆仑饭店拥有646间豪华宽敞的客房，是商务或休闲游客的明智选择。

在经过长期的装修改造后，2009年昆仑饭店的住宿、餐饮、康乐设施一应俱全。昆仑饭店将继续保持良好的服务于居停于此的每一位客人。别致而现代化的顶峰俱乐部为行政楼层的客人提供全方位的个性化服务。顶峰俱乐部是昆仑饭店为行政楼层的客人打造的理想第二家园。顶峰俱乐部结合别致的旋转餐厅和酒廊于一身，拥有私人会议室，舒适的入住环境，为行政楼层的客人提供专享的优质服务及特权。行政楼层精致的客房和套房都设有大理石浴室，以及淋浴和盆浴分开的超大盥洗间。顶峰俱乐部的客人可享受专项服务，包括欢迎香槟及24小时贴身管家服务等。

饭店拥有13个豪华餐厅，揽尽天下美食，咖啡厅提供24小时服务。15个中小型宴会厅和可容纳800人的多功能厅，及拥有330个剧场形座位的会议中心，使北京昆仑饭店接待高档宴会和高规格会议的能力在京城居于前列。

1. 昆仑饭店大堂
   Hotel Kunlun Lobby
2. 顶峰俱乐部行政楼层前台
   Summit Club Executive Floor Reception
3. 大堂吧
   Lobby Bar

Located on the banks of the beautiful Liangma River, Hotel Kunlun is ideally situated in northeastern Beijing in the Central Business District, and is only a 20-minute drive from Beijing Capital Airport. The Hotel is located near the China International Exhibition Center, and is short commute to many offices for business travelers, as well as an easy walk to both the 2nd Embassy District and the 3rd Embassy District.

A five star luxury hotel managed by Shanghai's Jin Jiang International Hotel Management Co., Ltd., Hotel Kunlun is the first Chinese-managed hotel to be awarded five-star status. It has been named one of "China's 50 Top Hotels" and in 2009, was selected by National Geographic Traveler as "Best Business Hotel" on their Gold List, making it the only hotel Chinese-managed hotel to be awarded this honor.

Hotel Kunlun boasts 646 guest rooms and suites catering both business travelers and tourists. Each of the Hotel's accommodations, dining, and leisure facilities are newly renovated, and furnished with the needs of the discerning traveler in mind. The luxurious Summit Club is Hotel Kunlun's unique approach to an executive club floor, pampering the most discerning of our guests. The Summit Club combines a chic revolving restaurant and lounge, private meeting spaces, elite accommodations, and most importantly, friendly services, to ensure the comfort and satisfaction of executive guests. Exquisitely appointed rooms and suites include a marble bathroom that features both a separate standing shower as well as a relaxing bathtub; executive floor guests enjoy exclusive benefits including welcome champagne and 24-hour on-call personalized butler services.

Thirteen dining outlets offer cuisines from a plethora of flavors from around the world, and a 24-hour café offers around-the-clock casual dining. More than fifteen small and medium-size banquet rooms, together with a 800 sqm grand banquet hall and a 330-seat conference center with stadium-style seating, all contribute to Hotel Kunlun's exceptional capability for hosting international conferences and large-scale banquets.

1. 顶峰俱乐部前台
   Summit Club Reception
2. 昆仑饭店外景
   Hotel Kunlun Exterior

1. 玉台
   Jade
2. 锦园餐厅
   Jin Yuan Restaurant
3. 和平厅
   Peace Room
4. 溪谷村日本料理
   Keikoku Japanese Restaurant

1. 溪谷村日本料理
   Keikoku Japanese Restaurant
2. 上海风味餐厅
   Shanghai Flavor Restaurant
3. 锦园餐厅
   Jin Yuan Restaurant
4. 顶峰俱乐部会议室
   Summit Club Meeting Room
5. 炫台酒廊
   Mezzanine Lounge
6. 和平厅
   Peace Room

1. 总统套房会议室
   Presidential Suite Meeting Room
2. 中式套房
   Chinese Suite
3. 国际会议中心
   International Conference Center
4. 琅玕厅
   Langgan Room

1. 行政套房
   Executive Suite
2. 行政楼层盥洗室
   Executive Floor Washroom
3. 总统套房客厅
   Presidential Suite Sitting Room
4. 总统套房门厅
   Presidential Suite Foyer
5. 行政豪华房
   Executive Deluxe Room

北京日坛国际酒店是一家按五星级标准建造的商务酒店，坐落于北京东二环繁华的朝外大街与建外大街之间，该区域是北京最具国际化的国贸商圈、建外商圈与朝外商圈的中心。它南临始建于明代1530年的皇家私家园林——日坛公园及第一使馆区；北接朝外商圈和著名的北京工人体育场及三里屯酒吧街；东望CBD中央商务区；西附享誉国际的雅宝路市场。酒店坐拥高贵的皇家人文环境，地理位置优越，交通十分便利。毗邻长安街和东二环，自酒店至天安门广场仅10分钟车程，至北京首都国际机场仅30分钟车程。

酒店设置首层酒店接引大堂、五层酒店接待大堂、六层至十九层客房区。酒店拥有302间/套设施一流、优雅舒适、宽敞明亮的客房，其中有总统套房、商务套房、高级豪华间及277个豪华间。

酒店地中海西餐厅为您提供中西式自助餐，另有品种丰富的零点菜单供您选择。

爱琴海酒廊为您调制中西美酒，另有香醇浓郁的咖啡、精美的中西小点任您选用。

酒店拥有宴会厅、多功能厅、贵宾厅及小厅共计8间，可提供总共1,100平方米的会议场地，容纳8～300人的各种形式的会议宴会。酒店以一流的现代化设施设备，提供精益求精且多元化的会议宴会安排，专业的会议宴会策划与全程跟踪服务，专注每一细节，保证会议宴会的圆满成功。

1. 外景
   Hotel Exterior
2. 接引大堂
   Concierge Hall

位于酒店B1层的健身房为您提供健身服务,内有跑步机、哑铃、多功能健身器等,使您在住店期间得到全方位的锻炼。

另有位于酒店B1层的超大室内游泳池,在此您可以得到全身心的放松。

1. 冷餐会
   Buffet Party
2. 大堂
   Lobby
3. 电梯间
   Elevator
4. 大堂吧
   Lobby Bar

Beijing Ritan International Hotel is a business hotel designed according to five-star standards, is located between Chaowai High Street and Jianwai High Street in east 2nd Ring Road in Beijing. It is the centre of most international of business districts of Guomao, Jianwai and Chaowai. To the south, the Ritan Park — a royal private garden established in 1530 Ming Dynasty and the first embassy area are nearby, Chaowai business district, famous Beijiing Worker Stadium and Sanlitun Bar Street are located to the near north of the Hotel, to the east is Central Business District, and to the west is world well known Yabao Road Market. The Hotel has noble royal humanistic environment and superior geographic position, the traffic is very convenient. It is close to Changan Street and east 2nd Ring Road, only 10-minute drive from Tian'anmen Square and 30 minutes from Beijing Capital International Airport.

There are receiving hall in the first floor, hotel lobby in the fifth floor, guest rooms from the sixth to the nineteenth floor. The Hotel has 302 top-class equipped rooms, elegant and comfortable, bright and spacious, including

Presidential Suite, Business Suite, Super Deluxe and 277 Deluxe rooms.

In the Mediterranean Sea Restaurant, both Chinese and Western style buffet are provided, and there are also various dishes for you to order.

The Aegean Sea bar provides mellow wine, fragrant coffee and exquisite Chinese and Western pastry.

The Hotel has Grand Ballroom, Multi-function Room, VIP Meeting Rooms and meeting rooms, 8 in total. It could provide a conference space with an area of 1,100 square meters, which could hold various conferences and banquets for 8—300 people. The Hotel will provide excellent and diverse conferences and banquets, professional scheme for conferences and banquets, and butler service. We will pay attention to every detail to ensure conferences and banquets completely successful.

Located in B1 floor, gymnasium can provide you fitness service with running machine, dumbbell, multi-function fitness equipment, etc, which can take you all-round exercise.

Located in B1 floor, super indoor swimming pool can relax your whole body and soul.

1. 贵宾厅
   VIP Banquet Room
2、4. 大堂吧（爱琴海酒廊）
   Lobby Bar (Aegean Sea Lounge)
3. 周到的服务
   Service

1

2

1. 地中海西餐厅
   Mediterranean Sea Restaurant
2. 冷餐会
   Buffet Party
3、4、5. 自助晚餐
   Buffet Dinner

1. 宴会厅
   Grand Ballroom
2. 多功能厅（婚宴）
   Multi-functional Room (Wedding)
3. 会议室
   Meeting Room
4. 阳光走廊
   Sunny Corridor
5. 贵宾厅
   VIP Banquet Room
6. 健身房
   Gym
7. 游泳池
   Swimming Pool

1. 高级商务套间
Super Business Suite
2、5. 高级豪华套间
Super Deluxe Suite
3. 豪华间
Deluxe Room
4. 卫生间
Bathroom
6. 高级豪华间
Super Deluxe Room

五星级的首都大酒店是北京最早的高档饭店之一。它坐落于前门、王府井商业风景区内，临近故宫、天坛、景山等著名景点，步行至闻名遐迩的天安门广场仅需10分钟。酒店周边交通四通八达，横贯东西，纵穿南北，车行至北京首都国际机场仅45分钟。优越的地理位置、舒适的居住环境、便捷的城市交通，使之成为来京宾客的旅居首选。

首都大酒店由AB两座楼宇组成，总面积8.5万平方米。改扩建后，店内装修更显豪华气派，更具民族特色。酒店共有各式客房596间，多达10款房型供宾客选择，尤以故宫观景套房最为闻名。房间均配备宽带接口，满足宾客高速上网的需求。商务宾客享有更多个性及特惠服务。

酒店拥有7个特色餐厅，提供港式粤菜、东北、四川风味、意大利、东南亚和日式菜肴。纯正的中、西美食，可满足宾客不同口味需求。咖啡厅提供24小时送餐服务；威哥鲍翅酒楼由中国烹饪大师梁诚威主理，主营鲍翅燕系列和精品港式粤菜；四季厅供应早、午、晚中西自助美食；位于A座顶层的波洛尼亚餐厅是品尝意大利美食和观赏京城美景的绝佳去处；维罗纳酒吧环境休闲、幽雅，富于浪漫气息，是宾客举办酒会、闲叙或进行其他娱乐活动的理想场所。

酒店有16间多功能小宴会厅，可

满足10～20人的宴会需求；锦云宴会厅可容纳400人，可分隔为3个独立厅使用；紫云大宴会厅可容纳800人，配有一流的影音、灯光和同声传译设备，能满足各式大型会议的需求，亦是举办豪华中、西式婚宴的理想场所。祥云接见厅装修豪华，可容纳180人；还有供20～80人使用的中小型会议室7间；聚英阁商务酒廊特设多功能会议室2间，办公通讯设备齐全，方便商旅临时使用。训练有素的宴会服务人员可随时按照您的意愿提供专业和个性化的宴会、会议服务。

酒店装修改造后，康体设施全部更新，装备现代的健身房、室内游泳池、保龄球馆和台球室，随时恭候您光临。忙碌一天的宾客，还可以来到酒店健康俱乐部，由我们的专业护理师为您做保健按摩，彻底放松。喜爱轻歌曼舞或热闹气氛的朋友，可到设备一流、装修豪华的卡拉OK开心尽兴，度过美好难忘的时光。

首都大酒店紧邻北京文化、商业中心，以无与伦比的地理位置、鲜明的民族风格、深厚的文化底蕴和专业的服务水平，熔铸独特魅力。酒店以"用心、亲情、精益、规范"的服务理念和"专业务实、锐意进取"的企业精神致力于酒店建设，把旅途的便利、高品位的设施、优美的环境和精益的服务呈献给四海宾客。用真诚的微笑和周到细致的服务诠释首都风韵、首都品格和首都人的殷勤好客，首都大酒店是五洲宾客的温馨家园。

1. 酒店大堂
   Hotel Lobby
2. 酒店外景
   Hotel Exterior

A landmark on the bustling East Qian Men Street in the heart of Beijing, the five-star Capital Hotel is one of the earliest deluxe properties in Beijing featuring world class facilities and services. The Capital Hotel is a 10-minute walk from Tian'anmen Square and Forbidden City. Nearby are also many other interesting monuments and historical sites including the Temple of Heaven, Great Hall of the People and Museum of Chinese History. Modern in furnishing while traditional in style, the Hotel is an ideal choice for business, leisure and MICE travelers.

The Hotel features 596 well-appointed guest rooms, all Capital Club rooms offer fantastic city views. The best known are Forbidden City View Suites. Besides complimentary use of ADSL, iron & ironing board and other deluxe amenities in room, Club guests can also enjoy many other exclusive benefits.

1. 祥云厅
   Xiang Yun Conference Hall
2. 酒店外景
   Hotel Exterior

7 distinctive restaurants serve a wide variety of Asian and Western food: Sichuan, Italian, Japanese, etc. Coffee House provides 24-hour room service; Vigor Abalone Restaurant specializes in Abalone, Shark's Fin, Bird's Nest and fine Cantonese cuisine. Four Seasons Restaurant supplies buffet breakfast, lunch and dinner; Ristorante Bologna on the 20th floor of Tower A is an award-enjoying restaurant for authentic Italian flavor with panoramic city view; the Verona Bar, with a blend of elegance and comfort, is the ideal place for hearty talk, cocktail and light entertainment.

For business and social functions, there is a choice of 16 private function rooms and 7 small meeting rooms. Jin Yun Ballroom accommodates 400 people, divisible into three halls. Zi Yun Grand Ballroom accommodates 800 people, fully equipped with audio/visual equipment. Luxuriously furnished Xiang Yun Conference Hall accommodates 180 people. The two independent boardrooms inside the Capital Club Lounge are fully set with executive facilities for temporary office work or private meetings. Besides, our meeting and banqueting service team is always at hand to cater to your requirements.

Our Fitness Center & Health Club is perfect for a work-out, tone-up and relaxation. After renovation, the center is further expanded and all facilities are upgraded. Guests may make good use of our fully set-up gym, indoor swimming pool, billiards, bowling alley and outdoor tennis court. Or you may get relaxed and refreshed in Sauna, Steam Bath and massage rooms with professional care and therapies such as body massage, foot reflexology, etc. For those who like singing, dancing or disco, our luxuriously renovated and well-equipped Karaoke Night Club is of course the right place to go and have fun.

1. 锦云厅
   Jin Yun Ballroom
2. 波洛尼亚餐厅
   Ristorante Bologna
3. 小宴会厅
   Private Dinning Room
4. 四季厅
   Four Seasons Restaurant

Capital Hotel welcomes guests both domestic and overseas all year round. Our utmost goal is to create a home for guests with quality facilities, beautiful environment and excellent service. The sincere smiles and attentive service of the Hotel staff always bring you home the gracefulness, kindness and hospitality of the people in the capital city. Capital Hotel, a home away from home for guests all over the world.

1. 威哥鲍翅酒楼
   Vigor Abalone Restaurant
2. 紫云厅婚宴
   Zi Yun Grand Ballroom Wedding
3. 锦云厅婚宴
   Jin Yun Ballroom Wedding
4. 聚英阁商务酒廊
   Capital Club Lounge
5. 维罗纳酒吧
   Verona Bar
6. 雪茄屋
   Cigar Shop

1. 会议室
   Meeting Room
2. 紫云厅
   Zi Yun Grand Ballroom
3. 保龄球馆
   Bowling Alley
4. 游泳池
   Swimming Pool
5. 健身房
   Gym

1. 长和康乐水疗中心
   Changhe SPA
2. 首都套房
   Capital Suite
3. 娱乐会所
   KTV Night Club
4. 故宫观景套房
   Forbidden City View Suite
5. 中式婚房
   Chinese Style Wedding Room
6. 西式婚房
   Western Style Wedding Room
7. B座行政套房
   Executive Suite, Tower B

香格里拉北京嘉里中心大酒店在开业时就以其强烈的现代感打破了五星级饭店给人的固有刻板印象，饭店的前卫设计和所营造的高雅、活泼氛围使之很快脱颖而出，成为北京名副其实的时尚地标。

香格里拉北京嘉里中心大酒店——令人心仪的个性之所，开业以来颇具声望，得到诸多奖励，其中包括：2007年被《私家地理》杂志评为"中国百佳酒店"，2001年6月被《欧洲货币》杂志评选为"北京五家顶级饭店"之一，2003年和2004年连续获得美国优质服务科学协会颁发的"五星钻石奖"等。

饭店位于北京商务中心区，距机场仅30分钟的车程，其极具优势的地理位置使客人轻松来往于首都的商务、购物及旅游观光区－故宫，天安门广场，天坛，雍和宫，日坛公园，红桥市场，秀水街，友谊商店……

作为CBD商圈最活跃的酒店之一，香格里拉北京嘉里中心大酒店一直保持着强有力的竞争优势，从未停止过对卓越的追求，不断打造新鲜事物，为CBD注入着灵感与活力。饭店引以为自豪的"炫酷"酒廊，是京城最有名气与人气的社交之地。炫酷的成功令人信服与羡慕，虽已诞生多年，但至今仍然被许多新开业的酒吧所效仿。2006年，饭店倾力推出的"缤味"咖啡美食屋，每日提

供新鲜烘焙的面包、蛋糕、三明治和纯正意大利咖啡，备受周边外籍人士及讲究品味的北京时尚一族青睐。香格里拉北京嘉里中心大酒店也是北京首批实现客房免费无线上网的酒店之一，目前饭店提供带宽至20MB的高速上网设施，在业内遥遥领先。

饭店的487间客房和套房均设有四管空调、多功能插座、电脑/传真接口、"即插即用"宽带上网系统、根据人体生理结构特点设计的弧形写字桌、独特的浴缸和淋浴分置的浴室等，充满时尚家居的舒适和精巧。

豪华阁行政楼层占据饭店最高的5个楼层，为尊贵的商务客人提供无与伦比的超值奢华服务：24小时管家服务，随心所欲的宽带上网，根据客人要求提供独立号码的扫描/传真/打印机，有收音机和CD播放机及多种CD盘选择、大屏幕液晶电视、西服熨烫、自助早餐、晚间鸡尾酒和精致美点、全天无限量软饮。开放的豪华阁酒廊设有一个会议室和一个宽敞的休闲区域、3个电脑工作台、多至10处的宽带接入点、无线上网设施，为下榻豪华阁的客人提供殷勤的超豪华服务。

店内4间餐厅提供丰富的美食选择，令口味迥异的客人大快朵颐。在咖啡苑，各式东西方零点美馔和每日国际自助餐物超所值，由来自欧洲、印度等世界各地的获奖厨师倾情奉献；海天阁中餐厅提供正宗粤菜和川菜，周末点心自助备受中外客人欢迎；炫酷酒廊——香格里拉北京嘉里中心大酒店旗舰酒吧诠释着饭店的时尚形象，京城外籍人士和本地商界、娱乐精英经常光顾的指标性场所，被众多国际传媒人士评为"彰显个性，引领潮流"之所。

香格里拉北京嘉里中心大酒店的宴会及会议设施具有极高知名度。无论是明星云集的盛大晚宴还是商务会议或世界性大型会议，都选择这里举办。最现代化的会议硬件设施和充满创意的宴会及会议统筹服务团队，保证每次活动的成功举办。二层大宴会厅是北京最大的

1. 大堂
   Lobby
2. 前台
   Reception Desk

1. 嘉里健身楼梯
   Staircase in Kerry Sports
2. 外观
   Exterior View

大宴会厅之一，采用无柱设计，可同时容纳1,500人。位于四层的九龙宴会厅，可举办220人的宴会并与绿色盎然的屋顶花园连接，是举办婚宴的热点场所。此外，11间规格不同的会议室适合20至110人的小型会议或培训。

覆盖3层楼、占地6,000平方米（约64,560方英尺）的嘉里健身是北京最具规模的酒店健身场所，包括一流的健身房、35米长室内游泳池、两片室内网球场、多功能球类运动场（壁球／篮球／排球／羽毛球），235米室外缓跑径和滚轴溜冰场，室内及室外儿童游乐场等，均铺设保护地面，环境优美，绿色掩映。

总部设在香港的香格里拉酒店集团目前拥有香格里拉和商贸饭店两个品牌，共计62家饭店，客房量超过28,000间。香格里拉是五星级的豪华酒店品牌，提供高品质的设施和服务。

北京嘉里大酒店已经成为现代商务之行或旅游的理想下榻之所。

Shangri-La's Kerry Centre Hotel, Beijing has carved itself a distinctive position in Beijing as a five-star hotel offering business and leisure travelers the legendary Shangri-La hospitality within an informal, uber-chic environment. The stylish interior is matched by comforts of a modern home: it is WIFI-enabled across public areas, and all 487 well-appointed rooms and suites boast hedonistic offerings such as a full-sized ergonomically designed executive desk, and a unique shower and bath fixtures.

Wining and dining facilities are presented through four establishments offering a spectrum of options. At the Coffee Garden, world cuisines avail on the a la carte menu or at the daily buffet spread reputed for great value and extensive choice. The culinary team is composed of international specialists who whip up mouth-watering delights from South (East) Asia to Europe and beyond. The Horizon Chinese Restaurant offers genuine Cantonese and Sichuan cuisines, and

1. 九龙宴会厅
   Kowloon Ballroom
2. 大宴会厅
   Grand Ballroom
3. 宴会
   Banquet
4. 电脑上网区域
   Tech Zone
5. 会议
   Conference

showcases gastronomic specialties by guest chefs across China's diverse provinces. Centro Bar and Lounge is a hugely successful party address that boasts patronage by the city's local and expatriate elite.

The bar's success stems from its reputation for outstanding "bar-verages", an extensive international wine collection and live jazz entertainment by world-class foreign musicians. Bento & Berries, a new(er) addition to the Beijing city-scape, has come into its own as a trendy café serving gourmet café, sandwiches and line-up of luxurious cakes and breads at great value.

Fitness enthusiasts would argue that an account of Beijing would be incomplete without discourse of the Kerry Sports' extensive facilities, spread across an area of 6,000 square meters (64,560 sq. ft.). As Beijing's most comprehensive and well-equipped hotel fitness centre, the lifestyle complex encompasses a state-of-the-art gymnasium, a 35-meter indoor swimming pool and SPA, court facilities and viewing gallery for tennis, squash, basketball, volleyball and badminton, and a recreation room for billiards, snooker and table tennis. Last but never least, the top floor of the complex offers joggers and roller-bladers a 235 meter-long outdoor running track complete with protective surface matting.

An excess of 6,000-sqm of function space avails MICE organisers of intimate to expansive scales. The Grand Ballroom located on the 2nd floor and Kerry Events Centre on the 2nd floor accommodate up to 1,500 and 1,800 people respectively, whilst 11 function rooms on the 3rd floor accommodate groups ranging from 20–110 people. The 350-sqm Kowloon Ballroom that accommodates up to 220 or can be divided into two sections suitable for functions of 80–100 persons is elegantly bathed in natural light with a distinct air of privacy and lends itself well to any occasion. Across the walkway, the Rooftop Garden (240 sqm) with a capacity of 200 guests is the perfect venue for special outdoor functions.

Shangri-La's Kerry Centre Hotel, Beijing has

received various accolades, including Zagat Survey's "Top 10 Most Popular Hotels" in Beijing in 2008 and *Travel + Leisure China* magazine's award as "China's Top Hotels 2007" in April 2007. It also received the Hewitt Associates' awards as "Best Employer in Asia 2007" and "Best Employer in China 2007". Located in the central business district and just 30 minutes drives from the International Airport, the Hotel provides easy access to the commercial, shopping and historical sightseeing spots of metropolitan Beijing, including the Forbidden City, Tian'anmen Square, the Heavenly Temple, the Lama Temple, Ritan Park, the Pearl Market, the Silk Market and the Friendship Store.

1. 穆拉诺吊灯
   Murano Chandelier
2. 海天阁中餐厅
   Horizon Chinese Restaurant
3. 粤式点心
   Dim Sum
4. 豪华阁行政酒廊
   Horizon Lounge
5. 炫酷夜景
   Centro Bar Night
6. 炫酷白天
   Centro Day Time

1. 多功能厅
   Function Room
2. 商务中心
   Business Centre
3. 游泳池
   Pool
4. 网球场
   Tennis Court

3

4

1、2. 炫酷一隅
   Centro of an Angle
3. 总统套房
   Presidential Suite
4. 豪华间
   Deluxe Room
5. 豪华阁客房
   Horizon Club Room
6. 精选套房
   Specially Suite
7. 行政套房
   Executive Suite

北京中国大饭店矗立于北京外交及商务活动的中心地带——中国国际贸易中心商圈,与中国国际贸易展览大厅和国贸商场毗邻。酒店坐落于北京市最著名的大街上,毗邻紫禁城,常常有外交官、商人和休闲旅游人士光临,是出发游览北京的最佳地点。

附近有许多外国大使馆,从北京首都国际机场到酒店只有45分钟车程。中国大饭店716间客房及套房是经典、奢华和品位最纯粹的典范。

大饭店拥有北京市内最先进的会议设施和各类场地供客人选择,包括用于私人聚会的多功能室、可容纳800人的大宴会厅、可容纳2,000人的会议厅等。活动全程都将有酒店经验丰富的工作人员协助安排。

令世人瞩目的中国大饭店的大堂堪称贵族皇家设计的典范。酒店大堂中的最具标志性的建筑之一红色亮漆巨柱赫然矗立在大堂前沿,更加显示出其帝王般的显赫与尊贵。每一根柱子都配以大理石基座,柱头用金色叶片和埃及水晶石镶嵌,亮丽的大理石地面和两个玻璃天窗交相辉映。整个大堂以金叶为主题的装饰,一直延至屋顶藻井,金光闪闪的水晶吊灯宛如串串珍珠在大堂上空熠熠生辉。璀璨生辉的水晶吊灯,被闪烁的金叶装饰的顶棚,深红漆的巨型廊柱以及与其相辉映的大理石地面,无不衬

托出大堂的雍容华贵，融合了中西方高雅华贵的时尚理念，呈献给客人一个优雅温馨的全新世界。

中国传统古典家具风格在大堂中体现得淋漓尽致。前台与礼宾部的接待台以黑色为基调，上面镶嵌着珍珠与金叶，并勾绘着中国传统风景。在大堂酒廊中的超大型座椅与沙发带给宾客一种现代舒适感。

最近，中国大饭店被中国国家旅游局评为"中国白金五星级旅游饭店"，荣获此奖项的酒店在中国大陆地区仅有三家。同时，中国大饭店还被《Conde Nast旅行者》杂志年度读者评选为"亚洲最佳75强酒店"，并荣登期刊"黄金名录"，被《欧元》杂志、《Frommer旅行指南》以及《亚洲财经》评选为"北京最佳酒店"，被《亚太商务旅行》杂志评选为"北京最佳商务酒店"，以及被《福布斯》杂志评选为"中国最佳五十家商务酒店"。使中国大饭店成为广大宾客造访北京，下榻酒店的首选。

1. 外景
   Exterior
2. 大堂局部
   Part of Lobby

China World Hotel, Beijing, with its highly acclaimed restaurants, soars over the China World Trade Centre complex, including the China World Exhibition Centre and shopping mall, in the heart of the city's diplomatic and business district. Just moments from the Forbidden City, the Hotel sits on one of Beijing's most prestigious avenues, and is frequented by diplomats, businessmen and leisure travelers who wish to experience Beijing from an optimal location.

Located near many foreign embassies and only 45 minutes from Beijing Capital International Airport, the 716-room China World Hotel is the purest example of contemporary class, luxury and style in Beijing, China. Hotel guests can also take advantage from a host of other benefits that enhances the stay experience.

The Hotel is also home to Beijing's most state-of-the-art meeting facilities. Our experienced staff can facilitate virtually any type of event in one of our private function rooms, or a gala gathering in the 800-person ballroom or 2,000-seat Conference Hall.

The grand lobby of the 716-room Shangri-La's China World Hotel, Beijing is reminiscent of the halls of an imperial palace. With shimmering crystal chandeliers, a gold-leaf latticed ceiling and monumental red lacquered pillars offset by golden hued marble floors, the lobby boldly combines dramatic traditional Chinese design elements with contemporary furnishings to create a luxurious and welcoming space for hotel guests and visitors.

The lobby's custom-made furniture draws inspiration from classic Chinese furnishings. The reception and concierge areas feature custom-designed desks with black crackle finishes inlaid with mother of pearl and gold leaf depicting traditional Chinese scenes.

1. 红色主题派对
   Red Party Theme Party
2. 大堂
   Lobby

Oversized armchairs and plush sofas bring comfortable modernity to the lobby lounge.
China World Hotel, Beijing, with its highly acclaimed restaurants, soars over the China World Trade Centre complex, including the China World Exhibition Centre and shopping mall, in the heart of the city's diplomatic and business district. Hailed as one of the first three hotels in mainland China to be awarded with a Platinum Five Star rating by the China National Tourism Administration (CNTA), China World Hotel, Beijing has been named one of the world's best hotels by both *Conde Nast Traveller* and *Travel + Leisure*. China World Hotel, Beijing was also voted "Best Hotel in Beijing" by *Euromoney*, *Frommer's Guide* and *Finance Asia*; "Best Business Hotel in Beijing" by *Business Traveller Asia Pacific, TTG Asia, The Asset and Asian Legal Business*; ranked one of the "Top Ten Business Hotels in China – Golden Pillow Award" by 21st Century Business Herald; and named one of "The Top 50 Hotels in China" by *Forbes* and *Travel + Leisure China*; making it the leading address for discerning travellers visiting China's capital city.

1. 宴会厅
Grand Ballroom
2. 餐厅
Restaurant
3. 餐厅局部
Restaurant Detail
4. 京剧主题派对
Beijing Opera Theme Party
5. 俱乐部大堂
Club Lounge

1. 夏宫入口
   Summer Palace Entrance
2. 夏宫私人包间
   Summer Palace Private Dining Room
3. 大堂吧
   Lobby Lounge
4. 黑与白主题派对
   Black & White Party Theme Party
5. 中式套房餐厅
   China Suite Dining Room

1、2. 多功能厅
  Function Room
3. 俱乐部会议室
  Club Meeting Room
4. 大堂吧
  Lobby Lounge
5. 健身中心
  Fitness Centre
6. 网球
  Tennis
7. 游泳池
  Swimming Pool

1. 套房起居室
Suite Living Room
2. 豪华客房
Deluxe Room
3. 套房卧室
Suite Bedroom
4. 顶级客房
Premier Room
5. 行政套房起居室
Executive Suites Living Room
6. 行政套房卧室
Executive Suites Bedroom
7. 花园套房
Grand Garden Suites

在中国第三大的城市中，天津喜来登大酒店是国际品牌酒店中少数的五星级酒店之一，坐落在著名的天津电视塔旁。酒店之外环境郁郁葱葱、繁花盛草，四周环水，是天津酒店中真正的绿洲。酒店共有296间不同类型的房间，包括行政楼层总统套房和几十套服务式公寓，可以满足不同种类的需求。在餐饮方面，酒店有正宗的中餐厅和西餐厅，咖啡厅和两个酒吧。

从酒店出发到天津滨海国际机场仅需30分钟，到北京国际机场则仅需要2小时的车程，并且仅需乘30分钟火车便可轻松到达首都北京。酒店交通便利，宾客可轻松到达天津西青开发区、北辰开发区、武清开发区、津南开发区、东丽开发区、滨海开发区、华苑产业园区和塘沽泰达开发区。

天津喜来登大酒店宴会厅一贯保持高贵，优雅，舒适的风格，有着美丽的灯光效果以及宽阔的空间。宴会厅可提供多用途会议室选择，范围从容纳8人的小会议室到可容纳700人招待会、500人会议或450人就餐的大宴会厅，同时提供会议用的相关设备。宴会厅可隔为三个独立的功能厅（上海厅，天津厅和重庆厅），顶高4.2米。厅内大型落地窗带来的自然采光及视线内的优美环境更能体现喜来登宴会氛围的与众不同。天津喜来登大酒店宴会厅是举办公司活动，举

办展览及婚礼的绝佳场地。

绿洲水疗在轻松的环境中为您提供各式印度尼西亚及中国传统的按摩和美容服务。

国际健身中心包括器械室、封闭式健身操房、水力按摩浴、蒸汽浴、户外网球场、休息室、女士瘦身室、太空舱,以及美容美发等诸多服务项目,满足您的不同需求。

1. 酒店景观
   Tianjin City View from Hotel
2. 前台
   Front Desk
3. 大宴会厅
   Grand Ballroom

1. 花园婚礼
   Garden Wedding
2. 酒店景观
   Tianjin City View From Hotel

Surrounded by a pristine garden, Sheraton Tianjin Hotel is a source of comfort and relaxation on your next trip to China's third largest city. Even though we are only three kilometers from the Tianjin city center, you'll feel worlds away. 296 guest rooms, including Club Floor and serviced apartments, are fully equipped to meet your every kinds of needs. Sheraton Tianjin Hotel provides many dining options, ranging from international delights to an all-day buffet.

Our convenient location places you within easy reach from your most important destinations-just 30 minutes drive from Tianjin International Airport, 2 hours drive from Beijing International Airport, 30 minutes to Beijing city center by bullet train and within easy access to the central business district as well as the Xiqing economic development zones, Dong Li (Tianjin Port Free Trade Zone/Tianjin Airport Industrial Park) and TEDA economic development zones.

The Grand Ballroom of Sheraton Tianjin Hotel is based on the concept of comfort and elegance, special light effect and extended seating capacity. The Ballroom offers a selection of multi purpose conference rooms, ranging from small boardrooms to accommodate meetings from 8 people to the Grand Ballroom meeting capacity up to 500 persons, dinner capacity up to 450 persons and standing reception up to 700 persons. A range of audio-visual equipment is available. The Grand Ballroom can separated into 3 individual function rooms–Shanghai Room, Tianjin Room, Chongqing Room. The ceiling is 4.2 m, with the natural light coming from the windows.

It is a perfect venue to organize upscale Corporate Meetings, Exhibitions and the elegant Weddings.

Oasis SPA offers a wide rang of Indonesian or traditional Chinese massage and beauty treatments in relaxed surroundings.

International Health Center includes Gym, Sauna, Tennis Court, Steam Bath and SPA, Aerobics Room, Alpha machine and Beauty & Hair Salon.

1、5. 盘山葡萄烧烤西餐厅
   Panshan Wine & Grill Restaurant
2. 天宝阁中餐厅
   Celestiod Court Chinese Restaurant
3、4. 花园烧烤
   Garden BBQ
6、7. 重庆厅
   Chongqing Room

1、3. 盘山西餐厅
   Panshan Wine & Grill Restaurant
2. 重庆厅
   Chongqing Room
4. 燕园咖啡厅
   Terrace Café
5. 商务中心会议室
   Meeting Room in Business Center
6. 天津厅
   Tianjin Room
7. 北京厅
   Beijing Room

1. 行政贵宾厅
Club Lounge
2. 大堂吧
Lobby Lounge
3. 国际健身中心
International Health Center
4. 游泳池
Swimming Pool

1

1. 套房
   Suite
2. 水疗中心
   Oasis Spa
3. 豪华房
   Deluxe Room
4. 商务中心
   Business Center

大连凯宾斯基饭店坐落于大连市商业中心区，面对风景宜人的劳动公园，与繁华的购物中心仅有咫尺之遥，距大连国际机场仅20分钟车程。饭店拥有两座建筑：25层的贵宾楼和31层的园景楼。

大连凯宾斯基饭店是由大连振屹房屋开发有限公司投资兴建的，由凯宾斯基饭店管理集团管理。

大连凯宾斯基饭店400间设施完备的客房和套房时尚典雅、宽敞舒适，拥有液晶电视、淋浴间独立的宽大浴室和宽带网络接口等设施，并坐拥公园园景和城市美景。

共6层的行政楼层，拥有专属的行政酒廊和会议室，为最具鉴赏力的宾客提供特别尊贵的礼遇，宾客可在位于22楼的行政酒廊免费享用早餐、下午茶、傍晚鸡尾酒以及无线宽带上网等服务。

8个独具特色的餐厅和酒廊让您"一站式"享受到风格各异的美食、美酒。柏林咖啡厅以其开放式的厨房提供国际式自助餐和单点美食；时尚典雅的龙苑中餐厅提供精致的粤菜和大连菜；马可波罗意大利餐厅擅长于正宗的意大利菜和自制意大利面条；马可波罗意大利轻食坊以更加轻松、随意的氛围和方式提供美味的比萨和意大利面；普拉那啤酒坊提供店内自酿的德国啤酒、德式美食并伴以每晚国际乐队的精彩表演，普拉那啤酒花园在宜人的季节里提供户

外烧烤美食；作为颇具时尚品位的鸡尾酒廊，空中酒廊是餐后浅酌、社交小聚并观赏迷人夜色的理想场所；在大堂酒廊，宾客可以品尝各种饮品，伴着现场音乐享受轻松时光；凯宾美食廊提供新鲜自制蛋糕、面包和巧克力等特选美食，并独家侍奉"意大利"系列咖啡。

饭店拥有总面积超过1,000平方米的豪华典雅的会议宴会场所，包括一个可分为3个独立区的大宴会厅和6个多功能厅，能举办不同规模和形式的会议和宴会。

4,500平方米的阿拉伯风格的欧意希斯水疗中心拥有设备先进、完善的健身房、游泳池、桑拿浴、水疗房、美容和美发沙龙等，提供令人放松身心、恢复活力的全方位理疗服务。

大连凯宾斯基饭店还拥有商务中心、宝马豪华轿车服务、专业洗衣服务、购物廊，以及24小时客房送餐服务等各种服务项目。

作为正宗的欧式豪华饭店，大连凯宾斯基饭店绝佳的地理位置和无与伦比的凯宾斯基殷勤好客，是您休闲度假和商务旅行的首选。

1. 大连城市景色及饭店远眺
Dalian City View with Hotel
2. 饭店夜景
Exterior (night)
3. 大堂
Lobby

1. 行政酒廊
   Executive Lounge
2. 凯宾美食廊
   Kempi Deli
3. 饭店外景
   Exterior

The Kempinski Hotel Dalian is situated in the heart of the commercial and business district and opposite the Labour Park. It is only a 20 minutes drive from the Dalian International Airport and only few steps away from the shopping centre. It comprises a 25-storey Grand Wing and a 31-storey Park Wing.

Owned by Dalian Zhenyi Real Estate Limited Company, the Hotel is managed by Kempinski Hotels.

Kempinski Hotel Dalian has 400 contemporary designed guest rooms and suites which well-appointed with LCD television, spacious bathroom with separate shower and broadband Internet access. All rooms have a scenic view of the park or the city.

The 6 exclusive levels of Executive Floor complemented by an Executive Lounge with a private boardroom which offers extraordinary benefits for the most discerning guests who can relax at the Executive Lounge located on the 22nd Floor with complimentary breakfast, afternoon tea, evening cocktails and wireless broadband access.

The 8 distinctive restaurants and bars bring together an exciting variety of cuisines and themes all within one location. Café Berlin with its diverse international buffet which features a large open kitchen also features an extensive A la carte menu. Dragon Palace Chinese restaurant with its elegant and tasteful design showcases tantalizing Cantonese and Dalian cuisine. Marco Polo Ristorante specializes in authentic Italian cuisine and delicious homemade pastas. Marco Polo Trattoria exclusively prepares gourmet pizza and pastas in a more casual dinning setting. Paulaner Brauhaus offers home-brewed Paulaner beer and German cuisine with nightly performances of its international. During the summer months, Paulaner Biergarten fires up its outdoor BBQ. Sky Lounge is a modern contemporary cocktail lounge ideal for after-dinner drinks or just socializing in style whilst taking in the gorgeous vistas. At Lobby Lounge, you can unwind, sip drinks along with live music. Kempi Deli offers many specialized gourmet products such as homemade cake, bread, chocolates and serving only "Illy" Coffee.

The Hotel offers a total of over 1,000 square meters of meeting and banquet space including a Grand Ballroom which is divisible into three sections and six well-appointed Function Rooms are available for any size and configuration of events.

The "Arabian Style" Oasis SPA boasts a state-of-the-art equipped gym, swimming pool, sauna, treatment rooms, beauty & hair salon. It offers a range of treatment and services to compliment its holistic approach to relaxation and rejuvenation.

Kempinski Hotel Dalian also features a Business Centre, BMW limousine service, specialized laundry service, shopping arcade and 24 hours in-room dinning.

This European luxury hotel with its desirable location and unique Kempinski hospitality will be your best choice for both leisure and business.

1. 大堂酒廊
   Lobby Lounge
2. 马可波罗意大利轻食坊
   Marco Polo Trattoria
3. 柏林咖啡厅
   Café Berlin
4. 龙苑中餐厅大厅
   Dragon Palace Dining Hall
5. 龙苑中餐厅贵宾厅
   Dragon Palace Private Dining Room

1. 宴会厅门厅——鸡尾酒会
   Foyer – Cocktail
2. 大宴会厅——婚宴
   Grand Ballroom – Wedding Banquet
3. 多功能厅——西式宴会
   Function Room – Western Banquet
4. 多功能厅——剧院式
   Function Room – Theatre
5. 大宴会厅——教室式
   Grand Ballroom – Classroom
6. 董事会会议室
   Boardroom

1. 马可波罗意大利餐厅
   Marco Polo Ristorante
2. 普拉那啤酒坊
   Paulaner Brauhaus
3. 普拉那啤酒花园
   Paulaner Biergarten
4. 理疗房
   Treatment Room
5. 健身房
   Gym
6. 游泳池
   Swimming Pool

1、5. 小套房
Studio Suite

2. 豪华套房
Deluxe Suite

3. 豪华房
Deluxe Room

4、7. 总统套房
Presidential Suite

6. 贵宾房
Permier Room

上海东郊宾馆是世界瞩目之地上海浦东建设的一个能体现时代特征的五星级花园式国宾馆。东郊宾馆位于浦东金科路1800号，四周有多个花园别墅环抱，是浦东乃至上海不为多见的城市绿肺。宾馆总体由贵宾楼、礼宾楼、迎宾楼、悦宾楼及70幢欧美风格的别墅群组合而成，置身园中有世外桃源的感受。凭借优美的自然风景，秀丽的庭院风情，以及豪华的宴会设施，东郊宾馆赢得了诸多中外来宾的青睐。

东郊宾馆整体占地1,200亩，几乎完全被绿色所环抱，并拥有超过100亩的水系湖泊，园内浑然一派中国古典水乡景象。在宾馆的园林中漫步，会让每一位宾客感受到一步一景的喜悦，时而青草茵茵、阳光明媚，时而鸟儿低鸣、巨木苍天，时而溪水涓涓、鱼儿游弋，时而竹林摇曳、花香飘飘。

贵宾楼，是宾馆专门用于接待国家首脑下榻的重要场所。贵宾楼处于东郊宾馆的中心位置，它坐北朝南，正面朝向大片草坪和湖面，两侧及后部由浓密的竹林、树木相拥环抱。贵宾楼整体风格按照豪华而不失简约，高贵而不乏典雅，精致又不失华丽的建筑理念建造。

礼宾楼，是宾馆主要的会议、宴会接待场所。楼内分为上、下两层，其中贵宾厅位于一层，面积420平方米，布局庄严、肃穆，是官方会议、商业会议及宴会的主要场地；紫金厅整厅面积900平方米，采用

无柱设计，可同时容纳近600位来宾，装修风格呈现了东方文化的庄重与典雅，是举行商务会议、大型宴会及新人婚礼的绝佳场地；玉兰厅，装修风格婉约、尊贵，整厅无柱，面积460平方米，最多可容纳宾客200人。厅内光线明亮、宽敞通透，配有高质量影音系统。

迎宾楼，整体建筑反映泱泱大国的气度、深厚的文化底蕴以及浓郁的地域风貌。楼内自上贯下的大厅使宾客感受到卓尔不群的艺术效果。楼内的客房区配有180套客房，4种豪华客房类型，装修简约、内饰豪华，一切以客人的舒适程度和方便程度为核心服务宗旨，为各类会议、商务和旅游度假的宾客享用，可满足各类宾客的不同要求，让客人真正享受到与身份相符的居住环境与服务质量。

悦宾楼是面对所有宾客开放的休闲寓所。总面积2万平方米，分3个层面。设有羽毛球馆、室内外网球场、标准化游泳池、供儿童使用的戏水池、乒乓球房、保龄球馆、桌球室、沙弧球馆、器械完备的健身房、专业教练执教的瑜伽馆、棋牌室、灯光璀璨的歌舞厅。为所有宾客提供了静谧舒适的放松环境。

别墅区是东郊宾馆最具特色的一部分，东郊别墅以近乎豪华的手笔建造了70幢欧美风格的别墅。别墅建筑面积区内绿树繁茂、青草茵茵，景观布局错落有致，全木质结构打造8种不同地域风情的独幢花园别墅。别墅区内保安措施周密完善，各类餐饮、运动及康乐设施一应俱全，是目前上海境内外人士理想的生活居住之地。

Face别墅会所是东郊宾馆的一个点睛之笔，特色餐厅包括日本料理、印度菜、泰国菜、摩洛哥菜和法国菜、意大利菜等，同时Face酒吧独特的异域风情随时恭候每一位尊贵来宾鉴赏。

东郊宾馆是集天堂神韵、宜人春色于一体的度假之地，集高档硬件设施、上乘服务于一体的尊贵之地，这里是度假、会务、休闲的胜地。我们将更致力于努力发展成为上海乃至全国最一流的五星级花园宾馆。

1. 迎宾楼
   Guest-greeting Court
2. 大堂
   Lobby

1. 楼梯
   Stairs
2. 室内
   Indoor

Shanghai Dongjiao State Guest Hotel is a 5 star garden hotel located in Pudong Shanghai–a global focusing place and it is an expression of the characteristic of era. Dongjiao State Guest is located in No. 1,800 Jinke Rd, Pudong. It is surrounded by several garden villas which can be thought as a green lung of Pudong, even Shanghai itself. It is composed by Distinguished Guest Court, Protocol Court, Guest-Greeting Court, Guest-Pleasing Court and 70 villas of European-American styles where you will feel like retreat away from the turmoil of the city when you are inside the garden. Dongjiao State Guest Hotel has won a lot of favor from both Chinese and Foreign guests because of the graceful natural scene, beautiful and elegant appearance of the court yard and deluxe banquet facilities.

Dongjiao State Guest Hotel contains a landscape of 1,200 Mu which is mostly hemmed in greenery and the lake and the river system is over 100 Mu, which shows a completely appearance of classic Chinese Watery Town. Wandering inside the garden of the hotel, the guests will feel the delight to see different scene when they move one step further, once you can see overlapping grass and sun shines brightly, then birds singing on the trees reach into the sky, and you also can see fishes swinging in the trickling stream, bamboos swinging with wind, the pleasant smell of flowers spread all over the place.

Distinguished Guest Court connected with the Protocol Hall with a long corridor covers an area of 8,000 square meters. It faces at south, with big grassland and river at its front, and dense bamboo trees and other trees around its two sides and back. Inside, a standard layout, the middle space is a vertical multi-level space, typical of traditional southern China garden style, exquisite and sumptuous. The Meeting Hall with bright light, famous paintings and various art pieces, is an absolutely good place for important meetings. Presidential suite even includes study and meeting room. All the facilities let distinguished national leaders and government officials enjoy the best work and leisure time at Dongjiao State Guest Hotel.

The Protocol Court with its serious and luxurious exterior, high and low constructions are combined with the green environment beside it. Inside, two-floor high lobby is the

1. 室内
   Lobby
2. 悦宾楼
   Guest-pleasing Court
3. 室内走廊
   Corridor
4. 迎宾楼一层采悦厅
   Caiyue Hall

core construction, which combines the three functions of official meeting, business meeting and banquet together. Zijin Hall on the first floor covers an area of 900 square meters with no pillar design, let you feel big and bright, and is suitable for various big events. Fine and unique Chinese food gives guests lots of aftertaste and is another reason for them to enjoy so much at the hotel. VIP Hall, Magnolia Lilly Hall has advanced audio-visual equipment, and is the main place in Shanghai for meeting important guests and holding big meeting ceremonies.

The Guest-Greeting Court, the main area open to public shows the bearing of a great country, deep cultural details and rich regional style. Big halls from upstairs to downstairs inside the building make us feel the unique artistic effect. The golden color is the passionate collision of East and West. The guest room floor has 180 rooms with four types of luxurious guest rooms for various guests of meeting, business and leisure. Simple construction and luxurious decoration make the comfort and convenience of the guests its core service aim. It satisfies various requests from different guests and let the guests really enjoy the living environment and service quality equal to their identity. Caiyue Hall on the first floor is a self-service dining hall, where guests can taste various Chinese and Western food with relax. Living and relaxing here is absolutely your exclusive choice.

Guest-pleasing Court is the leisure place open to all the guests. It has a total area of 20,000 square meters with three floors. It has badminton hall, outdoor and indoor tennis court, standard swimming pool, and pool for kids, table tennis room, bowling hall, snooker room, shuffle board hall, gym with complete facilities, Yoga hall with professional coach, chess & playing card room, and bright ballroom. It is a very comfortable relaxing place for amusement.

Villa Area is the most colorful part of the hotel. It has the most luxurious 70 villas built on the 80,600 square meters of land. The total area of the villa is 23,000 square meters, with lots of trees and grassland and the total area of green is over 80%. Eight different regional types of single garden villa with all wooden structure, has the familiar style of the U.S., the Great Britain, France, Canada, etc. It has a thorough and complete security system, various dining, sport and leisure facilities, which is the ideal living place for national and overseas guests.

Face Villa Club is the shining point of the hotel. Its special dining includes Japanese, Indian, Thai, Moroccan, French and Italian food. And its unique exotic atmosphere is waiting for the respected appreciation of every guest at any time.

Dongjiao State Guest Hotel is a paradisiacal resort with delightful spring scenery, a honorable place with high level facilities and top class service, a sacred place for vacation, conference and recreation. We will dedicate more effort to make our hotel become the top 5-Star Garden Hotel in Shanghai and even the whole China.

1. 礼宾楼紫金厅
   Zijin Hall
2. 礼宾楼玉兰厅
   Yulan Hall
3. 礼宾楼贵宾厅
   VIP Guest Hall
4. 友谊厅
   Greeting Guest Hall
5. 歌舞厅
   Singing and Dancing Bar

1. 泳池局部
   Details of Swimming Pool
2. 游泳池
   Swimming Pool
3. 健身房
   Gym
4. 桌球房
   Snooker
5. 羽毛球
   Badminton
6. 戏水池
   Leisure Pool

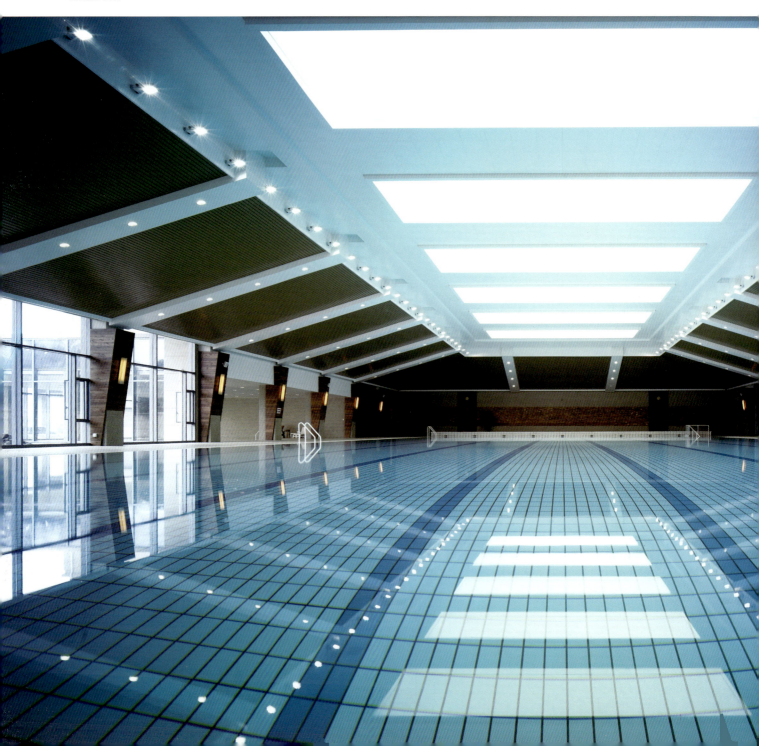

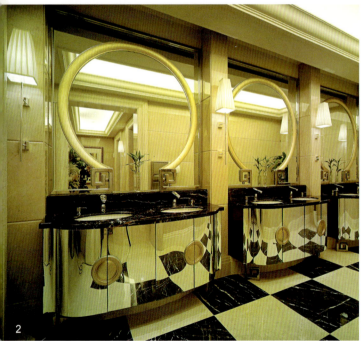

1. 大床房
   Gardon View Single Room
2. 室内
   Indoor
3. 局部
   Part
4. 贵宾楼
   Distinguished Guest Court
5、6. 外景
   Outdoor
7. 豪华大床房
   Deluxe Single Room
8. 悦宾楼
   Guest-pleasing Court

上海古象大酒店开业于2003年7月，位于繁华的市中心地段，坐落于上海著名的南京东路世纪广场正对面，一步之遥即是久负盛名的中华第一街——南京路步行街，步行即可到达闻名中外的外滩、人民广场和上海博物馆等商务休闲之处。周边汇集十几条公交线路及地铁1号、2号、8号线，交通非常便捷。

酒店拥有360间豪华舒适的客房及套房，设计高贵典雅。电梯先进现代，只有持房卡的客人通过插卡才能使用电梯到达任何客房楼层，大大提高了酒店内部的安全性。六至十二层是高级房楼层，各房间设独立的大理石盥洗室，客人可免费享用高速因特网。十五至二十二层为商务房楼层，配备商务房及套房等各类房型，设计高档完善，布置舒适温馨。二十三至二十七层为豪生俱乐部行政楼层，专为行政客人办理快捷的入住离店手续，并提供行政楼免费早餐、点心、礼宾服务、使用会议室等多项额外至尊优待礼遇。

总面积达788平方米的宴会场所，包括一个363平方米的无柱大宴会厅及6个大小不同的多功能会议厅。适合举办各种商务会议。还可根据要求将大宴会厅分隔，举办不同规模的会议，并可提供多款宴会佳肴。商务中心配有现代化的影音及会议服务设施，为商务客人提供完善的商务配套服务。

一楼的豪生咖啡厅宽敞舒适,这里推出丰盛的国际自助餐、零点菜单配以上等葡萄酒;精选多款优质海鲜、上等牛排,伴随独特巧克力喷泉和令人垂涎的甜品,加之周末晚间海鲜自助和丰盛可口的周日早午餐,让您尽享世界美食。

艺廊酒吧为您提供各种休闲食品、风味咖啡、经典/时尚鸡尾酒等多种饮品,是您与亲朋好友小聚的理想场所。您亦可在优美的乐声中享受温馨的下午茶或夜晚的闲暇时光。

维那吧提供各国葡萄酒、香槟、雪茄和小食。入夜时分,伴随无限美妙音乐,沉醉在优雅的夜色中。

美食屋每日提供各式新鲜糕点及大师自制欧式精选巧克力,另有各式现磨咖啡、茶和饮料。

位于酒店五楼的豪生水疗中心SPA中心装潢雅致,休息区采用中国古典茶室设计,在温热的气氛中充满高贵情趣。SPA配有三个独特的纵深木质浴盆,洒上玫瑰花瓣,宾客可在其中尽享洗浴的乐趣。各类按摩护理项目舒缓身心疲劳,重现充沛精神。

游泳池顶棚上的透明窗体采集丰富自然光线,在阳光下波光粼粼的水池将给您最舒适的游泳感受。泳池周围地板配有地热装置,即使室外冷峻严寒,也不妨碍畅游的愉快。

健身房空间宽敞,配有各类先进健身器械供您免费使用。专业的健身教练也会帮您进行科学、安全的锻炼。另外,健身房有专门的跳操房,练习瑜伽、跳健美操,都是不错的休闲体验。

1. 酒店入口 Entrance
2. 前台接待处 Reception

Found in July 2003, Howard Johnson Plaza Shanghai is ideally located right in the heart of Shanghai, just a step away from Shanghai's busiest shopping and entertainment center — Nanjing Road Pedestrian Street.

Owning accommodation of 360 spacious and elegantly designed guest rooms and suites with state-of-the-art facilities, the Hotel offers luxurious comfort and conveniences to discerning business travelers. The Howard Johnson Club, occupying the hotel's 23rd to the 27th floors, features exclusive benefits and services for the guests.

With 788 square meters of comprehensive function space, Howard Johnson Plaza Shanghai has a 363-square meter pillarless Grand Ballroom and six other function rooms for business and social events. Designed for flexibility, the Grand Ballroom can be divided into two or three smaller rooms. Complete Business Center services and contemporary audio-visual equipment and meeting aids are offered. A whole line-up of menus features a variety of international dishes to suit your guests' preference.

On the first floor of the hotel lies elegant and undisturbed Riviera Restaurant. Its half suspended design brings you beautiful scenes of the lobby. With melodic music, our international buffet daily takes you to experience a gastronomic trip around the sun-kissed Mediterranean, which is with the freshest authentic tastes that you can imagine. Our Sunday Brunch and Weekend Seafood Buffet are spectacular culinary treats.

Part of the vast and beautiful lobby, Pavilion

1. 自制精美蛋糕
   Home-made Cake
2. 大堂全景
   View of Lobby

1. 夜景外观
   Exterior at Night
2. 酒店大堂
   Hotel Lobby
3. 电梯厅
   Lift Corridor
4. 电梯
   Elevator

Lobby Lounge is just the place to relax comfortably with coffee, croissants or afternoon tea from morning to late night. Relax in the evenings and enjoy the best of Chinese & Western music.

Vinothek wine Bar has a wide collection of wines from some of the best vineyards worldwide. with cigars and delicate snacks, it is an ideal place to spend a cozy night.

Century Deli offers a daily fresh selection of cakes, pastries, and gourmet chocolates made by our in-house team of pastry chefs.

The resting area of Howard Johnson SPA, elegant and comfortable in a warm atmosphere. Indulge in a heavenly massage treatment will leave you feeling totally rejuvenated and refreshed.

Adopting transparent windows as ceiling, the glistening reflecting of the sun on the swimming pool brings you the extreme comfort and coziness. The floor around the swimming pool is equipped with floor heating system, which keeps inside warm even in the cold winter.

Various equipments such as cardio-vascular equipment, weight training stations are available in the spacious gym. Professional gym coach will tutor you to take exercises scientifically and safety. In addition, our gym is equipped with special room for yoga and aerobics.

1、2. 圣·拉斐奥
　　San·Rafael
3. 艺廊大堂吧
　　Pavilion Lobby Lounge
4. 美食屋
　　Century Deli
5. 自制巧克力
　　Home-made Chocolate
6. 豪生咖啡厅
　　Riviera café

1、2.健身房
　　Gym
3.玫瑰浴
　　Rose Bath
4.室内游泳池
　　Indoor Swimming Pool

1. 商务客房
   Business Room
2. 豪生世纪套房盥洗室
   Rest Room of Century Suite
3、5. 豪生世纪套房
   Century Suite
4. 商务豪华套房
   Business Deluxe Suite

4

5

花园饭店（上海），地处上海繁华的商业、文化、娱乐中心，是一座融古典高雅与豪华舒适于一体的现代化五星级酒店。在建于20世纪20年代的原法国俱乐部旧址上矗立起来的花园饭店（上海）既保留了古典优雅的欧洲装饰艺术的建筑精髓，又被赋予了新的时代气息，并融入近30,000平方米的葱绿、宁静的花园。似一朵静放的玫瑰，在繁华都市中恭候各位宾客的到来。

位于市中心枢纽地段的花园饭店（上海）与上海火车站以及虹桥、浦东两大国际机场之间均有高架快速道路相连，让您能更准确地把握出行时机；便利的轨道交通，为您市内旅游观光或商务出行提供更快捷的选择。您更可在毗邻的淮海路上感受时尚前沿的风采，体验动感大上海的韵律。

花园饭店（上海）拥有492间各式温馨的客房。豪华舒适的行政楼和静谧宽敞的行政沙龙为商务客人提供尊贵、贴心的服务；47套各类豪华套房可满足您个性化的需求。此外，酒店还设有各类高档服务设施包括：商务中心、三越商场、鲜花店、健身房、游泳池、网球场、保险柜、洗衣房、美容美发沙龙、泊车库等，为您营造豪华温馨、舒适宁静的入住环境。

花园饭店（上海）拥有5个餐厅、3个酒吧，您可在此品尝各地美食。一层

的玫瑰咖啡厅为您提供西式便餐。二层的"白玉兰"中餐厅以港式粤菜和上海菜见长。二层的"山里"日餐厅以纯正的日式料理享誉沪上。三十三层的餐饮楼层更融合了时尚美食："山茶花"铁板烧餐厅擅长极具观赏性的日式铁板料理；欧陆法式餐厅提供经典法式美食。此外您还可在位于一层的"绿洲"大堂酒吧会友小憩，或聊私事或洽生意，随心所欲；或在位于三层的"夜来香"酒吧感受法式浪漫，一览大花园的全景，轻松惬意；还可在三十三层的空中酒廊极目远眺，抿一口美酒，随着光影流动，放松心情。

花园饭店拥有10间大小、风格各异的多功能宴会厅，分别位于二层和三十二层。专业的宴会策划和训练有素的服务团队将满腔热忱地为您提供细致周到的服务。先进的视听设备、可升降的大屏幕以及各类辅助设备使您的宴会尽善尽美。此外，饭店还可以为您安排舞蹈、杂技、音乐等演出，更令您的宴会与众不同，使人难以忘怀。

二层共有大、中、小6个宴会厅，它们都由原法国俱乐部的老建筑改建而成，保留了法国古典装饰主义的艺术风格，于高雅中见气派，让来宾见识您的不凡品位。

尤其值得一提的是位于二层东侧的百花厅，它是花园饭店历史建筑中的精华。其最大的魅力之处是其大厅中央由彩色玻璃镶拼而成，中间为船底造型的顶灯。当灯光透过彩色玻璃照射下来时，整个宴会厅顿时万紫千红，氤氲缭绕。而罕见的7米多层高，更令整个大厅显得气宇非凡。这里是举办大型活动的首选，各类新品发布会、时装展示会也频频在此举行。四周的浮雕装饰以及落地大窗、剧院式包厢都彰显非凡的豪门气质而又不失浪漫，因此它也见证了无数对新人迈入幸福的殿堂。

位于花园饭店（上海）三十二层的空中宴会厅，因其地势之利而使宾客易高瞻远瞩，可将上海城市美景尽收眼底。三十二层的空中宴会厅运用了设计

1. 原法国俱乐部老建筑
   Former French Club
2. 大堂
   Lobby

装饰新理念,独到的灯光设计,使得每个宴会厅各显华贵靓丽。

整个建筑已被上海市政府作为历史文化遗产保护起来。回首其沧桑岁月,将带我们发掘一段弥足珍贵的过往。1926年一座由法国建筑师设计,馥郁着巴黎气息的"法国俱乐部"在此诞生。它融合了20世纪20～30年代最流行、最时尚的风格,然而其迷人的风采稍纵即逝。20世纪40年代,它曾为美国驻华海军所用。1949年新中国成立之后,收归国有,改名为"文化俱乐部",花园用作体育场地。1959年,毛泽东主席的短暂逗留为它增添了一层神秘的面纱。20世纪60年代,更名为"锦江俱乐部"。直至1984年,花园饭店(上海)项目开工,开始了对老建筑的加固修筑。1990年3月20日,花园饭店(上海)在众人的期盼中正式开业。时光流逝,追昔抚今,在这个汇集了艺术精华的地方,将我们对美好往昔的追忆拉回到久远的过去,成为永恒的灿烂。

The Okura Garden Hotel (Shanghai) is ideally situated in Shanghai's prestigious commercial, cultural and entertainment district. The Okura Garden Hotel (Shanghai) is a five star hotel that combines the best of classical elegance and modern comfort. Built in the 1920s, this is one of the most significant buildings erected by the French in Shanghai. The Okura Garden Hotel has infused contemporary sophistication into the old world charm of the former French Club, along with its 30,000 square meters garden. Like a rose in full bloom, the Okura Garden Hotel (Shanghai) stands to welcome its guests from all around the world. The Okura Garden Hotel (Shanghai) is in the heart of the city center and enjoys excellent expressway connections to the Shanghai Railway Station, the Hongqiao Airport and the Pudong International Airport. The subway system provides a convenient way for you to visit Shanghai and to shuttle around the city.
The Okura Garden Hotel (Shanghai) has 492 well-appointed rooms. The deluxe Executive Floors and the spacious Executive Salon

1. 花园俯拍
   Overview of Garden
2. 花园饭店(上海)全景
   Okura Garden Hotel Shanghai

provide business travelers with comfort, luxury and impeccable service. In addition, our 47 Luxurious Suites will meet the most varied needs of the well-heeled traveler. Other facilities in the hotel include a Business Center, the Mitsukoshi Shop, a Flower Shop, a Gymnasium, a Swimming Pool, Tennis Court, security boxes, laundry services, a Beauty Salon and spacious parking place to make you feel like you are home away from home.

The Okura Garden Hotel (Shanghai) has 5 restaurants and 3 bars where you can savor delicacies from around the world. The Coffee Shop Rose (1F) provides western style set meals, while the Chinese Restaurant Bai Yu Lan (2F) serves mouth-watering Cantonese and Shanghainese dishes. The Japanese restaurant Yamazato (2F) is renowned for its classic Japanese cuisine. The dinning floor on 33rd floor combines the best of simplicity and modernity. There, the Teppanyaki Sazanka specializes in Japanese-style teppanyaki cuisine, while the Continental Room serves up exotic French delicacies. With all these restaurants, the pickiest gourmet would be spoilt for choice. After your meal, you might want to relax with your friends at the Cocktail Lounge Oasis in the Lobby, or even negotiate your business dealings there. Experience French romanticism at its best at the Main Bar Ye Lai Xiang (3F) with its excellent view of the garden. The Wine & Cocktail Lounge Sky Bar (33F) on the top floor offers you a bird eye view of the city. A great place to relax and watch the stars go by as you sip on a glass of wine.

The Okura Garden Hotel (Shanghai) has 10 function rooms of various sizes and styles situated on the 2nd and 32nd floors. Our professionally trained meetings executives are on hand to provide you with the most detailed service. Our state-of-the-art audio-visual equipment and other facilities will give your meeting the special edge. The hotel is also able to provide you with dance, acrobatics, and other musical performances to make your meeting a most memorable one and to leave your guests with a lasting impression.

There are 6 banqueting rooms of various

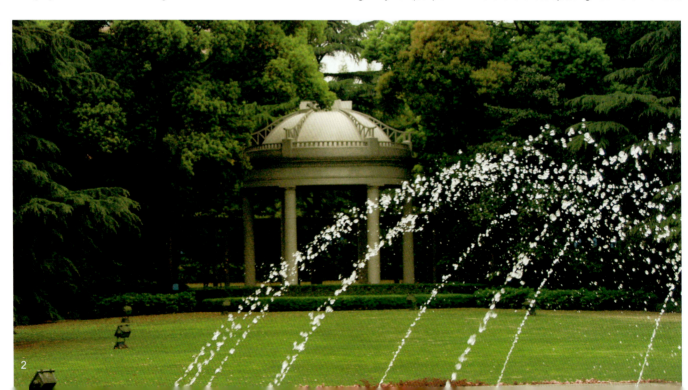

1. 花园证婚仪式
   Garden Wedding Ceremony
2. 生态花园
   Garden
3. 宴会厅——百花厅（晚宴）
   Banquet Room-Grand Ballroom (Dinner)
4. 宴会厅——康乃馨厅
   Banquet Room-Carnation Room

sizes on the 2nd floor. They were built for using by the former French Club and still retain its uniquely French décor and style. Its elegance and opulence provide an atmosphere of sophistication for your guests.

The Grand Ballroom situated in the east wing of the second floor is the most significant of the Okura Garden Hotel's long history. In the centre of the ceiling is a boat-shaped light made of tinted glass. This gives the Grand Ballroom an amazing glow. The height of the Grand Ballroom is over 7 meters, which gives it an added dimension in opulence. This is a premier venue option for large-scale events, product launches and fashion shows. The sculptures, the windows that extend from the floor to the ceiling and the theatre-style balcony all make the Grand Ballroom a very romantic place and so many couples have chosen to walk down the aisle here together.

The Okura Garden Hotel (Shanghai)'s banqueting facilities on the 32nd floor offers a splendid panoramic view over Shanghai.

As one of the old cultural heritages, this architecture has already protected by Shanghai Government. Looking back to the whole history it left us a valuable memory of the past time. As of 1926, this building was constructed as the French Club. It remains the most popular and fashionable style during 1920s to 1930s period of time. However, the glamour of this period was short-lived and soon vanished. The building was used by the U.S. Army on 1940s. Then after the establishment of the P. R. of China in 1949, it changed its name as People's Culture Palace with the garden as a sports field. Then in 1959, Chairman Mao stayed here for a period. From the end of 1960s the building was renamed as Jing Jiang Club. Till 1984 a renovation project was started to create the Okura Garden Hotel Shanghai with the cooperation of Shanghai Government. On March 20, 1990, the Okura Garden Hotel (Shanghai) opened on expectation. Now following the time passing by the hotel architecture emits the utmost artistic charm. It recalls the beautiful memory of the old time and stand on the world stage with permanent glamour.

1. 欧陆法式餐厅
   French Restaurant Continental Room
2. 宴会厅——百花厅
   Banquet Room-Grand Ballroom
3. 宴会厅——天龙厅
   Banquet Room-Dragon Room
4. 山里日餐厅
   Japanese Restaurant YAMAZATO
5. 玫瑰咖啡厅
   Coffee Shop ROSE
6. 绿洲大堂酒吧
   Cocktail Lounge OASIS

1. 宴会厅——凤凰厅（会议）
   Banquet Room-Phoneix Room (Meeting)
2. 宴会厅——茉莉花厅（会议）
   Banquet Room-Jasimine Room (Meeting)
3. 健康俱乐部健身房
   Gym of Health Club
4. 健康俱乐部室内游泳池
   Indoor Swimming Pool

1. 总统套房客厅
   Living Room of Presidential Suite
2. 豪华套房
   Deluxe Suite
3. 总统套房卧室
   Bedroom of Presidential Suite
4. 浮雕立柱
   Pillar with Relief
5. 原法国俱乐部楼梯
   Staircase of Former French Club
6. 二层前厅
   2nd Floor Foyer
7. 总统套房餐厅
   Dining Room of Presidential Suite

1951年6月9日，上海锦江饭店在茂名南路59号正式揭幕开张。占地3万余平方米，其中绿地面积1.65万平方米，是上海最负盛名、地理位置最优越的五星级饭店之一。

临近上海的购物天堂淮海中路，交通便捷，饭店距离新天地这个融合了历史、文化与娱乐的都市时尚之地仅10分钟路程，步行5分钟即可到达地铁陕西南路站或延安路高架，步行10分钟到达著名的南京路商业圈。

锦江饭店被美丽花园所环绕，锦北楼、贵宾楼和锦楠楼共有客房442间，贵宾楼、峻岭楼、另有公寓房和办公房共192套，锦江小礼堂则提供专业的会议、宴会服务。

上海锦江饭店开业至今已接待过500多位国家元首和政府首脑，见证过无数重大历史事件。

1. 锦江饭店全景图
   Jin Jiang Hotel
2. 峻岭楼
   Jun Ling Building

On June 9 1951, Jin Jiang Hotel was opened at No. 59 Mao Ming Road. Jin Jiang Hotel, one of the most famous hotels with best location in Shanghai at that time, covers an area of more than 30,000 square meters which includes a 16,500 sqm green area.

Situated close to Huai Hai Road, the Hotel enjoys convenient traffic, for example, only 10 minutes away from Xin Tian Di—a hotspot of entertainment where fashion meets history and culture, a 5-minute walk from South Shaanxi Road Station/Yan'an Road Highway and a 10-minute walk from Nanjing Road Commercial Circle.

Surrounded by beautiful garden, Jin Jiang Hotel has 442 guest rooms located in Cathay Building, Cathay Garden and Grosvenor House, and 192 service apartments and suites located in Grosvenor House, Jun Lin Building. Jin Jiang Grand Hall offers the professional meeting & banquet services to host a successful event.

As a state guest house, Jin Jiang Hotel has received more than 500 state heads and government leaders and witnessed many important historical events since its establishing.

1. 锦北楼正面
   Cathay Building
2. 锦楠楼大堂
   Lobby of Cathay Garden
3. 锦福会中餐厅走廊
   Corridor
4. 贵宾楼贵宾俱乐部
   VIP Club

1. 锦江小礼堂宴会厅
   Grand Ballroom
2. 锦北楼锦福会中餐厅
   Fortune Palace
3. 锦北楼锦江厅
   Jin Jiang Ballroom
4. 锦楠楼百事丽西餐厅
   Cathay Brasserie

1. 锦江小礼堂宴会厅
   Grand Ballroom
2. 锦楠楼百事丽西餐厅
   Cathay Brasserie
3. 锦北楼
   Cathay Building
4. 锦江小礼堂贵宾会见厅
   VIP Room
5. 锦楠楼大堂酒廊
   Lobby Lounge
6. 锦楠楼大堂书房
   Lobby Library VIP Room
7. 锦北楼梦咖啡
   Dream Cafe

1. 锦楠楼
   Cathay Garden
2. 贵宾楼
   Grosvenor House
3. 锦江小礼堂
   Jin Jiang Grand Hall
4. 室内游泳池
   Indoor Swimming Pool
5. 健身房
   Gymnasium
6. 桑拿浴室
   Sauna

1. 贵宾楼总统套房
   Presidential Suite
2. 锦北楼经典房
   Classic Room
3. 锦北楼经典套房
   Classic Suite

五星级上海浦东香格里拉大酒店成为亚太区最大豪华酒店集团——香格里拉酒店集团麾下规模最大的产业。自1998年开业以来，凭借优质的服务和良好的设施，酒店屡获殊荣，备受赞誉。2005年落成的紫金楼以及2009年面目一新的浦江楼奠定了浦东香格里拉无与伦比、卓尔不群的地位。

上海浦东香格里拉大酒店地处上海乃至全国的商业中心地带——陆家嘴金融贸易区，毗邻浦江东岸，俯瞰外滩风光，地理位置无与伦比。对岸的外滩，作为闻名于世的历史地标点，20世纪90年代初曾是上海最繁华的金融中心，而今其独特旖旎风光吸引来众多各地游客，展示着世纪交替时辉煌雄壮的建筑文明。

由纽约建筑师Kohn Pedersen Fox（KPF）设计的紫金楼于2005年9月26日正式开业，拥有375间客房和套房。其中高级豪华房面积达到54平方米（581平方英尺）以上。浦江楼拥有577间客房及套房。从宽敞、舒适的客房和套房眺望，可欣赏古老外滩、旖旎浦江或上海现代金融区的城市风光。位于浦江楼和紫金楼共有区域的是数家集世界时尚前沿设计于一体的餐厅和酒吧，拥有两个上海最大面积宴会厅的会议及宴会设施、[气] Spa、两间健身房、两间游泳池及一个室外网球场。

所有客房都设有全套香格里拉设施,包括宽带及无线上网、数据接口、国际长途直拨、卫星电视、茶水/咖啡冲泡设备以及24小时客房服务。

酒店引以为豪的盛事堂是酒店的第二间宴会厅,面积为沪上最大,可举办容纳1,700位宾客的鸡尾酒会。加上原有的大宴会厅和12间大小各异的会议室,酒店总共能够提供高达6,500平方米(69,965平方英尺)的室内外活动场所,可满足各类活动的需求。

10间风格迥异的餐厅、酒吧及酒廊均出自先锋时尚设计师的手笔,涵盖了多次获得国际大奖的设计界大腕Adam D. Tihany、Bilkey Llinas Design和Super Potato。

经典法菜、独特设计和醉人美景在酒店的标志性餐厅翡翠36餐厅及酒吧中融为一体。居高临下,位于酒店的三十六层,宾客可俯瞰都市和外滩全景。屡获国际殊荣的设计师Adam D. Tihany创造的独特建筑结构和设计令人称奇。

香格里拉招牌中餐厅桂花楼精选淮扬菜、川菜、本帮菜以飨大众,被美国酒店杂志社评为2009年度中国最佳酒店餐厅奖;被艺术家杂志评为2009上海最佳餐厅。

香格里拉[气]Spa以亚洲传统古方为本,根据五行概念设计,将金木水火土和阴阳和谐之气水乳交融。浦东香格里拉[气]Spa致力于营造出浓郁的"Spa中的Spa"的概念。[气]Spa曾被福布斯网站评选为全球十大最热门酒店Spa之一,2009年被 *Spa Finder* 读者票选为中国最受欢迎Spa。

2009年,浦东香格里拉浦江楼在历经20个月的装修后,以全新的面貌再次亮相,一案一几,雅致陈设,外滩风光,尽收眼底。

1. 上海浦东香格里拉劳斯莱斯奢华轿车服务
   Pudong Shangri-La, Shanghai-Rolls-Royce Phantom Limousine Service
2. 上海浦东香格里拉浦江楼豪华阁
   Pudong Shangri-La, Shanghai-River Wing Horizon Club Lounge

1. 热情好客香格里拉情
   Shangri-La Hospitality from the Heart
2. 上海浦东香格里拉外景
   Pudong Shangri-La Shanghai, Hotel Exterior

The five-star Pudong Shangri-La, Shanghai is one of the most highly regarded deluxe properties of Shangri-La Hotels and Resorts, Asia Pacific's leading luxury hotel group. Since it opened in 1998, the hotel has collated several awards and accolades for its fine service and facilities. With the addition of its Grand Tower in September 2005, the Pudong Shangri-La, Shanghai has been elevated to a class of its own, recognized the world over.The recently renewed River Wing now Presents a style of classical elegance with oriental touches after a 20-month refurbishment of its guest rooms and Horizon Club Lounge.

Pudong Shangri-La, Shanghai is located in the Lujiazui finance and trade district of Pudong (or East Shanghai), which is being developed to become the country's business hub. The hotel is ideally located on the eastern bank of the famous Huangpu River, overlooking Shanghai's legendary waterfront strip, the Bund. A historic landmark famous the world over, the Bund was Shanghai's financial center in the early nineties. Today it is a showcase of turn-of-the-century architecture.

Comprising two towers – River Wing and Grand Tower – the hotel showcases spacious, well-appointed rooms and suites with views overlooking the historical Bund, the mighty Huangpu River, as well as that of the futuristic Pudong financial district cityscape.

The Grand Tower, designed by New York-based architect Kohn Pedersen Fox (KPF) features 375 rooms and suites, including the Premier Room which offers 54 square meters (581 square feet) of comfortable space. Located between the Grand Tower and the River Wing which houses 578 rooms and suites, are a range of trend-setting designer restaurants and bars, comprehensive meetings and conference facilities with two of the city's largest Ballrooms, CHI, the SPA, two Health Clubs, two swimming pools and a floodlit outdoor tennis court.

All rooms enjoy the full array of Shangri-La amenities, which include complimentary broadband and wireless Internet, data ports

and IDD, satellite TV, tea and coffee making facilities and 24-hour room service.

Taking its pride of place is the Hotel's second ballroom–the China Hall – which is Shanghai's largest, with a capacity for up to 1,700 guests at cocktail receptions. Together with the Grand Ballroom and 12 meeting rooms of various sizes, the Hotel's meeting facilities offer a total of 6,500 square meters (69,965 square feet) of versatile indoor and outdoor event space.

Creating benchmarks in the Pudong and overall Shanghai entertainment scene are Pudong Shangri-La's 10 cutting-edge designer restaurants, bars and lounges showcasing the works of international award-winning interior design mavericks like Adam D. Tihany, Bilkey Llinas Design and Super Potato.

A dazzling combination of innovative cuisine, dramatic design and stunning views is Shanghai's iconic restaurant–Jade on 36–the Hotel's signature restaurant. Guests appreciate the unique architecture and design by award-winning Adam D. Tihany, with panoramic views of Shanghai and the famous Bund from Level 36, where Chef de Cuisine Fabrice Giraud showcases traditional French cuisine with a contemporary twist–culled from an extensive culinary experience in five Michelin-starred restaurants in Europe. Notably the one Michelin star Restaurant le Pain et le Vin in Brussels at which he was Head Chef from 1999 till 2001.

Pudong Shangri-La, Shanghai's signature Chinese Restaurant–Gui Hua Lou – serves a variety of Huaiyangnese, Sichuanese and Shanghainese cuisine. Opened in January 2006, diners may choose to be seated in the main dining area with views to the riverside promenade, or have the option of dining in one of five private rooms. It has won several accolades: 2009 Gui Hua Lou Awards "Top 50 Restaurants in China" (*Food & Wine Chin*) and "Shanghai's Best Restaurant 2009" (*Shanghai Tatler*), etc.

Shangri-La's signature CHI, the Spa at Shangri-La made its China debut at the Pudong Shangri-La in late 2005. Featuring some of the largest and most luxurious private Spa suites in the city, creating a "Spa within a Spa" atmosphere, it has been voted as "Favourite Spa in Mainland China" in the 2009 Spa Finder Readers, Choice Awards, "Top Ten Hottest Hotel Spas" by Forbes.com and the "Spa Interior Design of the Year" at the Baccarat Asia Spa Awards.

1. 浦东香格里拉自助餐厅怡咖啡
   Yi Cafe
2. 浦东香格里拉中餐厅——桂花楼
   Gui Hua Lou
3. 浦东香格里拉大堂酒廊
   River Wing Lobby Lounge
4. 浦东香格里拉滩万日餐厅
   Nadaman
5. 浦东香格里拉翡翠36餐厅
   Jade on 36 Restaurant

1. 浦东香格拉外滩全景苏州无锡桂林厅晚宴布置
   Suzhou, Wuxi, Guilin Rooms
2. 浦东香格里拉紫金楼行政酒廊
   Pudong Shangri-La, Shanghai-
   Grand Tower Horizon Club Lounge
3. 浦东香格里拉行政酒廊外滩全景图
   The Magnificent Bund View from the River Wing
4. 浦东香格里拉紫金楼游泳池
   Grand Tower Indoor Swimming Pool
5. [气] SPA双人SPA套房
   CHI, The SPA Double SPA Suite
6. 上海浦东香格里拉浦江楼豪华阁外滩全景房
   Pudong Shangri-La, Shanghai, Horizon Deluxe Room

上海柏悦酒店
PARK HYATT SHANGHAI

自古以来，诗人总喜欢以星星为题材，写出一首又一首委婉动人的诗。坐落于上海环球金融中心七十九至九十三层的上海柏悦酒店，把您与繁星之间的距离拉近。

"垂直型综合城区"位于浦东陆家嘴金融贸易区中心区的上海环球金融中心，楼高101层，492米，是世界上最高的大厦之一，也造就了上海柏悦酒店成为世界最高的酒店。这幢环保型的摩天大厦由兴建东京享负盛名的六本木新城的森大厦株式会社（Mori Building）负责兴建。

上海柏悦酒店的室内设计由屡获奖项的纽约设计师季裕棠（Tony Chi）先生及公司 Tony Chi and Associates设计。他的设计理念是具有现代中国特色的私人住宅式酒店，在体现富丽堂皇的家应有的舒适之余，亦注重传统中国几何学和建筑学。宾客将依次序由大门开始，行经大厅和房间，最后以庭院为终点。他把庭院想象为一个平静和宁神的圣地，让客人在这宁静的庭院中练习太极和下中国象棋。庭院将以自然的米色和天然物料为主，无论在感觉或是设计方面均保持及其讲究而低调。客人经过高达16米的酒店大门，边欣赏艺术长廊内一系列的中国现代艺术作品，边经由好像不受时空影响的电梯迅速被送到87层，到达酒店大堂。经过全天供应中西美食的大堂客厅，便到达充满欧陆风情的大堂餐厅，内设全套Bulthaup厨具

装备的开放式厨房,并设有可供10人就餐的"主厨餐桌",为客人提供专享盛宴。与大堂餐厅两端相连的分别是一个玻璃屋样的藏酒窖,珍藏了来自世界各地的400多种葡萄佳酿,和一个私密温馨的大堂酒吧。延续中国式私人住宅的理念,位于八十六层的沙龙共设有7间私人宴会厅及会议室。

当客人行至八十五层,则是安静闲适的水境,设有20米长的豪华泳池、水疗中心、健身室和一个太极园,每天清晨有太极大师在此言传身教,酒店总经理沈凯歌先生有时也会与客人一起领略这一传统中华武术的魅力。

如果说酒店的低层部分是平静的绿洲,而高层则洋溢着活力和刺激。于2008年底开业的世纪100,占据九十一至九十三层,是世界上最高的餐厅、酒吧和私人宴会场所。九十一层是可以容纳300位客人的餐厅,25米高的落地玻璃窗使整个空间更加开阔。多个开放式厨房提供中西日式美食,包括一个肉类厨房、配备4台巨型火炉的西餐厨房、配备烤鸭炉的中餐厨房、寿司吧、甜点区以及葡萄酒窖。

酒店的14间套房面积为130~194平方米(1,400~2,088平方呎)。8间特别套房内的主人睡房均备有两张特大床,浴室内设有特大浴缸,带有开放式厨房的私人宴会厅可为客人私人款待之用。每间套房均配有私人管家,酒店拥有一支由20个经过层层选拔、严格培训而成的全女生管家团队,为客人提供柏悦品牌享誉盛名无微不至的个性化服务。

1. 87层大堂客厅
   87 Floor Living Room
2. 87层酒店前台
   87 Floor Reception Desk

Since time immemorial, poets have romanticised and waxed lyrical about "sle-eping under the stars". Spanning the 79th through 93rd floors of the Shanghai World Financial Center (SWFC), Park Hyatt Sha-nghai is literally the highest hotel in the world.

Situated in the heart of the Lujiazui busi-ness district in Pudong, the 492-metre SWF is one of the tallest buildings in the world, housing 101-storeys. The eco-friendly skyscraper has been developed by Mori Building, which also built the highly successful Roppongi Hills complex in Tokyo.

The interiors of Park Hyatt Shanghai have been created by the award-winning New York-based designer Tony Chi of Tony Chi and Associates. His vision was to create a sophisticated modern-Chinese residence, designed with respect to traditional Chinese geometry and architecture, while providing all the comforts of a stately home. Guests will therefore travel through a sequence of "gates, halls and chambers", culminating in a courtyard where daily life congregates. Chi envisages a calm and spiritual sanctuary where guests can practice Tai-Chi or play Chinese chess in the courtyards. The spaces are therefore understated in both mood and design, with a predominance of earth tones and natural materials. Entering through a dramatic 16-metre high entrance gate, guests then traverse through a series of hushed galleries displaying contemporary Chinese art, leading through to elevator "cabins", which whisk them up a giddy 87 floors to the reception chamber. A tranquil Living Room, serving Western and Chinese comfort food all day, leads into an elegant European Dining Room, featuring an open Bulthaup kitchen and a 10-seater chef's table, available for tailored suppers. Adjacent to the Dining Room is a glass-walled wine library, housing 400-wines from around the world, and an intimate leather-

1. 86层沙龙
   86 Floor Salons Courtyard
2. 酒店外观
   Exterior

1

lined circular Bar.

Continuing with the philosophy of the Chinese private residence are the Salons on the 86th floor below. Below that, on the 85th floor, guests will encounter Water's Edge, a relaxation zone featuring an overflowing 20-metre infinity pool, a Wellness Studio with two treatment rooms, and a gym. There is also a Tai-Chi "courtyard", where a master will lead Tai-Chi sessions every morning. There, guests will be able to meet the charismatic General Manager of the hotel, Christophe Sadones, who will occasionally take part in the martial art sessions.

While the lower floors of the hotel will be an oasis of tranquility, the upper floors, opening at the end of the year, are being designed to reverberate with energy and excitement. Spanning floors 91 through 93, 100 Century Avenue is the highest bar of the world, restaurant and private dining room, and is primed to be the ultimate wining and dining destination in Shanghai. On the 91st floor, a 300-seater super-restaurant features in the sprawling space with 25-metre floor-to-ceiling windows. Serving Western, Chinese and Japanese cuisines, the multiple show

2

kitchens will include a charcuterie, a western kitchen with four dramatic charcoal grill ovens, a Chinese kitchen featuring a duck-roasting oven, a sushi bar, a pastry counter, and a wine cellar.

The hotel's 14 suites measure 75 to 180 sqm (807 to 1,938 sqft) and each of the eight speciality suites feature two king-size beds in the master bedroom, an oversized tub in the bath chamber, and a private dining room with an open kitchen for private entertaining. Each suite comes with its own private butler-one of a team of 20 all-female butlers that have been hand-picked to deliver the incomparable discreet and personalised service that's synony-mous with the Park Hyatt brand.

1、4.87层酒吧
  87 Floor Bar
2、礼宾部
  87 Floor Bell Desk
3、酒店前台
  87 Floor Reception Desk

1、2. 87层大堂茶阁
　　87 Floor Pantry
3. 87层主厨餐厅
　　87 Floor Dining Room Chef's Table
4. 92层世纪100西式酒吧
　　92 Floor 100 Century Avenue Music Room
5. 86层沙龙III
　　86 Floor Salon III
6. 86层沙龙II
　　86 Floor Salon II

1. 87层大堂客厅
   85 Floor Dining Room
2. 85层水境——水疗中心
   85 Floor Water's Edge Spa Treatment Room
3、4. 85层水境——无边界泳池
   85 Floor Water's Edge Infinity Pool
5. 85层水境——太极园
   85 Floor Water's Edge Taichi Courtyard

1. 柏悦套房
   Park Suite
2. 85层水境——更衣间
   85 Floor Water's Edge Changing Room
3. 93层宴会厅休息区
   93 Floor Banquet Room Lounge Area
4. 85层水境——理疗室
   85 Floor Water's Edge Spa Treatment Room
5、9. 柏悦客房
   Park Room
6、10. 外交官套房
   Diplomat Suite
7. 柏悦豪华房浴缸
   Park Deluxe Room Bathtub
8. 主席套房
   Chairman Suite

上海大酒店由上海烟草（集团）公司下属上海王宝和大酒店有限公司投资建造，位于上海最繁华的南京东路外滩商务休闲圈内，与"中华第一街"南京东路步行街的中心地段——世纪广场毗邻。交通四通八达，与多条地铁线相邻；步行可达人民广场、外滩等主要观光景点，优越的地理位置使您尽享购物、美食、观光、娱乐、交通便捷之益。上海大酒店外观稳重大气，设计风格独特，装潢豪华惊艳，格调优雅高贵，与一街之隔的姐妹酒店——上海王宝和大酒店呈双星同辉之势。

酒店占地6,713平方米（地上16层及地下3层）总建筑面积达60,131平方米，由法国何斐德设计师事务所和华东设计院设计，HBA（香港）设计师事务所进行装潢设计，外观稳重大气、设计风格独特、格调优雅高贵、装潢豪华惊艳。酒店拥有353间豪华客／套房，以及沪上首屈一指的复式总统套房，空间宽敞，豪华典雅。全新开业的上海大酒店配备先进的楼宇自动化技术及独到的门禁系统，拥有40平方米以上的豪华客房及其10平方米以上的宽敞卫浴空间，干湿分离的双台盆全进口卫浴设施，大屏幕液晶电视，为商务客人提供便捷和保障的具有不间断充电功能的保险箱等高端设施。

酒店一层大堂酒廊拥有开阔的挑高空间，伴随着流淌的音乐，是商务会谈、亲友小憩的理想场所。环境幽雅的

咖啡厅除每日提供自助早餐外,更在晚间供应美味超值的中西式自助晚餐,尽显上海都市的浪漫情调。二层高档奢华的法国餐厅,由50年厨龄的法国Maitres Cuisiniers协会顶尖厨师Mr. Robert Lucien Caillault担任总厨,他曾在日本大仓饭店集团工作长达10年,为法国菜在日本的普及和推广作出了巨大贡献。他将为宾客奉上正宗的法式大餐和上选葡萄酒。三层的宝粤轩配有零点餐厅及可分割式贵宾包房,特邀现任法国国际厨皇美食协会会员主席、"香港食神"龙甜师傅的得意门生、当代香港厨艺大师——林炎发先生亲自掌勺正宗港式粤菜。林先生此次加盟上海大酒店宝粤轩,将分享他精湛的厨艺,诚邀您品尝粤菜之精华,体验美食之艺术。酒店的最大亮点便是那悬浮于楼体中央的椭圆形大宴会厅——上海厅,在夜间宛如明珠,晶莹剔透,是现代与经典的完美结合。除无柱式和7米超高空间的设计概念外,还配备最领先的高科技会议设备。7种可变色灯光以及遥控式追光灯可根据客人要求提供极具个性化的会场氛围。400多平方米的宽敞序厅空间,加之多种不同规格和设计风格的宴会厅,成为各类商务会议和主题宴会的绝佳选择。五层集合了室内游泳池、健身房、桌球房、美发中心等健身休闲设施。酒店六层的行政俱乐部除了拥有独立接待中心、专用餐厅、小型商务中心、会议室外,还拥有一个内庭式露天平台,为繁忙的商务客人提供一个闹中取静的悠闲之所。

更值得一提的是,酒店拥有沪上首屈一指的复式总统套房,并配有一处闹中取静的空中花园。另外还设有商务中心、礼宾部、10部最新一代的奥迪斯高速客用电梯等。除了2.8米挑高空间可停放各种大型车辆的地下一层车库外,在寸土寸金的黄金地段更拥有超过170个车位的地下一至地下三层停车库。

上海大酒店将与坐落于南京东路——外滩钻石地段的各大国际品牌酒店一起,形成超豪华酒店区域,共同迎接世博,展现上海的都市魅力。

1. 大堂
   Lobby
2. 大堂酒廊
   Lobby Lounge
3. 商务中心
   Business Center

Invested by Shanghai Central Hotels Co., Ltd. which is under the Shanghai Tobacco (Group) Corp, Grand Central Hotel Shanghai locates in the most flourishing central area of Shanghai within the Bund business and recreation circle and adjoining the Century Square that lies in the central area of the Nanjing Road Pedestrian Mall, known as "The First Street of China". As the hotel site east access to all direction and adjacent to many subway lines, our honored guest could walk to many main sightseeing resorts such as the People's Square and the Bund. This superior geographical location provides great convenience in shopping, sightseeing, entertainment and transportation. The hotel covers an area of 6,713 square meters. It has 16 floors on the ground and 3 underground floors. The total built-up area is up to 60,131 square meters, designed by Frderic-Rolland Design Studio and the Designing Institute of East China. Its internal decoration is designed by HBA (Hong Kong) Designer's Studio. The appearance of Grand Central Hotel Shanghai is composed and formal; its design unique and special and its taste graceful and noble, and its decoration luxurious and attractive. The hotel owns 353 luxurious guest rooms suites, which boast big space, luxurious and refined furnishing and the best duplex president suite of Shanghai.

1. 上海厅婚宴
   Wedding Ceremony
2. 宝粤轩
   Bo Yuet Hin
3. 上海厅
   Shanghai Grand Ballroom
4. 酒店外景
   Hotel View

The first floor of hotel is the lobby, coffee shop and lobby lounge. The French restaurant lies in the second floor, and on the third floor is the Chinese restaurant Bo Yuet Hin headed by famous Hongkong chef. On the fourth floor, there are the multi-function rooms of different specifications. Among them is a large oval-sized 7-meter high pillarless banquet hall with no column support – Shanghai Grand Ballroom, which suspends in the middle of the building like a pearl and a highlight of the hotel. On fifth floor is an ensemble of many recreation facilities such as swimming pool, gymnasium and billiards room and hair-dressing centre etc. The sixth floor includes an executive club which not only has independent reception counter, small-scale commercial center, meeting rooms, but also an roof courtyard that offers a relaxing and quiet place isolated from noisy neighborhood to our busy commercial guests.

Moreover, the hotel also has the excellent Presidential Suite which includes a quiet garden. Besides, the business center, concierge, 10 latest Otis high-speed guest elevators and underground three-floor parking area, all these are well equipped with complete support facilities.

The Grand Central Hotel Shanghai will form an area of super luxurious hotels together with all other international hotels located in the Nanjing East Road — the heart of the city, in order to greet the World Expo 2010 ShangHai China. It is a showcase of Shanghai, for the glamour of this beautiful city.

1. 紫金厅
   Crystal Hall
2. 贵宾厅
   VIP Room
3. 大堂酒吧
   Lobby Lounge
4. 金百合厅
   Iris Room
5. 翡翠厅
   Jade Hall
6. 法国餐厅
   L'ile de France

1. 大堂
Lobby
2. 宝粤轩——包房
Bo Yuet Hin—Vip Room
3. 行政楼层
Executive Floor
4. 进门长廊
Entrance

1. 酒店夜景
　Night View
2. 酒店装饰
　Decoration
3. 健身房
　Gym
4. 桌球房
　Billiards
5. 游泳池
　Swimming Pool

1. 豪华套房　　　　3. 商务套房——书房
   Deluxe Suite　　　 Business Suite-Study Room
2. 卫生间　　　　　4、5. 豪华商务房
   Bathroom　　　　　 Deluxe Room

上海虹桥迎宾馆坐落于上海虹桥开发区与古北新区交界处，与万商云集的上海国际展览中心、国际贸易中心以及世贸商城相隔咫尺之遥，距虹桥国际机场、浦东陆家嘴金融贸易区和都市中心区域也仅仅15分钟的车程，宾馆附近的高架道路更是让您在40分钟内便捷地驱车抵达浦东国际机场。

上海虹桥迎宾馆是一座极富特色的五星级花园式酒店，是上海东湖集团旗下的重要成员酒店。2003年1月虹桥迎宾馆被正式评定为五星级旅游涉外饭店，跻身五星级饭店行列，在宾馆的发展历程中树立起一座里程碑。

上海虹桥迎宾馆是上海最著名的国宾馆之一，曾迎来五大洲的150余位国家元首、高层政要和知名人士，如中国前国家主席江泽民、美国前总统布什、英国前首相布莱尔和日本前首相中曾根等贵宾。

上海虹桥迎宾馆拥有数块风格迥异的完整草坪，其中最大的皇家草坪能够容纳近1,000人，是举办草坪婚礼及室外大型活动的理想场地；宾馆拥有216间客房、50多栋各式风格的别墅、16套公寓、5个餐厅与酒吧、12个气派非凡的多功能厅。无论是商务旅行、休闲度假、盛大庆典、公司宴请、私人雅酌，还是喜庆婚礼，虹桥迎宾馆都是您最佳的选择。

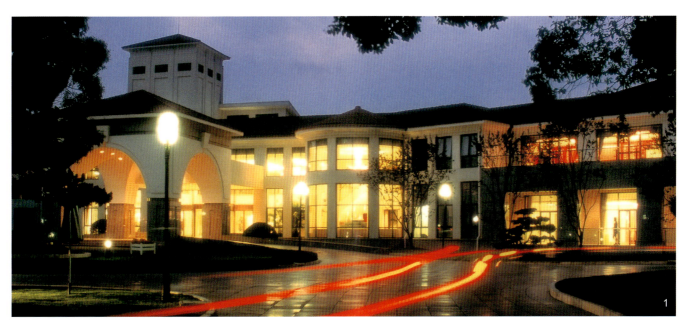

虹桥迎宾馆得天独厚，近20万平方米的园林犹如大花园，形成了都市中罕见的皇家园林，气派非凡。参天大树傲然耸立，园林精品点缀其中，在绿荫的映衬下织成一幅赏心悦目的画面。数百颗香樟、雪松、银杏等珍贵古树在都市中再现了森林，其中令人叹为观止的是5株70年以上树龄的雪松，古拙奇特，伸展苍劲，给人以沧桑之感；还有超过50年树龄的银杏、超过40年树龄的榕树，都具有极高的观赏价值。它们像饱经风霜的老者无声地诉说着悠远的历史。

这里是为政要名流、商业巨子倾情设定的时尚坐标；这里是一座汇聚群英的皇家花园；这里是为各界精英人士提供的高端社交平台；这里是跨国公司高层偕其家人共享的温馨家园；这里是您精彩生活的必然之选，也是您独具匠心的人生驿站。

1. 主楼夜景
   Night Scene of No. 6 Building
2. 宾馆航拍图
   Hotel Overall View

1. 行政楼大堂
   Lobby of Executive Building
2. 主席楼会见厅
   Meeting Room of Chairman Building

Shanghai Hong Qiao State Guest Hotel is located in the Changning District. It is in the western part of Shanghai and is another 'pearl' of Shanghai and its ideal location is situated in the Hong Qiao Economical and Technical Development Zone. Within walking distance, there are Shanghai International Exhibition Center, Shanghai Mart, and Shanghai International Trade Center. The hotel is also a mere 15-minute drive from Hong Qiao International Airport and downtown. Also, the drive only takes 15 minutes to Pu Dong Lujiazui Commercial Area and 40 minutes to Pu Dong International Airport via highway.

Shanghai Hong Qiao State Guest Hotel is a unique 5-star garden style hotel. It is one of the major garden hotels within the Dong Hu group. Endorsed by the National Tourism Administration of the People's Republic of China, the Shanghai Hong Qiao State Guest Hotel is officially acknowledged as a 5-star hotel in January 2003. It is the recognition affirmation of our guest hotel's outstanding operation, management, definitely facilitates and development in the future. It placed a milestone for Shanghai Hong Qiao State Guest Hotel development with no doubt.

The Hong Qiao State Guest Hotel is one of the most famous State Guest Hotels in Shanghai which has received more than 150 Presidents, State Guests and Celebrities, such as former President of China Jiang Zemin, former President of U.S. George W. Bush, former Prime Minister of Britain Tony Blair and former Prime Minister of Japan Yasuhiro etc.

The Hong Qiao State Guest Hotel is proud to have the largest garden within its premises. The biggest is the Royal Garden which can accommodates 1,000 people. It is the ideal place where can hold wedding and large activities outside. Our hotel not only has 216 lavish hotel rooms, but also has 50 different

1. 东湖轩中餐厅
   East Lake Chinese Restaurant
2. 行政酒廊
   Executive Lounge
3. 花园回廊酒吧
   Scenery Bar
4. 2号楼小宴会厅
   Banquet Room in Presidential Building

styles villas. In addition, we also have 5 restaurants and 12 banquet and conference rooms. Whether it is business travel, leisure vacation, the grand celebration or happy wedding, Hong Qiao State Guest Hotel also is your best option.

The advantaged garden of about 200,000 m² of Hong Qiao State Guest Hotel looks like a royal garden. Tall trees stand haughtily and the elaborate garden works form a picture against green shades, pleasing your eyes and mind. With several hundred camphor trees, cedars, gingkoes and some other rare ancient trees of hundred year, the forest in city reappears, in which, the most surprising is the five cedars of longer than 70 years, so age-old looking and fancy, stretching vigorously, giving you an impression as if they have experienced many vicissitudes of life; additionally, some other trees, such as gingkoes of longer than 50 years, banyans of longer than 40 years are of very high decorative value.

This is an ideal place which sets fashion coordinate for political elites and business giants. This is a royal garden which draws elites from all walks of life. This is a high-end social platform for celebrities. This is even more a warm homeland for high-level personnel in JV with their family. This is the choice for colorful life for certain and the post station in life showing ingenuity.

1. 龙虾
   Lobster
2. 360°景观多功能厅
   360° Multi-function Room
3. 六国峰会菜肴
   Dish for the Six-Country Summit
4. "晓"日餐厅
   "Akatsuki" Japanese Restaurant
5. 石头酒廊
   Rocky Lounge
6. 2号楼总统套餐厅
   Dining Room of Presidential Suite

1. 国宴厅
   State Banquet Room
2. 总统楼大会见厅
   Grand Meeting Room in Presidential Building
3. 总统套房房间装饰
   Decoration of Presidential Suite
4. 法拉利活动
   F1 Event
5. 草坪婚礼
   Garden Wedding
6. 健身中心
   Clark Hatch Fitness Center
7. 前厅部员工
   Front Office Staff
8. 宴会服务员
   Banquet Waitress
9. 中餐厅服务员
   Waitress of Chinese Restaurant
10. 总厨
    Chef
11. 房务部员工
    Housekeeping Staff

1. 行政房
   Executive Room
2. 总统楼总统套夫人房浴缸
   Madam Bathtub in Presidential Suite of Presidential Building
3. 总统楼夜景
   Night Scene of Presidential Building
4. 2号楼总统套房
   Presidential Suite of No. 2 Building

上海金茂君悦大酒店位于88层金茂大厦的五十三至八十七层，曾被2000吉尼斯世界纪录千禧年版评为"世界最高酒店"。拥有555间豪华客房的上海金茂君悦大酒店地处浦东高速发展的商业金融区陆家嘴的中心，离上海国际会议中心大酒店仅5分钟，距豫园和外滩著名的邻江大道只有10分钟路程。从酒店到虹桥国际机场只需30分钟，到浦东国际机场只需50分钟。

金茂大厦由中国金茂（集团）有限公司筹建，由芝加哥著名的建筑公司Skidmore、Owings 和 Merrill 设计，高度为420.5米。大厦里最具特色的是上海金茂君悦大酒店内的一个从五十六层起共33层楼高的中庭。酒店的内装修都是由美国佛罗里达州的Bilkey Llinas设计咨询公司设计的。

上海金茂君悦在现代艺术中融入了中国传统文化。客房豪华漂亮，均可欣赏到申城美景。客房中配有CAT5高速个人电脑接驳、两条电话线路和语音留言信箱。超大浴室内有单独的淋浴间和浴缸。淋浴间装有高科技三喷头淋浴塔和防蒸气镜（便于进行个人修饰）、玻璃洗脸盆和双面衣柜。酒店有嘉宾轩套房34间、外交官套房8间、总统套房2间及主席套房1间。作为凯悦集团在中国的旗舰，上海金茂君悦大酒店为国际商务游客提供了一流的服务和齐全的酒店设施。

嘉宾轩拥有8个楼层的行政套房，全天礼宾部服务，是商务客人的理想住处。嘉宾轩的客人在贵宾厅享用早餐、晚间鸡尾酒和全天候供应的茶点的同时可以观赏外滩风景。嘉宾轩还为住客提供免费会议室。

上海金茂君悦大酒店的商务中心位于五十四层的大堂里，该中心为客人开展商务活动提供全套设施和秘书服务，包括传真发送、电传、电脑、文字处理、摄影、翻译、打印和包裹包装。商务中心还可以按客人的要求印制名片。商务中心提供私人工作区域按小时或天出租。考虑到国际时间区之间的时差，商务中心提供24小时全天服务。

下榻于酒店的客人在紧张的工作之余可以享受位于酒店五十七层的健身和娱乐设施。绿洲健身中心是"世界上最高的健身俱乐部"之一。除享用俱乐部中的整套健身设施外，客人在室内游泳池游泳时还可以观赏上海全景。

上海金茂君悦大酒店有多个餐厅及酒吧供商务客人随意挑选，其中包括粤珍轩——广东餐厅、食在56（汇集多种风味的餐厅，日珍——日本餐厅、意庐——有砖砌的匹萨烤炉的意大利餐厅、烧烤餐厅和天庭—— 位于三十三层中庭底部的酒廊）、九重天酒廊——"世界最高的酒吧"之一，位于八十七层的空中酒廊、钢琴吧、咖啡厅、有5个中亚餐柜的食府小吃街。

金茂俱乐部上海餐厅位于酒店八十六层，是沪上最高档的上海菜餐厅，精美的菜肴和个性化的服务令人难以忘怀。

酒店有各种宴会和会议设施。其中包括能容纳395人的金茂音乐厅、1,200人大宴会厅、800人的嘉宾厅及10个多功能厅，均装备先进的艺术多媒体器材及声像设施。

1. 浦东夜景
   The Night Scene of Pudong
2. 前厅
   Forecourt
3. 九重天酒廊
   Cloud 9

Grand Hyatt Shanghai has been included in the 2000 Millennium edition of the Guinness Book of Records as the highest hotel in the world. Crowning the prestigious 88-storey Jin Mao Tower the hotel commences on the 53rd floor and rises to the 87th floor. The 555-room Grand Hyatt Shanghai is located in the centre of Lujiazui, Pudong's business and financial area. Located in the prosperous Pudong business district, Grand Hyatt Shanghai is just 10 minutes from 'The Bund', the city's famous waterfront showcasing turn-of-the-century architectural masterpieces and Yu Yuan Garden. Shanghai Hong Qiao International Airport is a 30-minute drive and from Pudong International Airport approximately 50 minutes away.

Jin Mao Tower was developed by China Jin Mao Group Co. Ltd., and designed by world-renowned architects, Skidmore, Owings and Merrill of Chicago, and soars to a height of 420.5 meters (1,380 feet). The most dramatic architectural feature of the Tower is a 33-storey atrium inside of Grand Hyatt Shanghai, starting on the 56th floor. The interior design of the Hotel is by Bilkey Llinas Consulting of Palm Beach, Florida.

Featuring contemporary art deco combined with traditional Chinese imagery, the guest rooms are spacious and all with stunning views of Shanghai. All guest rooms have broadband Internet access; CAT 5 high-speed modem computer dataports; two-line telephones and voice mail message system. The oversized bathrooms are appointed with separate bath and shower feature high-tech "shower-towers" with 3 shower heads, heated mirrors in the shower cubicle (convenient for shaving while you shower), clear glass sinks and double sided wardrobes. The hotel has 17 Grand Suites, 17 Grand Riverview Suites, 8 Diplomatic Suites, 2 Presidential Suites and one Chairman's Suite.

Eight floors of exclusive Grand Club accommodation are provided at the top of the Hotel, ideal for business travellers seeking an even higher level of personalized service. All-day concierge is provided to guests who can enjoy complimentary continental breakfast, evening cocktails served with deluxe hors d'oeurves and coffee and tea in the comfort of their private two-storey high Bund View Grand Club Lounge. Complimentary Internet access and an executive Boardroom is available for Grand Club guests.

Located on lobby level 54, Grand Hyatt's Business Centre provides a full range of office equipment and confidential secretarial services, such as translation, printing and parcel wrapping. Business cards can also be printed and delivered upon guest requests. The Business Centre also offers private work areas for rental on an hourly or daily basis and a conference room which seats up to ten persons. To allow for differences in international time zones, the Business Centre is open 24 hours a day, 7 days a week.

1. 晨曦初照
   Greeting the Dawn
2. 金茂大厦
   Jin Mao Tower
3. 璀璨景致
   Night View from Hotel
4. 大堂
   Lobby

1. 嘉宾厅
   Crystal Ballroom
2. 金茂俱乐部
   Club Jin Mao
3. 粤珍轩
   Canton

To wind down after a day of hectic business dealings, the business traveller can appreciate Grand Hyatt's fitness and recreational facilities that are located on Level 57—CLUB OASIS. In addition to comprehensive health club facilities and SPA treatments, guest can enjoy swimming in the "sky pool" while enjoying the breathtaking panorama of the Shanghai skyline.

Grand Hyatt Shanghai offers the business traveller an extensive selection of restaurants and bars in which to enjoy and entertain. Facilities include CANTON–Chinese restaurant, ON FIFTYSIX (a collection of eateries on level 56 featuring KOBACHI–Japanese restaurant, CUCINA–Italian restaurant with brick oven pizza, THE GRILL–offers freshest seafood and succulent prime grade meats, PATIO–a lounge at the base of the 33-storey atrium and Wine Bar–boasts the most extensive wine selection in town). CLOUD 9–the Sky Lounge, an all time night owl's favorite Bar on the 87th floor, PIANO BAR, located on Level 53 of the Jin Mao Tower boasting breathtaking views of the city, GRAND CAFÉ–24 hour restaurant, FOOD LIVE–a food court of 5 Asian and Western counters with a casual Chinese restaurant.

CLUB JIN MAO, located on the 86th floor, is Shanghai's most prestigious Shanghainese restaurant offers the finest facilities for entertaining and relaxation Club Jin Mao's exquisite and authentic cuisine and highly personalized services are available to public. The Hotel's extensive banquet and conference facilities include a concert hall / auditorium with seating for 390, a Grand ballroom for 1,200 people, a Crystal Ballroom for 800 and eleven separate meeting rooms. State of the art multimedia and video conferencing are available.

1. 钢琴吧
   Piano Bar
2. 意庐
   Cucina
3. 天庭
   Patio
4. 宴宾厅
   Drawing Room
5. 董事会议厅
   Boardroom
6. 金茂音乐厅
   Concert Hall
7. 繁星厅
   Polaris

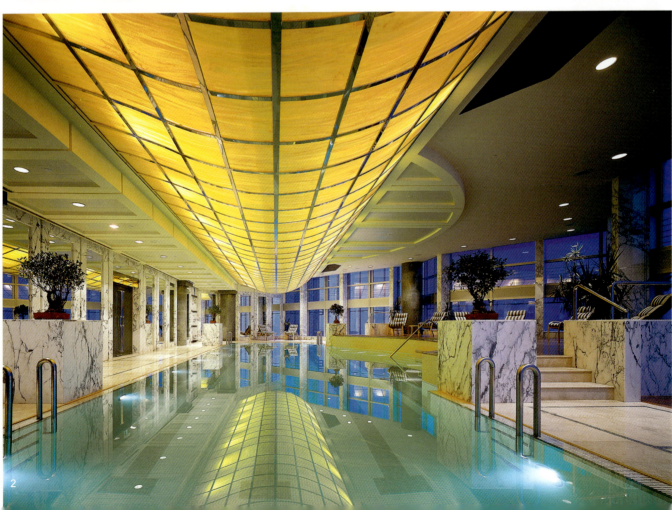

1. 嘉宾轩
   Grand Club Lounge
2. 游泳池
   Sky Pool
3. 水疗按摩室
   Relaxation in Spa
4. 绿洲健身中心
   Club Oasis
5. 套房浴室
   Suite Bathroom

1. 主席套房
   Chairman Suite
2. 君悦客房
   Grand Room
3. 外交官套房
   Diplomatic Suite
4. 中式总统套房
   Chinese Presidential Suite

中国一流饭店 珍藏版
China's First Class Hotels
Collection Edition

《中国一流饭店》编委会 编
Compiled by the Editorial Board of *China's First Class Hotels*

中国建筑工业出版社
China Architecture & Building Press

III

目录
Content

4 上海锦沧文华大酒店
Shanghai JC Mandarin, Managed by Meritus Hotels & Resorts

16 上海龙之梦丽晶大酒店
The Longemont Shanghai

26 上海浦西洲际®酒店
Inter Continental® Shanghai Puxi

36 上海瑞吉红塔大酒店
St. Regis Shanghai

48 上海斯格威铂尔曼大酒店
Pullman Hotels and Resorts, Shanghai Skyway

60 上海四季酒店
Four Seasons Hotel Shanghai

70 上海兴荣豪廷大酒店
Plaza Royale Oriental Shanghai

82 上海豫园万丽酒店
Renaissance® Shanghai Yuyuan Hotel

94 兴国宾馆
Radisson Plaza Xing Guo Hotel Shanghai

106 苏州金鸡湖凯宾斯基大酒店
Kempinski Hotel Suzhou, China

118 富阳国际贸易中心大酒店
Fuyang International Trade Center Hotel

126 罗星阁宾馆
Luoxingge Hotel

138 世贸君澜大饭店
Zhejiang Narada Grand Hotel

150 宜兴宾馆
Yixing Hotel

160 厦门悦华酒店
Yeohwa Hotel Xiamen

172 南昌凯莱大饭店
Gloria Grand Hotel Nanchang

180 郑州索菲特国际饭店
Sofitel Luxury Hotels, Zhengzhou International

192 武汉香格里拉大饭店
Shangri-La Hotel, Wuhan, China

200 广州白云国际会议中心
Guangzhou Baiyun International Convention Center

　　无论您此次旅行是为了商务洽谈，还是休闲旅游，糅合中西文化的上海锦沧文华大酒店——时尚舒适的地标，为您提供五星级的尊贵合适和无微不至的关怀。酒店位于南京路的中心地带，毗邻上海展览中心，恒隆广场、城市航站楼、地铁二号线均近在咫尺，交通便利，往来便捷。

　　这里拥有515间宽敞舒适的客房、技艺精湛的厨师们烹饪的国际美食、丰富的休闲娱乐选择、理想的会议场所、新近完成的无柱形设计的大型宴会厅（其总面积为845平方米），还有5个格局各异的会议室，设施齐全的健身俱乐部、网球场、游泳池和水疗中心……上海锦沧文华大酒店让您尽享奢华和关怀。

　　步入大堂，映入眼帘的是位于正前方的有5层楼高的巨幅手绘的《郑和下西洋》的漆画，被两边金箔镶嵌的旭日和波涛的画面所衬托，蔚为壮观。

　　无烟的君华贵宾俱乐部位于酒店二楼，氛围优雅，为您提供如家般的温馨服务。倚窗而坐，可将南京西路的美景尽收眼底。具有良好隔声设备的会议室、宽敞明亮的休闲酒廊、开放式厨房……所有的一切，不正是具有鉴赏力的您所需要的吗？

　　位于同一楼层的商务中心，设施一流。每一位商务人士的需求都能在这里得到满足。安静的工作室、快捷的宽带

上网、可供租用的手提电脑、国际直拨长途／国际订户拨号、旅行社服务等一应俱全，为您提供便捷的一站式服务。

在藏丞坊扒房我们为您精挑了上海最好的牛排，锦华宫中餐厅有闻名沪上的广式点心、紫云庭的自助餐、银涛廊咖啡厅和凝云阁雪茄吧各式美味，面面俱到，聚集您的各式美食体验。

装修改建后的文华健身俱乐部和中国首家欧式水疗中心——佳丽雅水疗中心占地面积3,000平方米，为你提供全新的健身体验和超越的优质服务，包括宽敞的二层楼健身房、桑拿和蒸汽浴设施、20米的室内游泳池、2个露天网球场和舒适的水疗馆。

Whether you are traveling for business or pleasure, the 5-star Shanghai JC Mandarin is the mark of modern comfort and convenience, which blends the best East and West. It is right in the middle of the business and shopping district on the famous Nanjing Road, just adjacent to the Shanghai Exhibition Centre, Shanghai Centre and Plaza 66. Shanghai Airport Bus Terminal, Metro Line 2 and entry to Shanghai's integrated system of highways are just a stone's throw away.

515 spacious rooms and suites, international gourmet cuisine by master chefs, an abundance of recreational options, viable conference venues, pillar-less Grand Ballroom covering 845 sqm and 5 stylish meeting rooms, fully equipped fitness centre, tennis and SPA…the JC Mandarin offers luxurious comfort and meticulous care.

Guests and visitors are able to see the grand lobby redesigned to feature a magnificent 5-storey, hand-painted lacquer mural of Admiral Zheng-Ho surrounded by many golden-foiled picture of morning sun and unwavering waves.

Meritus Club Lounge located on the 2nd floor is elegantly furnished and smoke-free, offering the busy executives' comforts away from home and office. With astounding views of prestigious Nanjing Xi Road, and equipped with three soundproofed meeting

1.酒店外景
Night Scene
2.银涛廊咖啡厅
Park Lane Coffee

rooms, spacious lounge and an open kitchen, and exclusive privileges … What else would a discerning traveler need?

The Business Centre on the same floor makes every businessman's dream come true. Workstations, broadband Internet access, computer laptops for rent, IDD/ISD and travel services etc. are all available at this one-stop service centre.

To round up your dining experience in the heart of Shanghai, we host a diverse range of cuisine from the best available steaks in town at Wine Bar & Grill, Mandarin Pavilion for Cantonese cuisine, Tatlers Restaurant for buffet to "al fresco" Park Lane Café and Cuba Cigar Lounge.

The Fitness Centre and the first European Wellness SPA in China with a total of 3,000 square meters offering you a brand new experience, a new level of service, including a spacious double-story gym, sauna and steam baths, a 20-metre heated indoor swimming pool, two open air tennis courts and the soothing SPA.

1、2.酒店大堂
Lobby
3.酒店外景
Night Scene

1. 文华宴会厅
   M Ballroom
2、3. 藏丞坊西餐厅
   Wine Bar & Grill
4. 锦华宫中餐厅
   Mandarin Pavilion Chinese Restaurant

1、2. 文华宴会厅
Mandarin Ballroom
3、5、9. 紫云庭西餐厅
Tatlers
4、7. 藏丞坊西餐厅
Wine Bar & Grill
6. 凝云阁雪茄吧
Cuba
8. 锦华宫中餐厅
Mandarin Pavilion Chinese Restaurant
10、11. 会议室
Meeting Room

1、3. 凝云阁雪茄吧
Cuba
2. 健身中心
Gym
4. 游泳池
Swimming Pool

1. 豪华房
   Deluxe Room
2. 君华贵宾房
   Meritus Club Room
3. 君华行政套房
   Meritus Deluxe Suite
4. 高级豪华房
   Grand Room
5. 总统套房
   Presidential Suite

The Longemont Shanghai
上海龍之夢麗晶大酒店

上海长峰房地产开发有限公司在中国揭幕了首家豪华五星级酒店——上海龍之夢麗晶大酒店。酒店拥有盛大高贵的建筑设计、绝佳的地理位置和世界级的服务设施，是上海著名地标之一。

上海龍之夢麗晶大酒店拥有511间客房及套房，由长江三角洲地区规模最大的民营企业之一的上海长峰房地产开发有限公司投资兴建，并由公司旗下新成立的龙之梦酒店管理集团进行管理。

上海龍之夢麗晶大酒店坐落于延安西路，毗邻市中心商业区，周边交通便捷。高达53层的壮观建筑拥有经典而时尚的设计风格，宾客可将城市美景尽揽眼底。

酒店由国际知名建筑公司和设计公司进行建筑设计和内部装修。511间精心设计的豪华客房和套房，处处体现着现代与经典的完美融合。独特的建筑设计保证了每一间客房都能欣赏到绚丽的城市景观。房内专业的商务空间，配有42英寸超大等离子电视、iPod音响系统、高速互联网接入以及宽阔舒适的卫浴空间。酒店还拥有上海浦西地区最大的会议及宴会场地，可灵活满足各项会晤和活动的需求。

酒店同时提供各地精致佳肴。优雅别致的就餐环境，配上无可挑剔的食物，保证您的行程趋于完美。全日餐厅提供中西风格的自助餐点或精致套餐，为您

全天恭候。如果您想体验更原汁原味的美食和气氛，阿米奇意大利餐厅将是不错的选择，主厨先生将为您烹制传统地道的意大利美食。皇朝尊会中餐厅提供顶级粤菜，天家则为您奉上新鲜的特色金枪鱼日本料理。大堂酒廊和雪茄吧则是忙碌一天后放松身心的最惬意场所。

在这里还能享受各项休闲设施，包括2间室外网球场、1间30米长室内恒温采光游泳池、设备齐全的健身中心及全球知名的迪卡拉水疗中心为您呈现极致奢华体验。

1、2.行政酒廊
The Club Lounge

The Summit Property Development Co. opened its first luxury hotel in China-The Longemont Shanghai. With its spectacular architecture and design, premier location and world-class facilities, the Hotel is one of Shanghai's top landmarks.

The 511-room hotel is owned by the Summit Property Development Co.–one of the largest privately-owned development companies in the Yangtze River Delta. The Company announced the official introduction of its new foray into the deluxe hotel market with the re-branding of the Regent Shanghai to The Longemont Shanghai. The Summit Property Group currently operates properties including offices, apartments, and hotels.

Rising over Yan An West Road with stunning views, this 53-storey hotel is within easy access to Hongqiao Airport and Pudong International Airport, and only minutes away from the central business and shopping districts of Shanghai.

The Longemont Shanghai is designed by world-renowned architects and interior designers. The contemporary yet classic hotel features luxurious rooms and suites, functional work areas, large 42-inch plasma TV screens, iPod docking stations, high-speed Internet access and spacious bathrooms with oversized designer baths. All guest rooms have stunning views over the city's striking skyline. The Hotel also offers the largest meeting space in Shanghai Puxi area. The Hotel hosts a wide array of exquisite cuisines served in pleasant atmosphere and beautiful surroundings. All-day-dining restaurant offers the choice of a buffet and a la carte menu for breakfast, lunch and dinner. For a more sophisticated alternative, there is also the Italian boutique restaurant Amici providing authentic traditional Italian cuisine. Royal China serves Cantonese cuisine and Tenya, the Japanese restaurant offers tuna specialty. The Lobby Lounge and Cigar Bar offer guests a much welcomed place to relax at the end of a hectic day.

Guests can enjoy some of Shanghai's best leisure facilities: two outdoor tennis courts, a 30-metre indoor heated swimming pool, a well-equipped gym and a world-class Dikara SPA.

1.酒店大堂
 Hotel Lobby
2、3.美食阁
 Tongs Deli
4.酒店大楼
 Hotel Building

1. 大宴会厅
   The Grand Ballroom
2. 大堂酒廊
   Lobby Lounge
3. 全日餐厅
   O^2 on 2 All Day Dining Restaurant
4. 雪茄吧
   CO2 Cigar Bar
5. 大宴会厅前厅
   The Grand Ballroom Foyer
6. 阿米奇意大利餐厅
   Amici Italian Restaurant

1. 皇家套房
   Imperial Suite
2. 会议室
   Meeting Room
3. 健身中心
   Health Club
4. 游泳池
   Swimming Pool

1. 行政套房
   Club Suite
2. 总统套房
   Presidential Suite
3. 贵宾房——大床房
   Premium Room—King Size
4. 贵宾房——双床房
   Premium Room—Twin Size

上海浦西洲际酒店位于市中心商业区,地理位置优越,交通便捷。上海火车站、城市轨道交通和地面高架道路组成的交通网络四通八达。距浦东国际机场仅60分钟车程,或驱车30分钟便可抵达虹桥国际机场。

酒店拥有533间豪华客房和套房,分设于两栋独立的玻璃帷幕大楼内。时尚典雅的客房内为商务宾客配置了高速国际互联网接驳、47英寸液晶电视,浴室的镜子内还另置有一台15英寸的液晶电视机。独栋的洲际俱乐部楼设有112间俱乐部客房和套房,以其至尊礼遇满足每位商务人士的不同需求,个性化的服务是洲际俱乐部的独特之处。

总面积超过3,125平方米的综合性会议设施包括一间可容纳700人的大宴会厅,三间可分别接待200～400人的会议中心,14个的多功能厅和一间319座的多功能剧院。如此庞大规模的会议与宴会场地,在浦西地区别无他家。酒店还配备了先进的视听设施、高速无线宽带接入、完备的技术支持,服务精良的专业团队,同时拥有全套秘书服务的商务中心,为各种类型的会议和宴会活动提供了全方位的支持。部分会议设施配有独立的出入口,为贵客提供了更多的私密空间。除了先进的硬件设施外,酒店还提供一系列创意活动,包括主题派对、精选咖啡茶歇和游船包价等。同

时便捷的地理位置和超值多样的婚宴包价,已成为沪上举办婚宴的新热点。

酒店设有五间风格迥异的中西餐厅及酒吧。翠庭中餐厅以其质量上乘的粤菜和本帮菜,还有细致周到的服务,成为社会名流和商业人士宴请宾客的首选场所。怡亭意式全天候餐厅采用极富创意的"世界厨房"理念,使宾客在享受饕餮美食的同时欣赏厨师们的精彩厨艺。精华500牛扒房为宾客提供诱人的炭烤美食和醇香馥郁的名酒佳酿。鲤鱼日餐厅内设有烧烤、寿司吧、铁板烧、清酒吧及独立包房,让您领略和食的精美别致、淡雅健康。在林荫大道酒廊观赏现场乐队的精彩演绎,聆听不同曲风,让疲惫的身心得以舒展,让思绪无限蔓延,伴您度过美好温馨的午后和夜晚时分。此外,酒店另配有先进齐全的健身中心、室内游泳池、户外网球场及全新概念的洲际水疗馆,为客人在繁忙的工作之余,提供一个惬意完美的放松空间。

"客人挚爱的杰出酒店"是上海浦西洲际酒店的服务宗旨。

1. 林荫大道大堂酒廊
   The Avenue Lobby Lounge
2. 酒店大堂
   Lobby

The InterContinental Shanghai Puxi is the first International luxury brand in the Zhabei district. Ideally situated in the Shanghai's central business district with walking distance from the Northern transportation hub, the InterContinental Shanghai Puxi is expected to be an ideal launching point for business and leisure.

"The new hotel features one of the largest allocations of meeting and convention space in the Puxi area. Its state-of-art meeting facilities with a wide range of venue sizes set new standards for modern convention centres, making the InterContinental Shanghai Puxi the perfect choice to host international conferences, wedding ceremonies and other special events", said Gilles Hervieux, General Manager of the InterContinental Shanghai Puxi.

Each of InterContinental's 533 rooms and suites, located in two glass towers, are exquisitely appointed with conveniences essential to one's comfort and pleasure. At a minimum floor area of 45 square metres, the rooms provide ample space where guests can unwind in total luxury. To facilitate a diverse and world-class dining experience, four new specialty restaurants at the InterContinental

1. 外景
   Exterior
2. 林荫大道大堂酒廊
   The Avenue Lobby Lounge
3. 大宴会厅
   Grand Ballroom

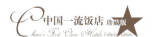

1. 鲤鱼日式餐厅
   Koi-Japanese Restaurant
2. 怡亭全日餐厅
   Ecco All Day Dinning
3. 洲际俱乐部酒廊
   Club Lounge
4. VIP接待室
   VIP Reception

Shanghai Puxi cater to a range of tastes: action stations and international favourites at Ecco, contemporary Chinese at Jade, authentic Japanese cuisine at Koi, alongside prime steaks and luscious grills at Prime 500. The Avenue Lobby Lounge is a chic and relaxed corner of the InterContinental Shanghai Puxi, offering drinks, snacks, afternoon tea and live entertainment every night. In addition to a 25-metre indoor swimming pool and a well-equipped fitness centre, SPA InterContinental launches a comprehensive range of both traditional SPA rituals and modern foot reflexology, complimented by Jacuzzi, sauna, steam room.

The Hotel is managed by IHG (InterContinental Hotels Group), one of the world's largest hotel groups by number of rooms. IHG owns, manages, leases or franchises, through various subsidiaries, over 4,200 hotels and more than 620,000 guest rooms in nearly 100 countries and territories around the world. IHG owns a portfolio of well recognised and respected hotel brands including InterContinental® Hotels & Resorts, Crowne Plaza® Hotels & Resorts, Holiday Inn® Hotels and Resorts, Holiday Inn Express®, Staybridge Suites®, Candlewood Suites® and Hotel Indigo®, and also manages the world's largest hotel loyalty programme, Priority Club® Rewards with over 43 million members worldwide.

1. 剧院厅
   Auditorium
2. 洲际水疗中心
   SPA Inter Continental
3. 游泳池
   Swimming Pool

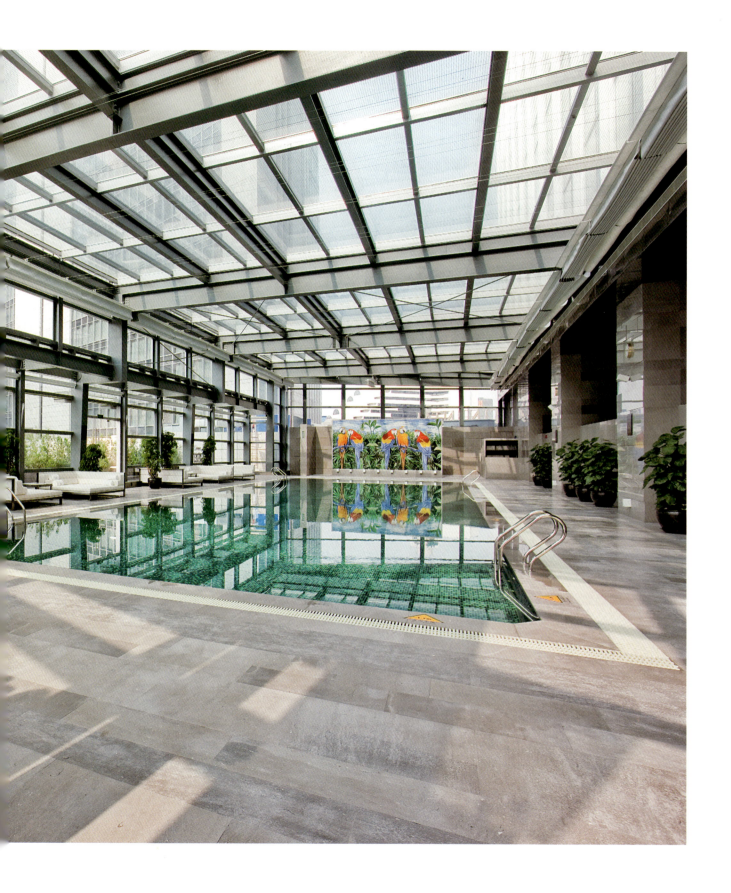

1. 俱乐部房
   Club Room
2. 俱乐部套房
   Club Suite
3. 浴室
   Bathroom
4、5. 豪华房
   Deluxe Room
6. 客房卫浴
   Bathroom

上海瑞吉红塔大酒店

上海瑞吉红塔大酒店位于上海浦东金融贸易中心地区，距离上海的文化和娱乐景点仅几分钟路程；距离两座国际机场分别仅有约35分钟车程，且毗邻城市文化旅游景点、会展中心、2010世博会址，随时为商务休闲旅客提供最优质的服务。酒店为到访上海这个亚洲大都市的游客提供一流的豪华住宿享受。屡获殊荣的上海瑞吉红塔大酒店以其无与伦比的简约典雅的氛围、专业的个性化服务以及独特的私人空间环境恭候客人光临。

酒店在保持了向宾客提供与众不同的个性化服务的优良传统的同时，又不忘创新。从您进入酒店到步出酒店大门的期间，酒店诚意为你提供全程服务。每一位宾客的个人喜好将在为您提供服务时就会被详细地记录下来，并据此为宾客提供舒心的服务。酒店将提供24小时传统的专职管家服务，随时为宾客提供细致而周到的私人服务。

所有入住上海瑞吉红塔大酒店的客人均可免费享受一系列贴身服务，如：由专职管家恭迎入店并做房内入住登记，住店期间，随时享用送至房内的咖啡或茶水，抵店时服装熨烫（不超过2件），每日新鲜水果及鲜花，选择宽泛的报纸和杂志，以及健身设施和大型室内游泳池。除了独具特色的服务理念外，酒店为客人提供了世界顶级的餐饮

体验。客人不仅可以享用到由屡获殊荣的意大利厨师长呈现的现代派意大利美食或是选择美式大陆佳肴，还可以在两间风格迥异的酒廊进行休闲放松。同时，酒店拥有超过1,000平方米的会议场地、24小时商务中心及设施完善的健身美容中心。

近日上海瑞吉红塔大酒店再次入选行业内领先的旅行杂志 Travel + Leisure 所评选的"全球500佳酒店"，并以最高分荣列上海地区榜首，以及被美国《酒店》杂志中文版评选为2009中国年度酒店奢华酒店十强。上海瑞吉红塔酒店是来往上海的商务人士享受豪华舒适住宿的最佳选择。

1. 大堂接待处
   Reception Area
2. 意大利餐厅
   Danieli's Italian Restaurant
3. 婚宴台设
   Wedding Table Setup

Situated in the heart of the financial and business district of Pudong, Shanghai, The St. Regis Shanghai is only minutes away from cultural and entertainment spots, around 35 minutes from both the Pudong and Hongqiao International Airports. The St. Regis Shanghai offers a unique first-class luxury experience for upscale travelers visiting Asia's dazzling international metropolis. Understated elegance, highly personalized service and a discreet sense of exclusive privacy await every guest.

St. Regis carries a legacy of innovation while continuing the rich tradition of distinctive personalized service. From the first point of contact to the moment the guest departs for his or her next destination, the guest will receive signature St. Regis Butler Service. Each individual guest's personal preference is carefully noted from previous stays and recalled to suit his or her comfort. The Legendary St. Regis Butlers are on 24-hour standby to provide meticulous and discreet personal service.

Every guest at The St. Regis Shanghai can enjoy a range of complimentary benefits including in-room check-in and check-out, pressing of garments upon arrival (2 pieces), fresh fruits and flowers delivered daily, and choose from a selection of over 600 International newspapers also delivered daily. Featuring more than 1,000 square meters (11,000 square feet) of meeting space, a comprehensive 24-hour Business Center, contemporary and award-winning dinning venues, and complete fitness and SPA facilities, The St. Regis Shanghai stands ready to pamper even the most discerning business travelers.

The St. Regis Shanghai has recently been recognized by the industry leading magazine *Travel + Leisure* in its 2009 January issue as one of the "500 World's Best Hotels" and Shanghai's No.1 hotel and also was recognized as one of "China 2009 Luxury Hotel Top 10" by *HOTELS China* Magazine for the second year in a row.

1. 池畔宴会
   Poolside Gala
2. 酒店外观
   Hotel Exterior

1. 酒店大堂
   Hotel Lobby
2. 圣思园国际餐厅
   Saints International Restaurant
3. 阿斯特宴会厅婚宴布置
   Astor Ballroom Wedding Banquet

1. 专职管家服务
   Signature Butler Service
2. 阿斯特宴会厅
   Astor Ballroom
3. 香槟庆典
   Champagne Celebration
4. 董事会议室
   Boardroom
5. 行政酒廊
   Executive Lounge

1. 瑞吉SPA
   St. Regis SPA
2. 魅力
   Seductive
3. 宽敞的卫生间
   Spacious Bathroom
4. 健身房
   Athletic Club
5. 室内泳池
   In-door Swimming Pool

1. 豪华房
Deluxe Room
2. 一丝不苟的至尊服务
Uncompromising Service
3. 东方套房
Mandarin Suite
4. 瑞吉贴心服务
St. Regis Hospitality Service
5. 首善之地
Address

6. 管家服务
Butler Service
7. 专职管家
Chief Butler
8. 开香槟仪式
Champagne Ceremony
9. 上海套房
Shanghai Suite
10. 皇家套房
Imperial Suite
11. 超豪华套房
Grand Luxury Room

随着商业的飞速发展，上海已成为一座繁华的大都市，它不平凡的历史和蓬勃的活力构成了一种独特的魅力，令其蜚声海内外。黄浦江两岸的建筑如画卷一般展现了这座城市的过去和未来，既有浦西的老式建筑和历经岁月、风貌依然的外滩，也有被誉为中国的"曼哈顿"、极具21世纪现代化特色的浦东。

在上海市中心的卢湾区，毗邻繁华的徐家汇商业区，坐落着一座国际化高档酒店——上海斯格威铂尔曼大酒店。酒店高52层，将城市景观尽收眼底，坐拥青葱翠绿的私家花园，为行色匆匆的宾客提供休闲放松的天堂。酒店地理位置优越，设施完善，服务周到，为您带来独特难忘的住宿体验。

从抵达酒店的那一刻起，您就会时刻感受到酒店休闲舒适的氛围。上海斯格威铂尔曼大酒店承袭"轻松入住，优越尽享"的品牌理念，为宾客提供无微不至的服务。酒店拥有645间宽敞舒适的客房和套房、6间餐厅和酒吧、17间一流的会议室、设施完善的健身中心、室内游泳池和水疗中心，并配备了最新的移动技术，让您随时与外界保持沟通。

酒店空间宽敞、装潢精致，处处摆设有经过精心选择的高雅艺术品。宾客可以尽情享受私人空间的舒适和私密。每间客房和套房均配备了最先进的技术设备，让您能够随时与家人和同事保持联系。客房空间宽敞，布置合理，充分考虑了下榻居住的舒适

性。每间客房的设计都非常注重营造安静的环境,让客人能够高效地工作,充分地放松和休息。当然,从客房眺望还可以欣赏到迷人的城市全景。入住行政客房和套房的客人还可享受部分行政俱乐部酒廊的服务。

在酒店中心这里有着"美食的天地"。融各种饮食文化、创意食材、厨艺展示和一流烹饪于一体,酒店将为您呈现独一无二的味觉盛宴。每家咖啡厅和餐厅都有着独特的风格;无论是湖畔咖吧随意尽兴的简餐和美丽的花园景观,还是华府轩中餐厅正宗的上海本帮菜。我们的大厨将把他们对美食的热爱和追求传达给每一位客人。

每天晚上,酒店的城市景观餐厅和酒吧将体现出完全不同的风格,营造精致优雅的用餐环境。融汇中西的各类美食为您打造无与伦比的饕餮盛宴,从馔巴黎海鲜自助餐厅现代风格的美食,到酒店标志性餐厅丽仕厅世界各地的创新美食。来到酒店的五十层,在充满火热激情的望景酒吧品一杯美酒,欣赏辉煌的城市景观,让自己彻底放松。

一流的活动需要一流的环境。而城市的天际线就是最好的背景。酒店拥有16间灵活多用、经过精心设计的会议室和一间可容纳550人的宴会厅,是您举办各类活动的理想场所,无论是精致豪华的婚礼、高管团队会议、公司员工晚宴、主题产品发布,还是高雅的鸡尾酒会,这里都可胜任。

我们技术先进的设施、专门定制的解决方案和24小时的周到服务必将确保您的各类活动顺利进行。我们的会务经理能够为您处理每一个细节,注重创新和细致,我们的IT解决方案经理则能够为您提供所需的各种多媒体和技术设施。

在当今快节奏的生活中,上海斯格威铂尔曼大酒店始终关注每位宾客的需求、隐私、休闲和活力。我们的水疗中心不仅为客人营造了私密的空间,更有舒适放松的一流环境。水疗中心能够为您带来多种感官享受的超凡体验,缓解您身心的疲劳,令您活力百倍。水疗中心融两种文化于一体,将中国传统的保健文化与现代化的美容健康技术相结合。

宾客可步行或骑自行车游览城市的独特

1. 酒店正门
   Main Entrance of Hotel
2. 酒店大堂
   Hotel Lobby

1. 亚都汇中庭
   Zaffraan Lobby
2. 酒店全景
   Day Exterior of Hotel

风貌，了解普通上海人的日常生活。清晨就出发，到附近的公园去，与成百上千的中国人一起晨练，打一套太极拳或气功，跳一段交谊舞或有氧操，抛却一切烦恼，享受美好生活。当然，您一定不想错过上海的地标性建筑，例如人民广场、外滩和468米高的东方明珠塔，或抽一天时间去杭州或苏州一游。

当您游览一天，尽兴而归后，上海斯格威铂尔曼大酒店是您休息放松的港湾，您可以尽情享受室内恒温游泳池、健身中心或水疗中心所提供的服务。在这片城市绿洲享受舒适快乐的生活，恢复精力，重现活力。

Shanghai, where the art of commerce has given rise to a prosperous cosmopolitan city, is as famous for its history as it is for its incredible dynamism. Set on the Huangpu River, the city's past and future are revealed in its architecture, from the classical buildings of Puxi and its legendary bund to the striking modernity of 21st century Pudong, the Chinese "Manhattan".

Right in the heart of this city, in the renowned Luwan District and nearby to the business district of Xujiahui, is the upscale international Pullman Shanghai Skyway. A 52 storey skyscraper, set amidst its own lush garden with dramatic skyline views and offering a haven for busy travellers, where the authenticity and energy of its location transforms a stay into a unique and unforgettable experience.

An ambiance of relaxed sophistication embraces you from the moment you arrive. Spreading its iconic message of "Check in, Chill out". Pullman Shanghai Skyway is a

full service hotel offering 645 well appointed rooms and suites, 6 restaurants and bars, 17 premium conference spaces, full fitness, indoor swimming pool and SPA facilities and the latest mobile technologies to stay connected.

Spacious interiors, quality finishes and hand selected artworks appear throughout the Hotel. Guests have the freedom to enjoy the intimacy and privacy of their own space. Each guest room and suite features the latest in technology to stay permanently connected with family and office, as well as a balance in space where a sense of comfort is just as important. Each room design exudes its own quiet energy in which to work, relax or rest. And of course the panoramic views of the city are given. For Executive rooms and suites there is also the added benefits of the Executive Club Lounges.

At the heart of the hotel is its "world of dining". Blending food cultures, creative ingredients and a touch of culinary showmanship with live cooking, dining in the Hotel is a captivating experience for the senses. Each café and restaurant has a distinctive style; from the casual dining of the Lakeside Café with its garden views to the classic Shanghainese dishes of the Hua Fu Chinese Restaurant. Our chefs share with every guest their passion for food.

In the evening the Hotel's skyline restaurants and bars are transformed, offering a truly sophisticated dining ambiance. Fusion cuisine is the inspiration behind their menus, from the modern interpretation of dishes in the Zaffraan Buffet Restaurant to the stunning elegance of the signature restaurant Le Ciel, an innovative international a la carte restaurant. Drift onwards to the sultry Blu Bar on the 50th floor where lounging with spectacular city views is tailored made for relaxation.

Great events take great surroundings. The city skyline is an inspiring backdrop. With 16 flexible

1、2.华府轩中餐厅
  Hua Fu Chinese Restaurant
3、4.亚都汇自助餐厅
  Zaffraan Buffet Restaurant

well designed meeting rooms and the Hotel's spectacular Grand Ballroom, accommodating up to 550 people, the Hotel is the perfect venue for every type of event, whether a grand wedding, an executive team meeting, incentive dinner, themed product launch or cocktail party. Each event is supported by hi-tech facilities, tailor-made solutions and round-the-clock service to guarantee its smooth execution. Our Event Manager is ready to handle every detail with creativity and precision and our IT Solutions Manager is ready to deliver all the multimedia and technology requirements.

In a fast paced world the focus at Pullman is on each individual's needs and desires; privacy, relaxation and rejuvenation. At the SPA, guests find not only a private space but a gentle atmosphere with maximum comfort where they can exist by themselves. Conceived to soothe and harmonize and to nurture a deep feeling of replenishment, the SPA experience is a complete multi-sensory journey. Linking two cultures, the SPA seamlessly blends the traditions of Chinese well-being with the knowledge and expertise of modern beauty.

Guests can explore the city on foot or by bike and watch how the shanghinese go about their daily lives. Head out early in the morning to the nearest park and join thousands of Chinese doing their morning workout of Tai Ch'i, Qi Gong, ballroom dancing, aerobics – anything goes. Of course the city's iconic landmarks such as People's Square, The Bund and the 468-metre-high Oriental Pearl Tower plus a day trip to Hangzhou or Suzhou are not to be missed.

And when you return from the day the mood at Pullman Shanghai Skyway is soothing and relaxing, with an indoor heated swimming pool, fitness centre and spa all available for you. Take time out in this urban oasis to recharge and rediscover your vitality.

1、6.丽仕厅
Le Ciel International A La Carte Restaurant
2.贵宾接待室Ⅲ
VIP Room Ⅲ
3.绿洲厅
Oasis Hall
4.行政酒廊
Executive Lounge
5.望景吧
Blu Bar

1、2. 仕格厅
   Grand Ballroom
3. 水疗中心
   Being SPA
4. 健身中心
   Fitness Centre
5. 游泳池
   Swimming Pool

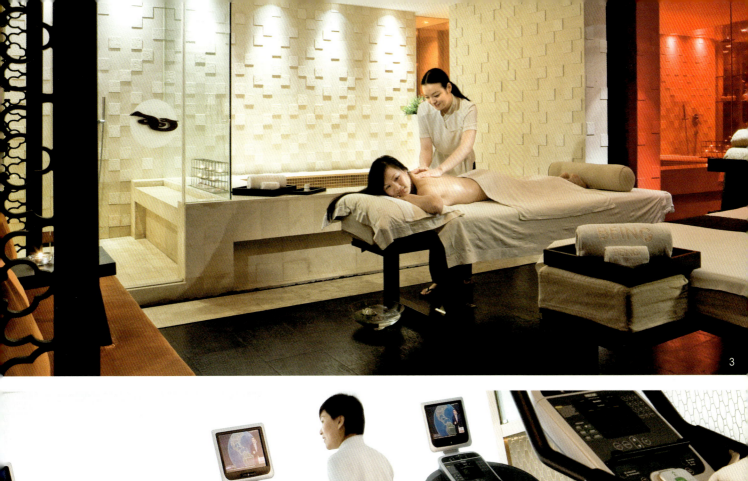

3

4

5

1、8.总统套房 Presidential Suite	3、5.酒店全景 Day Exterior of Hotel	6.钻石吧 Diamond Bar
2.湖畔咖吧 Lakeside Café	4.水疗中心 Being Spa	7.斯格威高级房 Superior King Room

上海四季酒店拥有421间客房，坐落于上海的市中心，步行就可到南京路和淮海路繁华的购物、娱乐和商业区。仅仅进入上海7年的四季酒店，已经连续两年被美国Travel + Leisure杂志评为上海第一大酒店。

宽敞的酒店客房象征了舒适与豪华。极具品位的现代化设计彰显了中西方文化交融的魅力。所有酒店的客房里都放置了L'Occitane的私人洗浴用品，还配有可容纳17寸笔记本电脑的超大室内保险柜。37层的行政俱乐部是适合商务客人享用的天地，为宾客提供齐全的秘书服务，也有丰盛的早餐和多款鸡尾酒及精美小食等着您。

上海四季酒店提供众多餐饮选择，为宾客提供国际大都会式的用餐体验。咖啡厅全天提供丰盛的自助式午餐和晚餐。氛围温馨的新太郎是诠释经典日式料理的日式餐厅。作为一个谈心聚雅的上佳场所，新太郎以其温婉简约的环境和匠心独具的潮流艺术装饰，成为追求时尚休闲用餐人士的最佳选择。

牛排馆是深受国际美食家好评的一家西餐厅。一流的牛排、海鲜和烧烤让每个光临餐馆的宾客都过口难忘，而餐馆的美酒总能满足不同宾客的口味。这里还因为经常举办各类名酒品尝晚会而深受宾客的喜爱。

四季轩餐厅由来自香港的袁瑞生大

厨掌舵,为宾客演绎经典粤菜,本邦菜肴以及精美的午式点心。大堂酒吧拥有令人放松身心的氛围,为您全天供应精美小食,休闲下午茶和多款鸡尾酒。

沁SPA,占据酒店整个六层,是一处宁神和心、复原兴气的清净之所。结合古代中国智慧及现代专业技术,您将享受专为您量身定制的芳疗呵护,契合您的生活理念。酒店的室内游泳池和健身中心也同样是您放松娱乐的场所。先进的健身设备和专业的健身顾问的指导使您可以在这里轻松愉快地完成您的健身项目。

酒店商务中心为明智的商务旅客提供全方位的服务。周到齐全的秘书服务、新一代的视讯会议设备、配备互联网接口的工作区以及商务会议厅,使商务之旅如虎添翼。

四季酒店员工以宾客需求为尊,为宾客提供最热忱、悉心、周到的服务。会议和宴会设施拥有1,160平方米(17,404平方英尺)的宽畅会议场所,7个多功能厅每个都配有高级室内照明和独立休息室。位于三层剧院式大宴会厅最多可以容纳800名宾客,是适合举办婚宴和大型公司活动的场所。外送宴席服务为家庭和公司聚会提供周全详尽的菜单。

无论是商务旅游还是休闲旅游,上海四季酒店都以其豪华舒适,体贴入微的个性化服务,使得更多的宾客拥有令人难以忘怀的体验。

1. 大堂景致
   Lobby
2. 大堂酒吧
   Lobby Lounge

1. 酒店外观
   Hotel Facade
2. 宾客抵店
   Guest Arrival

The 421-key hotel is located within walking distance of the most exclusive shopping, entertainment and business hubs of Nanjing and Huaihai Roads. Only into its 6th year in Shanghai, China, Four Seasons Hotel has already been voted as the No. 1 Hotel in Shanghai for 2 consecutive years by *Travel + Leisure*, USA.

Spacious guest rooms epitomise comfort and luxury. Tasteful contemporary décor exudes East West aesthetics. L'Occitane private bath label is a standard in all rooms and suites, as is an in-room safe that fits a 17" laptop. The 37th floor Executive Club Lounge is an exclusive haven for business travelers. Full-service secretarial support, an extensive breakfast buffet in the mornings and evening cocktail with a fine selection of horsd'oeuvres await you.

Six choices in cuisine offer a truly international dining experience. All-day dining Café Studio serves up an impressive lunch and dinner buffets of International treats. An a la carte menu of selected Italian fare highlights exquisite culinary finesse. With a contemporary Japanese bistro-style concept, Shintaro offers Japanese favorites in a casual elegant setting. Tastefully furnished and ornately decorated with a collection of prized avant-garde artwork, it makes a perfect dining destination if comfort and informalities are what you would appreciate for a leisurely dinner.

Steak House is another premier dining address that has been winning kudos and accolades from International food critiques. Known for serving up choice cuts of meat, fresh seafood and succulent grills, the wine list at this restaurant is extensive and has something for every gourmand. Steak House is also a regular venue for exclusive wine dinners.

Helmed by master chef Sam Yuen hailing from Hong Kong, Si Ji Xuan offers an extensive menu of classic Cantonese fare including afternoon dim sum and selected Shanghainese specialties.

With an ambience that is most relaxed, the Lobby Lounge has been a favorite respite for light meals, a leisurely afternoon tea and relaxing evening cocktails.

For Relaxation and Recreation, there is an indoor pool, a 24-hour well-equipped Fitness Centre with fitness consultants to take you through individual fitness program. For those feeling the boulders on your shoulders, let our SPA therapists set you on a journey to ultimate bliss with an extensive range of therapeutic treatments. Voted one of Asia's 10 Best Spas by *Travel + Leisure*, USA, the SPA at Four Seasons Hotel Shanghai is one of few in Shanghai that offers classic Balinese-style massage.

Serving the discerning business travelers is a full-service Business Centre where complete secretarial services and new-generation audio-visual equipment are available for rent. Other advantages include private workstations with high-speed broadband Internet connectivity and a boardroom for business discussions.

Business meetings are made memorable by Four Seasons staff, all eager to fulfill every need. Banquet and Conference facilities at Four Seasons Hotel Shanghai offer over 17,404 square feet or 1,610 square meters of meeting space in 7 function rooms, each with natural daylight and individual foyer for coffee breaks and cocktails. On site too, is a column-free Ballroom that accommodates up to 800 persons, ideal for wedding banquets or large-scale corporate engagements. Outdoor catering services with choices of menus prepared flawlessly by Four Seasons Shanghai's foremost chefs are available for home and office parties.

Whether visiting for business or leisure, the comfort and warmth of Four Seasons Hotel Shanghai make for an experience that is unforgettable.

1. 宴会厅
   Ballroom
2. 行政会议厅
   Meeting Room
3. 行政俱乐部
   Executive Club

1. 沁SPA接待厅
   Qin The SPA Reception
2. 双人芳疗室
   Qin The SPA Couples Treatment Room
3. 单人芳疗室
   Qin The SPA Single Treatment Room
4. 东方设计衣橱
   Qin The SPA Oriental Cabinet
5. 沁SPA双人豪华间
   Qin The SPA VIP Room

1.豪华房
Deluxe Room
2.四季行政套房
Executive Suite
3.特级房
Premier Room
4.沁SPA前台莲花
Qin The SPA Lotus
5.针灸服务
Qin The SPA Acupuncture
6.至尊翔龙按摩中使用的天然石
Qin The SPA Blue Stones Used in Imperial Dragon Massage Treatment

上海兴荣豪廷大酒店距离上海金融枢纽——新国际博览中心仅几分钟之遥，距离上海虹桥国际机场仅30分钟的车程；前往上海浦东国际机场也只需40分钟。豪华的设施、便利的交通、宽阔的视角使得酒店成为商旅休闲的最佳场所。

523间客房和套房豪华、宽敞、时尚，室内设计雅致，家具舒适精致。客房内宽大的落地玻璃窗视野宽阔，使您纵览黄浦江之美景。大面积的豪华浴室令人驻足，独特的大型花洒使疲劳的身心享受沐浴的快乐，且独一无二的电控玻璃更提升了空间的私密度。我们专业的贴身管家全天候为您提供无微不至的专业服务。

我们国际化的厨师团队以其精湛的厨艺让您尽享饕餮盛宴，体验来自世界各地的美食。传统风格的尚荣府中餐厅无疑是您品尝地道粤式佳肴和上海本帮菜的最佳场所。华美的餐厅装饰为您打造理想的就餐环境，使其与美食珠联璧合。坐拥于原石，木栅间，享受一份和式静谧的氛围，这里就是我们的J日本料理餐厅。在寿司/海鲜吧、点心台和日式烧烤吧，您可尽情选择自己喜爱的美食。

这里拥有堪称上海滩最大的水疗SPA馆，设有16间单独的贵宾包房，当您体验完整个疗程之后，您会感受到香薰精油所带来的无限舒适与惬意。我们国际化标准的室内游泳池将使您在繁忙的工

作之余得到全身心的放松。

11间大小不同的多功能会议室将满足您对不同会议规模的需求。高速互联网接口、笔记本电脑、投影仪等高科技设备一应俱全。我们优质快捷的同声翻译服务将确保您不耽误工作中的每个细节。酒店为举办会议和宴会提供将近2,000平方米的场地，其中包括面积为723平方米的无柱大宴会厅和260平方米的廊道。我们资深的专业会务团队将满足每场会务的不同需求，使您的会议圆满成功。

Located along bustling Pudong Avenue, only minutes away from the financial hub of Shanghai, the Shanghai New International Expo Centre and with easy access to modern expressways leading to both domestic and international airports make the Plaza Royale Oriental Shanghai the perfect Destination for business and pleasure. Standing at an impressive 140 metres high and towering over the famous Yangpu Bridge, the world's fourth largest cable-stayed bridge, the hotel boasts 360 degree views of modern and old Shanghai.

Our 523 tastefully-decorated guest rooms and suites are lavishly appointed and exude a unique boutique ambience. The Plaza Royale Oriental Shanghai offers enhanced services and amenities, and each of the luxuriously designed rooms reflects a level of comfort and quality for which Plaza Royale is defined. Floor to ceiling windows frame beautiful panoramic views of the Huangpu River and City scapes; bedside controls at your fingertips; deep and comforting beds; spacious bathrooms featuring rainforest showers; designer bathroom toiletries and personalized butler services dedicated to make your stay perfect.

Discover the stylish and refined atmosphere of the "Plaza Royale Oriental" in any of our restaurants or bars, with a choice of the "Café Royale" featuring an impressive

1. 酒店夜景
   Night View of Plaza Royale Oriental Shanghai
2. 酒店大堂
   Hotel Lobby

open kitchen serving up a wide variety of exquisite flavours from around Asia and complimented with international classics. Our "Lobby Lounge", a heart beat from the main hotel lobby, features light food, and our very own "classic" high tea, washed down with a comprehensive range of wines beers, spirits and freshly prepared teas or coffees and live entertainment to soothe and refresh. Savor the best in regional Chinese cuisine in a choice of 12 private rooms, form Cantonese, Sichuan and Shanghai, personally prepared by our Hong Kong Master Chef, in the elegant surroundings of the "Shang Rong" Restaurant. Discover the taste of Japanese cuisine; visit our "J" restaurant, complete with tatami tables and teppan grills. Any of our restaurant menus can be carefully served up in the comfort of our rooms with style and panache through our in-room dining, should you desire and we would be delighted to create your own favorite dishes 24 hours a day.

The SPA features the largest and most luxurious facilities in Shanghai, complete with elegant bathing, herbal steam facilities and a host of rejuvenating therapies. Each one of the 16 private treatment rooms has been carefully designed to create a timeless environment where you can indulge your senses, soothe your body and revitalize your spirit.

Combining luxurious décor with the latest audio visual technology in a sophisticated hotel environment, the 723 square meter Grand Royale Ballroom is located on the 3rd floor, and complimented with a 260 square meter foyer, accommodates up to 400 guests with elegant banquets dinner or up to 600 people for cocktail receptions. A choice of eleven versatile function rooms of various sizes, fully adaptable to suit your specific needs for multi-purpose events also equipped with the latest audio/visual facilities, high speed Internet and video streaming capabilities further enhance our ability to flex to your needs, are also available. Our professional Catering Team is well prepared to serve you.

1. 皇家宴会厅——婚礼
   Grand Royale Ballroom – Wedding
2. 酒店夜景
   Night View of Plaza Royale Oriental Shanghai

1、3、4.皇家宴会厅——婚礼
　　Grand Royale Ballroom – Wedding
2.J日本料理餐厅
　　"J" Japanese Restaurant

1、2、4.尚荣府中餐厅
Shang Rong Fu
3.悠廊大堂酒吧
Lobby Lounge
5.皇家宴会厅——剧院式
Grand Royale Ballroom-Opera
6、7.精美食物
Delicious Food

1. 皇家行政酒廊
   Royale Lounge
2. 豪廷咖啡厅
   Café Royale
3. 台球室
   Billard Room
4、5. 游泳池
   Swimming Pool

1

2

1. 豪廷套房——卧室
   Royale Suite-Bedroom
2、3. 江景房——客厅
   River View Room-Sitting Room
4、5. 豪华豪廷客房——卧室
   Royale Deluxe Room-Bedroom

上海豫园万丽酒店是由上海豫园大酒店有限公司拥有、万豪国际集团负责管理的。设计别具一格的上海豫园万丽酒店坐落在浦西黄浦区河南南路，毗临豫园。豫园是具有中国传统特色的园林建筑，其间亭台楼阁、精致湖景、拱桥石舫交相呼应，是上海唯一保留下来的明代花园建筑。豫园周边地区是上海有名的古城，这里也有很多其他旅游景点，例如城隍庙、湖心亭茶楼，以及著名的中国传统手工艺品购物中心——豫园商城。

上海豫园万丽酒店拥有340个风格时尚的客房，其中包括14个套间。客房的设计用色奔放、颇见巧思，例如采用玻璃作为围板的浴室等。还有部分客房的浴缸更是设置在起居室的中央，以便客人在沐浴之时可以尽情观赏新、旧上海的景致。

酒店的大堂及公用区域设计新颖、宽敞舒畅，其空间具有高度的灵活性，客人在此可潇洒自如地工作或休憩，不论是进行小型会议，抑或是两三知己欢聚，再或是自斟独酌，皆可各适其式。

上海豫园万丽酒店把万豪获奖无数的"泉"SPA（Quan SPA）首度引进至上海。它位于酒店的最高两层，置身其间可饱览沪市景色，其设施包括一个健身房、"一望无际"的泳池、室内SPA花园及休憩区域。这个特色"泉"SPA是由捷

克著名获奖建筑师Borek Sipek设计的。他一向以个性化、色彩浓郁及妙着纷呈的风格而闻名。"泉"SPA的设计富有时代感，拥有10间理疗室，提供别具特色的室内热水浴及Vichy Showers 理疗服务。顾客可以选择单人、双人房间，另设豪华足底按摩区域。此外，除了"泉"SPA 品牌独有的按摩油外，该水疗服务中心还提供专用于面部及身体护理的法国著名品牌Algotherm的产品。

在餐饮设施方面，上海豫园万丽酒店拥有两家餐厅及一家酒吧，其豫园咖啡厅提供各式国际美食及有机食品；万丽轩则提供新派中菜；豫吧是品尝美酒及各式鸡尾特饮的好去处。

上海豫园万丽酒店是"万豪礼赏奖励计划"的成员，目前已有超过3000家万豪国际酒店加入了该计划，会员在这些酒店消费可获得奖励积分或航空奖励里程。

The stylish Renaissance Shanghai Yuyuan Hotel on Henan South Road is located in the Huangpu district of Puxi. Located nearby is Yuyuan, a traditional Chinese park complete with beautiful pavilions, miniature lakes, bridges and rock formations. It remains the only Ming-era garden in Shanghai. The area surrounding Yuyuan is known as Old City and is home to local attractions such as the Temple of the City God, the famous Huixinting Tea House and the Yuyuan markets, a bazaar of stores that sell traditional Chinese arts and crafts.
The modern hotel showcases 340

1. 前厅
   Front Office
2. 可观赏豫园景观的大堂
   Lobby with Yu Garden View

contemporary guest rooms, including 14 suites. Guest rooms are designed with touches of whimsy and bold color including glass-enclosed bathrooms. Select guest rooms feature cheeky bathtubs located in the living area of the guest room offering expansive views of old and new Shanghai.

The Hotel offers guests expansive and innovative lobby and public spaces, eliminating traditional architectural barriers. The adaptable spaces enable guests to smoothly transition from work to play, offing areas where guests can meet and work in small groups, take private time out, or enjoy a relaxing drink or bite to eat.

Boasting the first award-winning Quan SPA in Shanghai, the Hotel's SPA forms part of a Wellness Zone with gymnasium, infinity edge pool, indoor SPA garden and relaxation areas spread out over the top two floors of the Hotel with breathtaking views across the Shanghai city skyline. Designed by award winning and prominent Czech architect Borek Sipek, renowned for his individual, unusual, colorful and rich designs, the SPA presents a distinctly contemporary ambience and has 10 treatment rooms with a mix of in-room hot tubs and Vichy Showers, single and dual occupancy rooms and a luxurious Foot Lounge. Algotherm from France provides the SPA's premium skin care range for facials and body treatments in addition to the Quan signature massage oils.

The Hotel boasts two full-service restaurants and one bar. The Yu Garden Café serves international and organic cuisine and the China Bistro offers contemporary Chinese cooking. The Yu Bar is part of the innovative public space and offers an extensive wine and cocktail menu.

The Renaissance Shanghai Yuyuan Hotel along with over 3,000 Marriott-affiliated hotels worldwide, participates in Marriott Rewards, the guest reward program that allows members to earn their choice of points or airline miles for every dollar spent during each stay.

1. 楼道
   Floor Corridor
2. 酒店外景
   Hotel Exterior

1、2.宴会厅——豫园宴会厅
Yu Garden Grand Hall
3.万丽轩
China Bistro
4.万丽轩的包间
Private Room in China Bistro

1、2、3.行政酒廊
Club Lounge
4.豫园咖啡厅
Yu Garden Cafe
5.鸡尾酒
Cocktail
6.外滩观景晚餐
Band View Dinner

1. 会议室
   Boardroom
2、9. 泉水疗花园
   Quan SPA
3. 私人理疗室
   Treatment Room
4. 泉水疗
   Quan SPA
5. 水疗
   Treatment
6、7. 水疗疗程
   SPA Treatment
8. 水疗欢迎茶
   SPA Welcome Tea

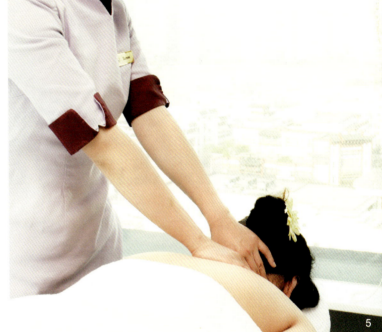

1. 总统套房起居室
   Living Room in Presidential Suite
2. 总统套房主卧室
   Bedroom in Presidential Suite
3. 总统套房盥洗室
   Bathroom in Presidential Suite
4. 套房
   Suite
5. 万丽景观房窗边风景
   View near the window
6. 室内按摩浴缸
   In-room Hot Tub
7. 豪华房
   Deluxe Room

兴国宾馆
Radisson
RADISSON PLAZA XING GUO HOTEL
SHANGHAI

闻名遐迩的国宾馆上海兴国宾馆，现已成为极具知名度的国际五星级精品酒店。酒店位于上海市中心领馆区，拥有得天独厚的地理位置，延安路高架近在咫尺，车行至虹桥国际机场仅15分钟，至浦东国际机场45分钟，至商业中心仅5分钟。出行购物、饮食娱乐极为方便。酒店还配备了现代化的高新技术：避免二次污染的中央吸尘系统，加之整个酒店坐拥市中心70,000余平方米的大花园和别墅群，为客人提供远离尘嚣的悠然和静谧，被誉为"真正的绿色花园酒店"。

上海兴国宾馆有历史悠久的故事，拥有20多幢风格迥异的法国、英国、德国、美国、西班牙、加拿大式的别墅楼，也因之而曾被誉为上海市中心最大的别墅宾馆，宾馆占地总面积7万多平方米，绿化覆盖率达到80%以上。所有的老别墅陆续建造于20世纪二三十年代，解放前分别为德士古石油洋行、太古洋行等官僚资本家和民族资本家的办公和住宅处，其中最为知名的一号楼别墅建于1934年，这座雍容典雅的英式皇家建筑，是由著名的苏格兰建筑师克拉夫·威廉·埃利斯爵士遥控设计，是当时赫赫有名的英商太古洋行大班的住宅。1952年以后，上海第一任市长陈毅等领导曾在此下榻。1956年划归新成立的市委办公厅招待处，初名为第一招待

所,后改名为兴国招待所,主要接待市委安排来沪的中外贵宾,毛泽东等老一辈无产阶级革命家都曾多次下榻。

2001年上海兴国宾馆在大花园内建造了一座融中西方建筑风格为一体的现代化楼宇,并加盟卡尔森国际酒店集团的营运管理,成为沪上知名的五星级国际商务酒店。新建的这座16层高的楼宇颇具现代风格,内部设计成功地体现了中西合璧的风范。共有190间设计典雅的客房和豪华套房,所有客房都配备高速因特网接口,客房内提供免费上网等个性化服务以满足商务客人的特别需求。酒店拥有多个风格迥异的餐厅和酒吧,提供纯正的中西式佳肴,为客人带来完美的餐饮享受。颇具现代化的宴会/会议设施一应俱全,包括会议中心、宴会厅,接见厅及影剧院等多个大小各异的多功能会议室,并配有同声翻译系统。酒店还有多个户外花园场所,适合举办花园婚礼、鸡尾酒会、野餐烧烤等露天活动。另外,酒店还拥有一个具有透明天顶和花园景观的克拉克国际连锁健身中心,配有世界一流的健身设施及个性化的服务,向客人传递一种令人愉悦的健身理念,使人得到平衡、健康、更有活力的生活。

酒店服务融合了中国传统特色——友好、微笑和高效。员工接受过专业的系统培训,从客人抵达至离店的整个过程提供超越客人期望的服务,使丽笙品牌被高度认可。

上海兴国宾馆是中国第一家由国宾馆跃居为参与国际竞争的国际品牌商务酒店,并且保持了国宾馆的服务特色。它体现了中与西、历史与现代的完美相约,也成功地反映了中国酒店业的发展与世界接轨。

1. 大楼夜景
   Night View
2. 酒店大堂
   Hotel Lobby

The famous guesthouse Shanghai Xing Guo Hotel has become a very well-known international five-star boutique hotel in Shanghai. It is situated within 70,000 square meters of historic gardens in the heart of the consular district, and equipped with a modern high-tech, the central vacuum cleaner system which can avoid secondary pollution. The Hotel towers over beautiful gardens and villas, providing a tranquil and welcome haven for guests to enjoy and relax. The Hotel is close to the major diplomatic, shopping, entertainment and historical areas. With its easy access from the Yan An elevated highway, it is just 15 minutes from Hongqiao International Airport, 45 minutes from Pudong International Airport and only 5 minutes from the central business district.

The historical Xing Guo Hotel is renowned for its villa complex built in the 1920s and 1930s. It is known as the largest hotel in garden and villa style in downtown Shanghai. The Hotel has more than 20 villas of French, British, German, American, Spanish and Canadian design, occupying 70,000 square meters of land of which 80% is covered by green, all the old villas were built in 1920s and 1930s. Among them, the villa one building is the most attractive and mysterious building in the garden complex. It is designed remotely by the well-known British architect, Sir Clough Williams-Ellis. The three-storeyed building once belonged to Butterfield & Swire, a British concern which used to monopolize the Chinese shipping industry in 1930s. After the foundation of the People's Republic of China in 1949, the Shanghai Municipal government took over this building, Chairman Mao once stayed in it in 1950s. Afterward, the villa complex turned into the Xing Guo Guesthouse receiving many leaders from the Beijing Government and other Chinese and foreign VIPs.

1. 花园景观房
   Garden View Room
2. 大楼日景
   Day Exterior of Hotel Building

1、4.花园
Garden

2.一号楼别墅
Villa 1

3.草地婚礼
Garden Wedding

In 2001, the Hotel completed a new 16 - storeyed building in the garden surrounding and joined the Carlson Hotels International Management Group, renamed as Radisson Plaza Xing Guo Hotel Shanghai. The new building reflects the charm and tradition of Europe in style and decor. Featuring modern architecture, the interior successfully blends Chinese and Western design. The Hotel's 190 guest rooms including suites are of luxurious and contemporary design and equipped with Radisson Plaza amenities to ensure 100% guest satisfaction. Business travelers will appreciate a high level of personalized service while enjoying free broadband internet access and business services. The Hotel has 4 restaurants and bars offering diverse dining options, a range of versatile conference and meeting facilities all equipped with simultaneous interpretation system. Additional, beautiful landscaped gardens are an idyllic setting for a wedding ceremony, cocktail party, barbecue and more. With the unique panoramic garden view, the Clark Hatch Fitness Center is your partner in pursuit of all-round fitness. The mission of the Clark Hatch is to infuse into the lives of members a total fitness philosophy in a pleasing, professional, and personal manner conducive to achieving the goals of members for more fit, energetic, and balanced lives.

Service throughout offers that special blend of Chinese hospitality – friendly, efficient and always delivered with a warm smile. Staff are trained to ensure that guests expectations are exceeded, from when they arrive to when they leave – a quality for which Radisson Plaza hotels are recognized.

Radisson Plaza Xing Guo Hotel Shanghai is the first State Guesthouse participation in International competition in the hospitality industry. The Hotel maintained the unique characteristics of the state guesthouse and reflected the successful development of the hotel industry in China.

1. 酒店大堂
   Hotel Lobby
2. 香樟园西餐厅
   Cafe Li Brasserie
3. 八号楼夜景
   Night View of Villa 8
4. 丽宫中餐厅
   Li Palace Chinese Restaurant
5. 行政酒廊
   Plaza Club Lounge
6. 泰芬吧
   Tavern Bar & Grill

1. 八号楼会议中心宴会厅
   Ballroom at Villa 8 Conference Center
2. 丽岳厅
   Board Room
3. 八号楼接见厅
   Villa 8 Conference Center
4. 健身中心
   Health Club
5. 游泳池
   Swimming Pool

1、7. 总统套房
　　　Presidential Suite
2. 服务员
　　Waitress
3. 厨师长
　　Master Chef
4. 销售经理
　　Sales Manager
5. 门童
　　Doorman
6. 洗衣房员工
　　Laundry Staff
8. 豪华套房
　　Deluxe Suite
9. 桑拿房
　　Sauna

苏州金鸡湖凯宾斯基大酒店位于苏州工业园区，金鸡湖和独墅湖美轮美奂的自然风景就环绕在酒店周围，27洞金鸡湖高尔夫球场近在咫尺。酒店能够提供多达3,000平方米的各类会议设施及各国风味美食，是商务及休闲旅客的理想住所。从上海虹桥及浦东国际机场，无锡机场和杭州萧山国际机场到达苏州都非常便利。

458间客房包含127间豪华双人房、70间套房、1间总统套房及4间外交套房，房间宽敞优雅，浴室以大理石装饰，从落地窗向外望去，即是苏州最秀美的天然湖泊或毗邻的高尔夫球场。所有房间均配备无线宽带上网、宽敞的书桌、可留言国际长途电话及可收看国内外节目的40英寸平板电视，并设有14小时客房送餐服务。

怡时咖啡厅让您在临湖的用餐环境中体验优雅浪漫的欧式奢华风情，新鲜多元的自助美食让您感受开放式厨房带来的无尽乐趣。凯宾美食廊为现代都市人贴心设计了精致可口、风味独特的蛋糕、面包及各色自制美点，让您把至尊美味带回家品尝。

望湖阁中餐厅提供地道的广东菜和淮阳菜。11间装修风格迥异的私密包间，充满活力热情的厨师团队，不管是商务宴请，或是朋友小聚，这里都将是你的最佳选择。

酒店拥有敬业且经验丰富的一流员工，能确保您的各项活动顺利进行。所有的会议室均配备无线宽带上网及最先进的视听设备。会议室共有9间，面积从120平方米至1,850平方米的宴会大厅不等。

酒店的商务中心24小时全天开放，为住客提供商务服务，包括秘书工作、传真、打印及复印。

酒店健身中心占地超过4,000平方米，拥有各种最先进的健身设施，包含水流按摩浴缸及50米长室内恒温游泳池，还有室内网球场和壁球馆。

Kempinski Hotel Suzhou Surrounded by the stunning natural scenery of Jinji Lake and Dushu Lake, is located within Suzhou Industrial Park. The hotel is adjacent to the 27-hole- Jinji Lake International Golf Course and offers 3,000 sqm of meeting and conference facilities and extensive international dining options, making the hotel ideally suited for both business and leisure traveller. Suzhou is served by Shanghai Hongqiao and Pudong International airports, Wuxi Airport and Hangzhou Xiaoshan International Airport.

The 458 spacious rooms including 127 Deluxe twin rooms, 70 suites, a Presidential Suite and 4 Diplomatic Suites are elegantly furnished with marble bathrooms and floor-to-ceiling windows offering stunning views over Suzhou's marvellous lakes and the golf course. All rooms are equipped with wireless broadband Internet access, a large desk, IDD telephone with voicemail system and a 40 inch flat screen TV with International and local channels. 24-hour room service is available.

The Season's Café, with full view of Dushu Lake and garden surrounding, presents a sumptuous selection of dishes from around the world at the Buffet by our Show Kitchen.

1、2.酒店外景
Hotel Exterior

The Kempi Deli is offering awide selection of delicious homemade cakes, bread,chocolates, cold cuts and sandwiches for you to take away.

Wang Hu Ge Chinese Restaurant serves exquisite Cantonses and Huai Yang cuisine. 11 individual private rooms with its very own style and concept catering to all occasions or choose to seat at the main ala restaurant where one can enjoy the impressive view over the lake.

Our dedicated and experienced staff will ensure your event proceeds smoothly. All meeting rooms are equipped with wireless broadband Internet access and the latest in audio/video technology. A total of 9 meeting rooms ranging from 120 sqm to 1,850 sqm Grand Ballroom.

The business centre is open 24 hours a day, offering confidential business services including secretarial, fax, printing and photocopying.

The Health & Recreation Centre occupies over 4,000 sqm, features state-of-the-art fitness equipment, Jacuzzi and an indoor 50-meter swimming pool. Also available are indoor tennis and squash courts.

1. 外景栈桥
   Hotel Jetty
2. 酒店大堂
   Hotel Lobby
3. 酒店外景
   Hotel Exterior

1. 大堂
   Lobby
2、5. 怡时咖啡厅
   Seasons Cafe
3. 大宴会厅
   Grand Ballroom
4. 望湖阁中餐厅
   Wang Hu Ge Chinese Restaurant

1、5、6. 普拉那啤酒坊
　　Paulaner Bräuhaus
2. 大堂吧
　　Lobby Lounge
3. 望湖阁中餐厅
　　Wang Hu Ge Chinese Restaurant
4. 怡时咖啡厅
　　Seasons Cafe

1. 外交套房
   Diplomatic Suite
2. 按摩水疗池
   Jacuzzi

3. 桌球室
   Billiard Room
4、6. 游泳池
   Swimming Pool
5. 健身房
   Fitness Centre

1、5.外交套房
  Diplomatic Suite
2.豪华湖景房
  Deluxe Lakeview Room
3、4.漾水疗
  Yang Spa

"天下佳山水,古今推富阳"。群山蜿蜒,春江水逶迤而行,带给了富春大地一川如画的绝色佳景。千年之前,汉末孙坚、孙策曾以此地为起点,驰骋沙场、称霸江东、名震中原,孙权继业创建吴国一代丰功伟业,成为后世所景仰之丰碑。一代代孙氏后裔在同一片天地间,演绎着生气和活力,把富阳精雕细刻成富春江畔融自然之美和人文之美的璀璨明珠。贞高绝俗的黄公望于此隐居避世,绘就传世杰作《富春山居图》;峨冠博带的罗隐,文采风流的郁达夫,生于斯而醉于斯……凡此种种,不一而足,自然山水的神韵和历史文化的积淀形成了富阳旅游的独特景观。

在这如诗如画的江湖之滨,一幢气派非凡的建筑临江而立、傲立其间,如一颗耀眼的明珠,与秀美壮丽的江景共同构成一副美丽的画卷,它就是富阳国际贸易中心大酒店,一座五星级的高品质旅游酒店。

这里地理位置优越,地处杭州富阳的政治、商业、文化中心,位于"三江"旅游线上,毗邻萧山国际机场,直面沪杭甬高速,是富阳旅游的重要中转站。游杭州、逛上海,给商务洽谈、旅游观光的八方来宾带来极大的交通便利。

漫步江边远眺,已被国贸中心大酒店的俊美线条所折服;走近酒店,更是惊叹于酒店的恢宏气势。极具现代美感、光

彩夺人的中心建筑主体,散发着令人惊叹的恢宏气势。在这座建筑面积达6.8万平方米的巨大空间里,包含了国际贸易中心大酒店、国际贸易中心大厦及超过6,800平方米的大型地下停车库等,其高度及广度,冠绝富阳。推门而入,富丽堂皇的酒店大堂、高贵典雅的餐厅、舒适恬静的客房气度不凡,可谓得富阳美景憩息之天时,富春山水相依之地利。登高远眺,富春江色一览无余、旖旎风光尽收眼底,高贵典雅的气质与富春江水一起,构成了国贸独特的品格。

无论是彰显尊荣地位的总统套房,还是如居家般惬意的标准客房;无论是尽享如醉风景的江景房,还是全球风云瞬息在握的行政房,国贸酒店超丰富的各类房型总能满足不同客人的入住需求,让顾客尽情体验品味生活的无限魅力。酒店客房均设置在九层以上,窗体采用豪华玻璃幕墙,视野宽广,鸟瞰四方,富春江美景尽收眼底。宽带网络接口,时尚典雅的家具,优美的人居环境设计,体贴入微的热情服务,让顾客在充分享受贵宾级待遇的同时,也感受到如家般的随兴生活。

10个不同规模的会议室,都专门配备了融合最新科技的会议设备以及训练有素的专职会议经理,可以尽力满足高档会议的一切所需。而其中的璀璨之星,就是一个面积为610平方米的大型多功能厅,其盛大璀璨、高贵典雅,令与会者尽显气派。

穿行酒店,在酒店大堂吧驻足小憩,享受富春江水与阳光的恬静;在高雅的雪茄吧畅谈人生,感受世界知名极品雪茄与红酒的尊贵与奢华;在豪华包厢觥筹交错,品尝顶级粤菜、杭帮菜及国际风味美食的饕餮盛筵……

酒店拥有六大餐厅,包括一个可容纳400人的富阳市最大的无柱式宴会厅,搭配时尚典雅、雍华尊贵的装潢,让每一位顾客随时感受国贸酒店的体贴与用心。从各种精美点心到各式海鲜美味,从各式的小菜到南北精选、正宗日本料理,再到东南亚、西式经典美味,都融合了新颖的现代口味与传统烹饪风格,让每一位顾客在杯盏相碰间回味国贸的美食之道。

1.大堂
Lobby
2.总台服务
Font Desk Service

酒店还设有大型KTV包厢、游泳池、健身室、桌球、乒乓球、桑拿、足浴、棋牌等娱乐设施,为工作与休闲寻找最佳的天平,让宾客尽情享受入住国贸期间每一天的快乐。灯火阑珊时的富阳国际贸易中心大酒店,移步换景,目眩神迷中儒雅不凡,让身为都市精英的你找到自己的精神家园。

五星级的酒店,五星级的服务。每一位光临国贸大酒店的顾客不仅仅能体验由"问候、礼让、微笑"贯彻始终的星级服务,更能领略到国贸中心大酒店所着力缔造的独具个性的酒店文化。汲取富春文化养分与力量,国贸中心大酒店正在用它的每一个亲切的微笑,生动谱写着一曲"用心,就能创造一切可能"的奋斗之歌!

未来的国贸,是富春江畔最为耀眼的一颗璀璨的明珠,必将焕发更加夺目的光彩!

"The landscape of Fuyang is unparalleled in the world". The beauty of mountains and the picturesque Fuchun River that travels across the city brings Fuyang splendid landscape. At the end of Han Dynasty, Sun Jian and Sun Ce started their career here and later Sun Quan became the founder and king of the Kingdom of Wu, which has been admired as a monument in Fuyang's long history. Their descendants from generation to generation has carved Fuyang city into a gorgeous pearl filled with both natural beauty and human beauty by Fuchun River with their vitality and wisdom. Renowned painter Wang Gongwang secluded himself here and created the masterpiece "Dwelling in the Fuchun Mountains". Luo Yin, one of the poets of the late Tang Dynasty, and Yu Dafu were both born here and fascinated by this enchanting place. In one word, the beauty of the natural landscape and the charm of the long history and rich culture

1. 送餐服务
   Room Service
2. 外景
   Hotel View
3. 西餐厅
   Western Food Restaurant
4. 套房细节
   Details of Standard Suit
5. 内景
   Interior View

has made Fuyang a top tourist city in China. Along the picturesque Fuchun River there stands an impressive building, Fuyang International Trade Center Hotel, a top five-star tourist hotel. Coupled with the magnificent riverview, this hotel has become a splendid pearl in this beautiful picture.

Situated in the political, commercial and cultural center of Fuyang city of Hangzhou, the hotel enjoys an ideal geographical location. As a stop of the "three river" tourist line, the hotel is adjacent to Xiaoshan International Airport and faces the Shanghai-Hangzhou-Ningbo Expressway. Being an important tourist transit, the hotel provides great convenience for people to travel in Hangzhou and Shanghai or to carry out business talks.

Both the outside and the inside of Fuyang International Trade Center Hotel are great appeal to tourists. Full of modern aesthetics, the gorgeous main building stands in all its majesty. The area of the building is 68,000m^2, covering International Trade Center Hotel, International Trade Center Plaza, an over 6800m^2 underground garage and so on, whose height and breadth are unparalleled in Fuyang city. The magnificent lobby, elegant restaurant and convenient rooms all reflect the harmony and beauty of the city. One can fully enjoy the view of Fuchun river and the Beautiful sights from a great height of the hotel. It is elegance and Fuchun river that best interpret the Hotel.

Be it Presidential Suite which highlights the status, standard room which makes the guests feel at home, riverview room where the guests can enjoy enchanting scenery or executive room in which the guests can easily obtain all information, the various rooms in the hotel can always meet different needs and let the guests fully enjoy themselves. All rooms are settled at the 9th or above floors. The luxury glass curtain wall enables the guests a wide field of view. Broadband network interface, elegant furniture, pleasant living environment and considerate service let the guests not only enjoy VIP treatment but feel at home.

Ten conference rooms of different scale are all equipped with high-tech conference facility and well-trained professional conference manager, which make it possible to meet all needs of high-end meetings. Among them, the most splendid one is a multi-function hall covering 610m^2, whose grandness and elegance can well embody the guests, status.

Walking through the hotel or having a rest stop at the hotel lobby can make you enjoy the tranquility of the Fuchun river and the sunshine; Talk about life in the elegant cigar bar, and feel the noble and elegant of the world-renowned cigar and the red wine; Enjoy the drinking, taste the top Candonese dishes, Hang Zhou dishes or even the

international cuisines in the luxury boxes⋯
The Hotel has six dining halls, including the biggest astylar in Fu Yang, which can contain 400 people. The dining hall, equipped with an elegant and distinguished decoration, can make every custom feel the thoughtfulness and carefulness provided by this international hotel at any time. Each dish, from the exquisite desserts to the various delicious seafood, the different dishes to the well-picked foods from the south or the north, the traditional Japanese foods to the classical delicious from the south-east countries or the western countries, are all integrated with the novel modern taste and the traditional cooking style. So that every custom when drinking can feel the specialty of our hotel's foods.

The Hotel is equipped with large KTV boxes, swimming pool, fitness room and provides some recreational facilities like snooker, Ping Pong, sauna, pediluvium and chess. This provides a well balance between working and leisure, and makes each custom feel the happiness of staying here everyday. When the lights reflecting, viewing the various vague scenery makes you the elite in this modern city, find your own spiritual home here.

The five-star hotel, with the five-star service, makes each custom here experience the star service of "greeting, comity, smiling", but also can get the special and personal idea of the International Trade Central Hotel's culture. Absorb the energy and power of Fuchun's culture, the International Trade Central Hotel is now using its every smile to write a struggling song vividly. That's " with our whole hearts, then everything is possible".

The future International Trade Central Hotel is the most shinning pearl of Fuchun river, and also it will give its most brilliant luster.

1. 会议室
   Conference Room
2. 西餐服务
   Dinner Service
3. 酒吧
   Bar

1.环境细节	2.咨客服务	3.礼宾服务	4.西餐江景	5.会议室	6.会议服务细节
Decoration	Greeting Service	Concierge Service	Scenery	Conference Room	Conference Service

罗星阁宾馆地处嘉善繁华商贸中心，闹中取静，是集商务会议、旅游休闲于一体的浙北地区首家挂牌五星级酒店。宾馆占地面积25亩，总建筑面积3万多平方米，整体布局体现江南园林风格，是古典和现代智慧的交融，亭台楼阁、小桥流水、长廊竹影犹如一处世外仙境……是商业会晤、婚嫁宴请、旅游休闲等的最佳去处。

罗星阁宾馆拥有舒适典雅的标准房、商务房、豪华房，以及各类套房200余套，房间以暖色调为主，风格独特。另外配有各类先进设备，为您进行商务会议、旅游休闲带来舒适方便，让您体验高品质生活，延续家庭温馨。

宾馆拥有50～400平方米不等的多个宴会厅，可同时接待800人以内的婚宴、高档酒会及宴会。在丹桂楼中餐厅，南北美食荟萃，宾客可在此体验完美味觉，尽享天下佳肴，在零点自助中享受怡然情趣。19个风格各异的豪华中餐包厢，可以为您提供五星级的顶级服务，让您倍感尊贵。西塘月色大堂吧，小桥流水，古乐流溢，中西饮品、咖啡、名茶、西点小吃一应俱全，在此品茶会友悠然自得。竹韵春天酒吧，装饰高雅，悠扬的音乐、轻松的氛围、美酒、咖啡，使您全身心放松，享受尊重服务。行政商务酒廊，环境舒适优雅，为行政楼层客人提供精美的下午茶点、

饮品服务，是成功人士会谈、休息的理想场所。6间大小不同、风格各异的会议厅，全部配备了音视频转播系统、高清晰投影设备、专业音响等先进完善的会议设施，能充分满足不同商务活动的要求，是举行商务谈判、新闻发布会、产品展示会、营销推广会、培训研讨会的最佳场所。

1. 外景
   Hotel View
2. 大堂
   Lobby

Luoxingge Hotel, Jiashan which located in the center of the town, is designed and constructed according to the five-star standard, and is an ideal residence for holiday or business trips. Hotel covers about 25 Mu in which the construction area amounts to over 30,000 square meters. Kiosk, pavilion, bridge, and corridor, make you hard to know that you are in the picture or the picture exists in your heart. With a feeling of home, guests will not only enjoy a pleasant and cozy stay, but also express their nobleness and elegance.

Luoxingge Hotel, Jiashan has totally over 200 rooms and suites, such as standard room, executive room, deluxe room and different kinds of suites etc. All the advanced equipments assure your utmost comfort.

Banqueting halls with different proportions from 50 square meters to 400 square meters can support 800 people banquet or cocktail party at the most. Osmanthus Chinese Restaurant: Dishes are made with top grade seasonal raw materials, and you can enjoy them that are exception in both vision and taste and are special for their delicate appearance and plain taste.

19 deluxe boxes of Chinese restaurant in different style will offer you exalted feast and top service. Moonlight on Xitang Café: Comfortable atmosphere, fantastic drinks, classical Chinese music makes you leisureliness. Bamboo · Spring Bar, is an excellent bar to relax in after a whole day hard work.Business Lounge, with comfortable atmosphere, fantastic drinks, is an ideal place to meet with friends or business associates, and enjoy your favorite libation including famous international teas and coffee. Luoxingge Hotel's 6 impressive function hall and meeting rooms, are all equipped with audio and video system, LCD projector, and high-quality sound & light system. A professional team of banquet and convention service personnel attends all corporate meetings, major conventions, and conference.

1. 园林细节
   Details of Garden
2. 大堂
   Lobby

1. 环境
Surrounding
2. 大堂吧服务细节
Details of Lobby Bar Sevice
3. 大堂细节
Details of Lobby Bar

1. 自助餐
   Buffet
2. 自助餐厅细节
   Details of Buffet
3. 中餐服务
   Dinner Service

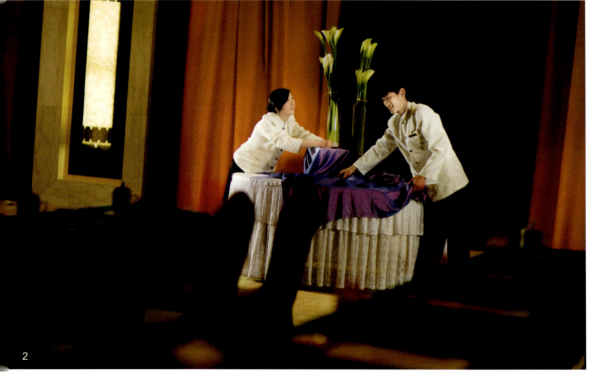

1. 行李生
   Concierge Service
2. 会议服务细节
   Details of Conference Service
3. 会议室
   Conference Room

1. 中庭园林
   Garden
2. 客房
   Guest Room
3. 廊
   Porch

浙江世贸君澜大饭店毗邻西湖风景区，位于杭州市金融、商业、旅游和文化中心，地处杭城最大的贵族商务区——黄龙商务圈的中心位置。这里环境优越，人文基础浓厚，商务配套全面，交通便捷，因此深受品牌公司、规模企业青睐。清雅的景色、便利的交通让商旅客人在迅捷完成商务拜访之余，还可自在享受休闲的乐趣。

饭店拥有392间/套豪华客室，并设计了多种房型满足不同客人的需求。揽窗远眺，宝石流霞，黄龙吐翠，尽收眼底，让人心旷神怡。为了让商旅客人享受在"家"的温情，在舒适的客房内，均配有生饮水装置；拥有宽带高速上网接口；并在个别套房内首次引进了厨房设备；而床上的中国传统丝绸软靠垫，使客房变得更为实用和温馨。

为营造独特的商旅氛围，酒店在丰富的文化内涵基础上，将文化氛围与硬件氛围有机地结合在一起。每一个步入酒店的客人都会被大堂上、回廊间、转角处精心布置的艺术装饰所吸引，宋、明、清时期的名人字画、陶瓷雕塑、明代马车、古代窗雕、纤维壁画、玻雕、木雕……处处皆景，散发着浓郁的人文气息，山水浙江的独特艺术魅力丝丝尽现，给酒店带来了独特的艺术生命。

在增强酒店环境文化内涵的同时，浙江世贸君澜大饭店注重以"人文"理

1. 全景
Panorama
2. 大堂吧
Lobby Bar
3. 大堂吧人物
Guest at Lobby Bar

念推动服务品位的提升。当客人进入房间，会发现床上已铺着他习惯的软垫；当客人生日时，会接到酒店温馨的祝福电话；当客人忘了关上车窗，酒店的安全人员会顶着寒风守在他的车旁……贴心精致的个性化服务使浙江世贸君澜大饭店成为商旅客人的最佳伙伴。

作为浙江省的会议场所集中地，浙江世贸君澜大饭店拥有大、中、小型会议场所12处，能满足商务谈判、产品展示、时装表演、新闻发布、高级中西宴会等多种商务活动的需要。场内设施齐全，功能完备、先进，并配备六路同声翻译、四路摄像电脑编辑及高清晰度背投影等系统，是浙江省最高规格的政务、商务和对外交流的重要活动场所之一。省内最大的无柱式宴会厅——"世贸厅"，设计高贵，可根据客人的不同需求，举办700人酒会或500人的中、西宴会及展览、时装表演等活动，更可分割为两个独立的宴会厅，为宾客提供更多的选择。

独具特色的系统化会议接待体系也向社会证明了浙江世贸君澜大饭店是浙江省内承办高标准大型会议、宴会的首选之地。开业至今，酒店已承办了如微软、IBM、诺基亚、可口可乐等一大批国际知名公司大中型会议，圆满完成了"全国旅游工作会议"、"亚洲高级别研讨会"、"首届世界佛教论坛"、"两岸关系研讨会"等大型活动的接待任务，吸引了不计其数的国内外政要、知名人士、巨商富贾。

风荷轩、丹桂楼分别位于浙江世贸君澜大饭店的三层和四层，这里不仅名肴荟萃，更是闻名遐迩的商务酬酢和高级饮宴场所。世贸君澜品牌名肴鲍鱼、鱼翅、燕窝、佛跳墙享誉杭城，来自香港的粤菜名肴大师郭祺先生凭借20多年的入厨经验，将粤菜饮食文化演绎成味觉艺术奇珍。不仅于此，酒店二楼云天阁适时推出的各类主题美食节也颇受商旅客人的青睐。从地中海风味到南北美风情，让客人们尽享国际美食盛宴。如今，当人们对美食的需求到了

1. 客房窗景
   Scenery Outside the Window
2. 大堂
   Lobby

"追求健康"的第三阶段，世贸君澜先把脉再定制的"健康药膳"，亦开始流行起来……

随着互联网（Internet）技术的飞速发展，浙江世贸君澜大饭店有效地利用现代信息产品，完善了各类信息配套构件，逐步健全了现代商务自助服务，实现了饭店各区域的宽带上网；而行政楼专用会议室、洽谈室、专用商务吧、图书阅览室等商务场所的设立，进一步提高了行政楼层接待层次。豪华、先进的商务环境使入住世贸君澜的宾客充分体验到了现代文明的迅捷舒适，为酒店打造商务酒店品牌打下了坚实的基础，并带来了源源不断的商务客源。

2004～2006年，浙江世贸君澜大饭店连续三年荣获杭州市"十佳星级饭店"称号，并与上海金茂君悦大酒店等十家酒店一起被评为首届"中外酒店'白金奖'——中国十大最受欢迎酒店"。2008年，浙江世贸君澜大饭店亦荣获"浙江省最佳品质饭店"、"2008年中国十佳会议中心"、"中国饭店业30年最具影响力饭店"等多项殊荣。

浙江世贸君澜大饭店先进完善的设施、科学成熟的管理、浓厚幽雅的文化气息和细致入微的个性化服务，让您尽享温馨的呵护、尽显成功的价值！

Zhejiang Narada Grand Hotel is adjacent to the West Lake Scenic Area, and it is located at the core site of Huanglong (Yellow Dragon) Business Circle, the largest noble business district in Hangzhou, which functions as the financial, business, tourism and cultural center of the city. It is blessed with wonderful environment, profound humanistic ground, well-equipped business facilities and convenient transportation. Therefore, it has won great favor from famous-brand companies and large-scale enterprises. Its graceful scenery and easy traffic can allow the guests to enjoy the pleasure of leisure at fulfilling business visit rapidly.

The Hotel currently has 392 luxury guest rooms. Meanwhile, it also provides guest rooms of various types to satisfy the needs of different guests. Overlooking through the window, you can command a superb panoramic view of the gorgeous sunglow covering Baoshi Hill or the striking verdure of Yellow Dragon Cave, which will send you carefree and joyous. In order to provide the guests with home-like feelings, the Hotel has installed an apparatus of direct drinking and high-speed broadband access in every comfortable guest room. In particular, some special suites have even been equipped with kitchen fittings for the first time. Meanwhile, the cushions made in traditional Chinese silk fabric on beds have made the guest room prettier and cozier.

For the purpose of creating a unique ambience of business trip, the Hotel has perfectly combined its cultural environment

with hardware equipment on the basis of enriching its cultural connotation. Every guest entering into the Hotel will be deeply attracted by the elaborately decorated hall, corridors and corners with extraordinary calligraphic works and paintings, ceramic sculptures, horse-trolleys of Ming Dynasty, ancient window carvings, fiber murals, glass-carvings, wood-carvings… everywhere can be a particular view, which gives forth strong humanistic aroma. The distinctive artistic glamour of Zhejiang mountains and waters are fully displayed, which brings the hotel a unique artistic life.

In the meantime of enriching its cultural connotation, Zhejiang Narada Grand Hotel also lay emphasis on the promotion of service quality by the conception of humanity care. When a guest enters his room, he will be delighted to find that his bed has already be covered with his habitual soft cushion; he will receive a warm-hearted phone call of blessings from the Hotel on his birthday; if he forgets to close the car windows, the security staff will safeguard his cars in chilly wind…The intimate and thoughtful services of Narada has made it the best companion of travelers on a business trip.

As a core venue for conferences in Zhejiang Province, Zhejiang Narada Grand Hotel has 12 various size conference rooms which can meet the needs of such diverse activities as: commercial negotiation, product demonstration, fashion shows, press release, and high-level banquets in both Chinese and Western styles. All the rooms are equipped

1. 云天阁
   Skylight Pavilion Café
2、4. 中餐服务
   Dinner Service
3. 中餐包厢
   Dinner Room

with: six sets of simultaneous translation, four sets of computer editing of video cameras and a high-definition rear projection system. All this ranks the Narada Grand Hotel as one of the highest-level sites for governmental affairs, commercial and foreign exchange activities. The nobly-designed "World Trade Hall", the biggest astylar banquet hall at the provincial-level, can house 700 people for cocktail parties or 500 people for Chinese or Western style banquets, exhibitions and fashion show. In addition, the hall can be divided into two independent banquet halls which provide more choices for guests.

The characteristic systematized conference structure has also proved that "Narada" is undoubtedly the first choice for hosting large-scale conferences and refined banquets. Since its establishment, the hotel has undertaken large and mediun-sized conferences of such world-renowned companies as: Microsoft, IBM, Nokia, Coca-Cola, "National Tourism Workshop", "Asian High Rank Seminar" and the First Session of World Buddhism Forum", which has attracted numerous politicians, celebrities and business tycoons from home and abroad.

Lotus Restaurant and Osmanthus Restaurant are situated at the second floor and the third floor respectively of Zhejiang Narada Grand Hotel, where various well-known fine delicacies are provided. Meanwhile, they are also famous for business communications and high-grade banquets. The notable foods including abalone, shark fin, bird's nest, Fotiaoqiang (sea food and poultry) in Narada always enjoy great reputation in Hangzhou. Mr. Guo Qi, a master cook from Hong Kong of Cantonese cuisine, is skilled at utilizing Cantonese cuisine culture to produce gustatory artistic works by virtue of his over-20-year cooking experience. In addition, various fine food festivals on proper occasions presented by Yuntian Pavilion Restaurant of the first floor also find favor

1、5.行政酒廊
Executive Lounge
2、3.行政酒廊服务
Executive Lounge Service
4.宴会专员
Banquet Service
6.厨师
Chef
7.云天阁细节
Skylight Pavilion Café

from travelers and guests. They can have the chance of enjoying delicacies of the whole world, varying from Mediterranean flavor to American taste. Nowadays, people's demand for fine food has entered into the third stage – seeking health. For that purpose, the wholesome medicinal food provided by Narada, which should be ordered after feeling the consumer's pulse (to know his physical condition) has become quite popular.

In keeping pace with the rapid development of Internet technology, "Narada" effectively utilizes modern information products, offers improved IT accessories and has implemented broadband Internet access in the Hotel; what's more, the establishment of conference rooms, negotiation room, special commercial bar and library in the administrative building advances the reception level of administrative floors. The luxurious and advanced commercial environment allows guests to experience all the modern comforts, which in turn has created a solid foundation for forging the hotel brand and brought customers back time after time.

Zhejiang Narada Grand Hotel was given the title of Hangzhou's "Top Ten Star-graded Hotels" three times from 2004 to 2006. In 2005, it was awarded "Platinum Award of Foreign and Domestic Hotels – China Top Ten the Most Populous Hotels"; in Sep. 2006, it was awarded Hangzhou "2006 Top 100 Credit Tourism Enterprises"; in 2007, it was crowned with the title of "2007 China Excellent Green Hotels".

Zhejiang Narada Grand Hotel will provide you with advanced facilities, technical staff and efficient management and personalized services all within a sophisticated, harmonious atmosphere in order to bring you great success.

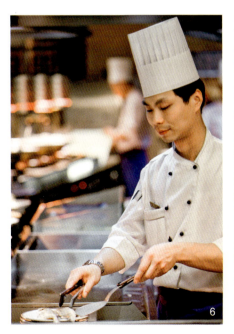

1、2.中餐包厢细节
　　Dinner Room Details
3.婚宴秘书
　　Wedding Service
4.行政酒廊服务
　　Executive Lounge Service
5.会议专员
　　Conference Service

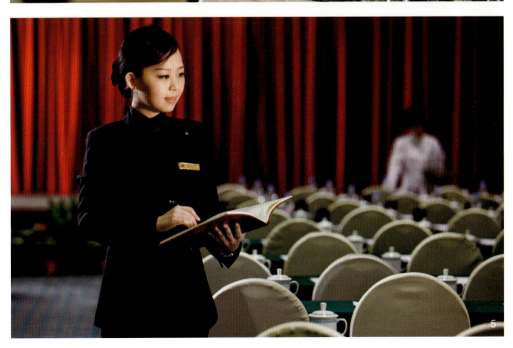

1. 游泳池细节
   Swimming Pool Details
2、3. 游泳池
   Swimming Pool
4、5. 客房
   Guest Room

宜兴历史上有名的宜兴宾馆，前身为国宾馆和清末民初邑人任藻清私家花园，现为宜兴市首家五星级饭店。

坐落于宜兴历史上著名的"岳堤"遗址上的宜兴宾馆，占地1.3万平方米，是宜兴环境最为优雅的宾馆，一弯氿水，三面环绕，竹影流水，飞檐青瓦，她是江南特有的中式建筑风格与现代时尚的氛围完美结合的典范。2003年，宜兴市知名房地产企业——兰山房地产开发有限公司入主宜兴宾馆，并于2005年出资2.2亿元人民币对宾馆全方位改扩建。扩建后的宜兴宾馆于2008年7月24日荣膺五星。

宜兴宾馆前身是宜兴望族任家溪隐花园，又名翡翠园，建于1921年，因溪隐园位临京杭国道（宁杭公路）过境段中间，因此为当时的南京政府青睐，作为招待从南京驱车去杭州的中外贵宾歇憩之所。1933年，国际联盟（联合国前身）李顿调查团曾在此小憩，并举行了记者招待会，溪隐园随招待会镜头在纽约、伦敦等欧洲国家广为传播。抗日战争爆发后，溪隐园遭受严重破坏，一片荒芜。直至1955年，经宜兴市人民政府重新修缮扩建，成为外宾招待所，主要接待国家和地方领导人，及各国外宾。

新宾馆外观造型错落有致，别有一派江南建筑格调。著名书法家尹瘦石手书的"宜兴宾馆"四个大字，代表着"教授之乡"浓重而又灵秀的大家之气。宾馆大堂金碧辉煌，恢宏大气，豪华而又典雅。大幅名家

紫砂壁画《荆溪十景图》、美术大师徐悲鸿先生的《憩马图》、著名绘画大师钱松岩先生的《黄山图》金箔画,超大规格的木制隔屏,特别是由500把紫砂茶壶和清乾隆年间的国宝大铁缸构成的中心艺术品,是把画与陶、人与景、现代与传统、历史与潮流诸元素巧妙融合的典范,有着大而不疏、华而不俗的超然效果,厚实的宜兴人文内涵无处不在鲜活地流淌,走进宜兴宾馆,似乎步入了一个笔墨丹青、古玩荟萃的大观园。

宜兴宾馆拥有271间客房,其中包括174间豪华客房,一个总统套间,一个行政楼层。行政楼层共有22间客房,并设有独立的行政酒廊,提供雪茄、酒品、茶饮及精美小吃。宾馆景观房备受青睐,倚窗而眺,西氿波光粼粼,铜峰青山叠翠,宛如一幅山水画映入眼帘,令人心旷神怡。

善卷厅、滆湖厅、蛟桥厅……以宜兴人文景观命名的21个豪华餐饮包间,是一房一典故,宴客之时便可了解宜兴这一有着2,000余年历史的江南名城。在这里,可以品尝地道的淮扬菜,还有名扬海内外,雅称"太湖三白"的白鱼、白虾、银鱼,以及各种山珍野味。争妍陶都的紫砂器皿、均陶、精陶、青瓷、彩陶"五朵金花",陶艺大师的稀世作品更会令君大开眼界,赞叹不绝。

西餐厅、大堂吧、咖啡厅巧妙分合,互为呼应,提供自助早茶、法式西餐及各式茶点。金海湾咖啡厅以"情调与咖啡"为主题,厅内烛光点点、琴音缭绕、醇香四溢,窗外氿水荡漾、树影婆娑、翠竹摇曳,内外情景相宜、相映生辉,营造了幽静清雅、灵动飘逸的宜人景致,恰似仙境在人间。

此外,经过全新改建的新宾馆,增设了可容纳400人的多功能厅、精品商场,以及芭堤雅桑拿中心、KTV、健身中心等休闲项目。

宜兴素以"陶都"、"洞天"、"竹海"、"茶洲"著称于世,位于市中心的宜兴宾馆宛若一颗镶嵌在宜兴大地上的璀璨明珠,是宜兴家喻户晓、为周边城市所熟知的五星名店。

1. 外景
   Exterior View
2. 总台服务
   Front Desk Service

The famous historic Yixing Hotel originated from private garden owned by Ren Zaoqing, a noble family in Qing Dynasty, up till now turned into the first five star hotel in Yixing.

Yixing Hotel is located on the historical site "Yue Dyke" occupying the land of 13,000 sqm. The Jiu-lake surrounding in three directions, the black brick and modillion over the bamboo shade make the hotel as the most elegance environment in Yixing. It was honoured a gloria model by combining the South China architecture style with modern pattern. In 2003, the famous Real Estate enterprise – Lanshan Real Estate Development Company Ltd. got to own this hotel and invested RMB 220 million for its overall renovation in 2005. The hotel was honoured 5-star rating in July 24th 2008.

The former construction of this hotel was the private garden of Ren's family, named "Brook Hiden Garden" or "Jade Garden" which was built in 1921. Due to its nice location between the two highways, Beijing—Hangzhou and Nanjing—Hangzhou, the former Nanjing Government kept a close watch on it, and set up it as the rest place for some VIP officials and foreigners on the trip from Nanjing to Hangzhou. In 1933, the Inspection Group lead by Lidun from the International allies (the former UN) once took rest here and held a press conference, the garden was widely spread on the photos taken by the conference over New York, London and Europe. During the anti-Japanese War, the Garden was violently destroyed and overall desolate.

The appearance of the new Hotel looks harmoniously with its special South-China architecture style. The Hotel name "Yixing Hotel" written by the famous calligraphist Mr. Yin shoushi is showing the strong spirit of "the town of professor". Decorated with the huge terra-cotta fresco "Ten sceneries in

1. 旋转楼梯
   Revolving Stairs
2. 外观
   Exterior View

1. 大堂
   Lobby
2. 包厢服务
   Loge Service
3. 扒房细节
   Grill Room Details
4. 西餐厅服务
   Western-style Restaurant Service

Jingxi", the painting "Resting Horses" drew by the famous artist Mr. Xu Beihong, the golden painting "Huangshan Mountain" drew by the famous artist Mr. Qian Songyan, the hotel lobby was dressed grand and splendid. The tremendous wooden screen with 500 pcs terra-cotta teapots and the famous vat in China made in Qing Dynasty composed a central art corner which creating a fantastic model with painting and terra-cotta, human and scenery, modernism and tradition, historic and current elements, achieving a unforgettable impression, huge but not loose, luxury but not vulgarity. The profound connotation of Yixing culture is showing over here and there. Stepping into the hotel lobby you would find yourself in a painting and antique gallery.

There are 271 rooms in the hotel including 174 luxury rooms, one presidential suite, one executive floor with 22 rooms and detached executive lounge serving cigar, wine and drinks, and some delicacy food as well. The river view rooms are well loved, from the window you may catch a nice painting in sight with the river and the mountains which refreshing you in jolly mood.

The 21 separated wing-rooms were named by local sceneries such as Shanjuan Hall, Gehu Hall, Jiaoqiao Hall…one room means one story, during the feast you would learn the history of this famous South-China town for more than 2,000 years. You could also enjoy the standard Huaiyang flavour here, including famous " Taihu Lake three whites" white fish, white shrimps and whitebait as well as multifarious food from mountains and sea. For the food vessel, some fine ceramic made by famous artist would make you surprising and exclaiming.

Western restaurant, lobby bar, coffee lounge laid out harmoniously serving breakfast buffet , western food and sorted cakes. Gold Coast Cafe lobby bar is running under the sentiment theme, sitting inside with candle light, music around, incense air, jade-like river over the window, bamboo and tree shade, you would have a illusion that you were lost in a fairyland.

Furthermore, after overall renovation the hotel built up a function hall for 400 pax, a kiosk, a Thailand Sauna Centre, KTV and Health Club.

Yixing is world-wide known for its "Capital of ceramic" ,"The lava cave", "The sea of bamboo", "The tea continent". And Yixing Hotel located in the centre of the city looks like a shining pearl enchased on Yixing territory, and meanwhile it is a very well-known 5-star rating hotel among the circumjacent cities.

1. 大堂
   Lobby
2. 西餐厅
   Western-style Restaurant
3. 大堂吧细节
   Lobby Bar Details
4. 扒房
   Grill Room
5. 扒房服务
   Grill Room Service

1. 行政套房
   Executive Room
2. 客房
   Guest Room
3. 客房细节
   Guest Room Details

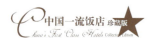

厦门悦华酒店
YEOHWA HOTEL
XIAMEN

Former Xiamen Mandarin Hotel

悦华酒店是福建省独一无二的首家五星级别墅式花园酒店，占地20多万平方米，1984年建店，以豪华商务、会议、接待为主，拥有423间／套客房、1,100平方米的无柱宴会大厅、不同规格的餐厅和会场，配套齐全，豪华气派，是"悦华"品牌的诞生地和旗舰店，拥有顶级接待服务文化的雄厚积淀。

悦华酒店拥有20多年会议和宴会服务的经验。这里曾经成功承办亚太经合组织APEC会议、世界500强跨国公司会议及中日韩三国部长级通信会议等最高规格国际会议。

馨悦楼的华庭千人多功能厅及其前厅总面积超过1,600平方米，大厅挑高6米，是大型专业会议和宴会的新选择。凌云阁是中型会议宴会区。凌云阁一层有525m^2的宴会大厅、二层有370m^2国际会议厅。

多种就餐选择，诱人的美食，聚集厦门顶级餐厅。无论是绿庭餐厅恢宏的景色、极品佳肴，还是各个咖啡厅、酒吧、酒廊友好的国际氛围，光临厦门悦华酒店，您一定会找到理想的美食。悦华酒店独有的"宴会菜"，总结了20年来各类高端商务宴会和顶级国宴服务所积累的经验，融汇中国八大菜系以及德、法、日、意等中外经典宴会菜肴，为客人量身定做，是装饰精美、口感健

康细腻、富含生态、时尚、文化、健康的美食，结合国宾级服务标准而形成的全新宴请新概念。

悦华酒店因曾接待众多世界著名的重要人士而广受赞誉。这里曾接待过美国前总统理查德·尼克松、新加坡前总理李光耀等政坛要客。

日式别墅群，是厦门酒店业唯一的日式风格别墅，是长住客家庭的理想家居。日式别墅为单体建筑，外观独特，每户都有自己的私家草地、花园和停车位；每栋别墅130～160平方米，为跃层式，楼上是2间主卧，楼下是1间客卧，还有客厅、厨房和餐厅，家庭配置应有尽有；所有别墅坐北朝南，自然采光充足。

作为都市绿洲，酒店绿化超过16万平方米，到处是"绿色"，给人予希望和活力，让您每天充满新鲜的能量。作为都市绿洲，蓝瓦白墙的楼宇、菠萝蜜树下的日式花园别墅、总统别墅贵宾楼群和超大生态花园错落有致地分布，所有空间非常宽敞，让您心情舒畅。馨悦园是厦门酒店业第一个大型生态花园，占地面积达7万多平方米，奇花异草，山水相间，种植不少世界珍稀植物，独一无二的1,690米店内花园运动跑道，仅对住店客人开放，私密安全，是您晨练、散步休闲和观赏的好地方。有氧运动的自然健康生活方式在这里得以精彩体现，让您随时亲近大自然，与大自然共呼吸，获取心灵深处那一份轻松和自在。此外，酒店还拥有2个配有夜间灯光的国际标准的露天网球场，完善的康体中心和娱乐中心，健身房、桑拿、按摩功能齐全，海神酒吧大厅和13间日式KTV包房，丰富健康生活。

1. 酒店全景
   Hotel's Bird View
2. 馨悦楼
   Xinyue Building

Xiamen Yeohwa Hotel is most famous for its ECO-GARDEN also known as the Best Urban Oasis and Original Ecological Environments with peace, beauty, elegance and warm styles.

Ideally situated in the center of Xiamen Bay where is the SEZ cradle, Xiamen Yeohwa Hotel is convenient to Xiamen International Airport, High-tech Torch Zone, Zhongshan Road, Ferry, Gulangyu Island and SM Shopping Arcade etc. all where are within 15 minutes drive.

There are totally 200,000 square meter space in our hotel, among of which the Xinyue Garden is the idyllic place for leisure, sightseeing and sporting covering 70,000 square meters. With the full—equipment facilities such as indoor water therapy swimming pool, 1,690 meter Garden Jogging Track and 2 international tennis courts, not only the aerobics you can enjoy, also the whole natural style environment and the

1. 海宇楼大堂局部
   Haiyu Building Lobby Details
2. 馨悦楼大堂
   Xinyue Building Lobby

1、6. 绿庭自助餐厅
   Green Yard Coffee Shop
2. 红夫人西餐厅
   Madame Rouge Restaurant
3. 悦华佛跳墙
   Yeohwa Fotiaoqiang
4. 贵宾休息区
   VIP Room
5. 日本料理
   Japanese Restaurant

fresh air you can feel.

The state-of-the-art gardens feature in Chinese traditional architecture style with blue emperor tiles and white walls. Totally 451 rooms including spacious rooms and suites, Xiamen Yeohwa Hotel offers a finest accommodation, facilities and services. Different from the traditional hotel pattern, an individual building of our executive floor- The Yeohwa Club with high speed Internet access, fax machine, wide selection of local and foreign channels providing the privacy and convenience to discerning travelers whether on business or for leisure, also Wireless High Speed Internet Access in all public area of our hotel . With the characteristics of peace, beauty, elegance and warmth, Xiamen Yeohwa Hotel makes the only urban oasis in town.

With over two decades banquet service experience, our hotel have successfully held many international meeting which included Asia Pacific APEC event, Top 500 worldwide company meeting, Telecom meeting by Ministers from China, Korea and Japan etc., including a conference meeting room with 1,100 square meters and the only synchronization transaction facility in town, International Conference Room with 370 square meters, Banquet Hall with 525 square meters and over 20 elegant meeting rooms, our MICE team offer a specialist service for your event and most importantly warm, friendly, attentive and catering experience.

Xiamen Yeohwa Hotel has essential cuisine arts from eight major Chinese cooking series and all kinds of classic dishes from the style of German, France, Italy and Japan etc. Our famous chefs create a stunning and lavishly cuisine to privileged banquet dining experience. The Yeohwa Fotiaoqiang

is the most famous dish with a legend in Fujian Province. We have Chinese, French and Japanese restaurants where dining in our luxurious restaurants with different decoration style and personal service, not only the delicious food but also the social prestige and nobility you can enjoy. The Yeohwa Hotel was honored to have the world famous VIPS' stay such as former President of U.S. Nixon, former Minister Mentor of Singapore Lee Kuan Yew and DELL CEO Michael Dell etc. The leaders of The CPC and China Central Government also visit here frequently. The twenty years' service experiences create the warm hospitality culture, which symbolizes the most outstanding level of the hotels. The Yeohwa Hotel is famous for the good reputation of star-spangled awards as one of four-star hotels in 1989, the first five-star hotel in Xiamen and Fujian Province, the unique Xiamen member of China Famous Hotel Corporation, the earliest member of Union International Les Clefs D'Or, the China Tourism Famous Brand in 2003 and one of the Foreign Investment Advanced Hotels in the year of 2005.

With full support by The C&D Group, Yeohwa Brand chain hotels are Booming. The five-star Quanzhou Yeohwa Hotel and Wuyi Mountain Yeohwa Hotel were opening successfully as the best hotel in Quanzhou and Wuyi Mountain city.

Xiamen Yeohwa Hotel is your next perfect MICE destination. You will be served with our top-ranked professionalism and expertise to make your events a great success.

Yeohwa-The Best Urban Oasis and what we make is different.

We are looking forward to welcoming you stay with us.

1. 红夫人西餐厅
   Madame Rouge Restaurant
2. 华庭外走廊
   Foyer of Mandarin Grand Ballroom
3. 亲切服务
   Warm Hospitality
4. 精致摆台
   Exquisite Setup

1、3、4. 商务中心
　　　Business Centre
2. 华庭多功能厅
　　Mandarin Grand Ballroom
5. 国际会议厅
　　International Conference Hall

1. 海宇楼行政房
   Haiyu Executive Room
2. 馨悦海景花园商务房
   Xinyue Sea-View Garden Deluxe Room
3. 花园商务大床房
   Xinyue Garden Deluxe Single Room
4. 花园商务双床房
   Xinyue Garden Deluxe Twin Room
5. 馨悦海景花园套房
   Xinyue Sea-View Garden Suite Room
6. 馨悦花园套房
   Xinyue Garden Suite Room
7. 套房卫生间
   Bathroom

南昌凯莱大饭店坐落于滕王阁之侧，隔江遥望世界第二的"南昌之星"摩天轮，步行5分钟即可到达城市商业中心。作为江西省首批五星级酒店之一，无论是商务旅行还是观光购物，南昌凯莱大饭店都是您的最佳选择。

饭店共有327间舒适的客房，全都配备宽带上网接口，可满足商务人士的需求。商务标准间融合了传统与现代元素，新更换的大屏幕液晶电视，为房间增色不少，配有整洁卧具的特大号床让客人安享睡眠。所有套房均有干、湿区域分离的卫浴空间，卫生间更配备了时下流行的各种洗浴设施。饭店有一面朝向赣江，因此入住江景房的客人可以欣赏到绝美的景观。在壮丽的赣江对面是南昌市的红谷滩新区，远远眺望亚洲第一高的摩天轮和林立的高楼，在夜晚灯火阑珊时，偶尔几艘豪华游船驶过，使宾客仿佛置身外滩。

一楼大堂的品味餐厅提供早、午、晚餐，经营东南亚美食与西餐经典菜式。这是首家提供国际半自助餐的西餐厅，宾客在这里可以得到品味美食与时尚的双重享受。大堂酒廊设有沙发椅与吧台，这里提供特制茶饮、西饼、特色小吃、现烤面包与糕点，每晚还有现场钢琴演奏，是商务会谈或与朋友聊天的首选场所。二楼以"船"命名的中餐厅富有中国古典韵味，大厅宽敞明亮、金碧辉煌，精致的水晶灯

与传统扬琴相映成画，富丽堂皇但不显俗气和张扬。宾客在这里可以享用到可口的粤菜和特色赣菜，并在周末享受正宗的港式早、午茶。

三楼与四楼的宴会厅也可兼作会议厅，均可容纳300多人。此外还有7个可容纳20～100人的小多功能厅，适合举办各种商务会议和研讨会。会议厅的整体装修风格稳重、高雅和大气，音像设施、投影设施等会议设备配备齐全，为各类会议提供完善的技术支持与专业的会议策划团队。

饭店的健康中心位于四层，健身设施配备齐全，并设有临江室内恒温游泳池。宾客如果在旅途中感觉疲劳，或是在运动中消耗了过多的能量，还可以在这里享受桑拿、按摩服务。客人入住饭店期间都可以免费使用健身设施和游泳池。

入住凯莱行政楼层，可直接在位于二十层楼的行政酒廊办理入住和退房手续，客人抵达时，酒店会提供免费熨烫衣、擦鞋服务。快捷周到的专享服务彰显客人的尊贵。入住行政楼层的客人除了可以在行政酒廊享用免费早餐以外，还可以享受下午茶、上网服务及每天1小时免费使用行政楼层会议室。行政楼层客房的市内电话及传真免费，还可以延迟退房。如果有需要，一对一的贴身管家随时恭候。

南昌凯莱大饭店是江西省首批五星级饭店之一，历年来先后在江西省及全国范围内获得"中国最优商务酒店"、"江西最佳品牌酒店"、"南昌市2008年度劳动关系和谐企业"等荣誉。

1. 大堂 Lobby
2. 大堂酒廊 Lobby Lounge

Gloria Grand Hotel Nanchang located at the city centre of Nanchang, and face to the Ganjiang River, besides with the Tengwang Pavilion and Ba Yi Bridge. It is the nearest 5-star hotel from the old urban Nanchang to the Changbei Airport, which is also only 5 minutes' distance on foot to Shengli Road of the city shopping centre.

There are 327 guest rooms in the Hotel. All rooms are fitted up with high speed Internet access, which fits in with the demand of business travellers. Some standard rooms are fitted up with new Big-Screen LED TV and comfortable King size bed. There is Bath Area of dry wet separation in all suites, within various of fashion equipments. Guests occupied in River-view Rooms could see the beautiful landscapes out of the window. On the other side of the Ganjiang River is the Honggutan New District of Nanchang. There Nanchang Star Ferris Wheel, the highest ferris wheel in Asia, is located there, with other magnificent buildings.

The Taste Cafe located on the 1st floor provide daily buffet breakfast, lunch and dinner with Asia and Western dishes. It is the first restaurant to provide semi buffet service, where you could enjoy nice food and romantic atmosphere. The lobby lounge has special tea drinks, cookies, snacks, fresh bread and cake. Every night, we have the live piano performance in our lobby lounge, it's the best place for you to invite our friends or partner. The Chinese restaurant located on the 2nd floor, named as Sampan Seafood Restaurant. Cantonese cuisine, local dishes, and also our Weekend Dim Sum are offered here.

The banquet rooms are located on the 3rd and 4th floor that can used as a conference rooms, accommodating up to 300 persons capacity for each room. Besides that, there are 7 function rooms with 20-100 persons capacity that can be used for all kinds of business conference and seminars.

The 4th floor has our Health Club, rully equipped fitness facilities and river view swimming pool. The sauna and massage are provided for you when you get tired from the trip or feel less energy. The fitness facilities and swimming pool are complimentary for all our in-house guests.

As E-Floor guests, you could enjoy the check-in/out served on the 20th floor E-Lounge, we also provide free ironing and shoes polishing upon your arrival. The E-Lounge provide daily breakfast for E-Floor guests and also can enjoy our afternoon tea service. Complimentary Internet access and 1 hour free use of the meeting room at E-Lounge. Free local calls, faxes and late check out at E-Floor. Butler service also could be served here if you need it.

As one of the ealiest 5-star hotels in Jiangxi Province, Gloria Grand Hotel Nanchang won the titles of "China's Best Business Hotel", "The Best Brand Hotel in Jiangxi", and One of "the Enterprises on Harmonious Labor Relationships in Nanchang 2008" etc.

1. 品味餐厅
   Taste Cafe
2. 外观（夜景）
   Exterior (Night Time View)

1. 品位餐厅
   Taste Cafe
2. 船餐厅大厅
   Sampan Chinese Restaurant Lobby
3. 大堂
   Lobby

1. 宴会厅课堂式会议
   Ballroom Room Classroom Meeting
2. 南昌III厅接见台型（夜景）
   Nachang Hall III (Nighttime View)
3. 游泳池
   Swimming Pool
4. 套房
   Suite
5. 总统套房客厅
   Living Room of Presidential Suite

郑州索菲特国际饭店是被誉为"欧洲先锋、全球酒店及企业服务集团"——雅高国际酒店集团管理的豪华五星级酒店，姊妹酒店超过4,000家，遍布全球140多个国家；是中原地区唯一上榜福布斯中文版2006、2007和2008年度的"全国最佳商务酒店"。屡获包括《大河报》颁发的"游客满意的十佳饭店"、河南省旅游局历年评选的"全省最佳商务酒店"、《东方今报》评选的"最具风尚酒店"、私家地理颁发的"中国最佳酒店"和建筑鲁班奖在内的多项殊荣。开业迄今，成功接待了众多国家的政界要人及王室成员，有泰国王后和诗琳通公主，挪威王子，塞拉利昂总统，香港及澳门的最高行政长官及NBA著名篮球运动员沙克·奥尼尔。

饭店因拥有气势恢宏、充满自然景观的大堂而蜚声海内外。2008年重新装修了包括会所楼层和商务楼层及会议室在内的全部设施。饭店楼高20层，有240间房间，另有2个风格独特的中西餐厅、2个休闲酒吧、1个夜总会、室内恒温游泳池、健身房、桑拿和水疗馆。整个饭店因宁静雅致的户外设计、超大透明的玻璃穹顶、错落有序的布局而营造出浪漫优雅的舒适氛围。

郑州索菲特国际饭店地处郑州市城东路和金水大道交汇的黄金地段，周边省级政府机构林立，金融商贸云集，仅10分钟车程即可到达郑东新区，15分钟可到达全国的铁路交通中枢——郑州火车站，距新郑国际机场也仅30分钟车程，交通非常便利。

饭店对面的紫荆山公园和环绕酒店的金水河畔,增加了住店客人的休闲乐趣。一日游的知名景点有驰名中外的少林寺、黄河风景游览区、古都开封和洛阳的龙门石窟。

郑州索菲特国际饭店,共有包括豪华客房、独立或连通的套房及负有盛名的总统套房在内的240间客房,其中包括129间豪华客房、25间会所客房、35间商务客房、2间残障人用房、44间套房、1间总统套房。饭店提供24小时礼宾接待服务、24小时送餐服务、机场接机服务和商务中心服务。所有房间的幽雅装饰和独特的法式情调让您有一种归家的感觉。

引领时尚的圆顶阁西餐厅每日向您提供正宗的西式佳肴;古朴典雅的粤唯先中餐厅为您奉上独创的新派粤菜及本地美味美食;12间高贵典雅、别具一格的VIP宴会厅房,7间从54平方米、可容纳14人,到448平方米、可容纳500人的会议场所满足您不同规格的商务会议和宴会需求,一流的宴会会议设施和完美的视听效果使这里可接待不同类型的宴会和会议,如:婚宴、新闻发布会、论坛峰会、鸡尾酒会等。客人可以选择不同形式的会场台型布置,如:剧场式、课桌式、U形台、圆桌式和鸡尾酒会形式。而能容纳2,000人的中厅更适于举办大型主题庆典。

斯诺克台球和美式花球案依环廊而立;全新概念的空间3酒吧带给您视觉和听觉的双重震撼,夜色降临时,宾客可在此小酌并欣赏调酒师的精彩表演;威尼斯康乐会所的室内恒温泳池、全套顶级品牌运动器材、形体训练室、桑拿和夜总会等设施,可为您放松疲惫的身心、舒展尘世心灵。汇集世界品牌的索菲特名品街让您尽享购物的惬意。

结婚对人的一生来说是最重要的时刻,为了给新人缔造一个经典完美的幸福瞬间,索菲特国际饭店精心准备了从人民币1,699~2,299元的具有五星特质的"索菲特完美婚宴"系列。别具一格的婚庆典礼、温馨豪华的婚宴布置、美味精致的喜筵佳肴,以及弥漫着醉人芬芳的香槟酒,绝对让您体会到顶级婚宴的精彩和索菲特独一无二的法式浪漫。酒店还为您免费提供中、西背景板,优质的音响效果,造型鲜花,幸福红

1. 饭店外景
   Hotel Exterior View
2. 大堂
   Lobby

毯等，这些都是为您的婚宴精心准备的。相信郑州索菲特国际饭店会用激情与完美装点您难忘的人生时刻。

郑州索菲特国际饭店的十八至十九层的独特的会所楼层是整个中原地区独一无二的。会所楼层分为会所客房、会所套房和会所精英套房。位于二十层的会所酒廊是专供会所楼层客人休息、品茶、聚会和享用早餐的场所，另有一间完美装饰的会议室可供您进行商务洽谈和小型会议。

Sofitel Zhengzhou International is the first choice for luxurious 5-star hotel accommodation in Henan province. Sofitel Zhengzhou International continues to receive various accolades and awards including *Forbes Magazine*'s 2006, 2007 and 2008, *Travel + Leisure*, "Best 50 Business Hotels of China", the "10 Best Business Hotels of Zhengzhou", as well as the much coveted "Most Elegant Hotel of Henan Province" award and the Luban Architecture award. Each day Sofitel Zhengzhou International welcomes many visitors from both home and abroad. In addition many dignitaries and celebrities have stayed or attended functions in the hotel since the opening in 1999 including the Queen of Thailand, the Crown Princess of Holland, the Prince of Norway, President of Sierra Leone, Chief Executives of the Hong Kong and Macau SAR, and the NBA Basketball Player, Shaquille O'Neal. In the 20 storey high tower, guests are offered a spectacular atrium lobby area with 240 elegantly appointed rooms and suites. Sofitel Zhengzhou International combines a high standard of comfort and service with a wide range of culinary choices and leisure options for the discerning traveler. It features two exclusive designed restaurants, two fashionable bars, one nightclub, indoor heated swimming pool, gymnasium, sauna, Decleor SPA and extensive banquet and

1. 完美婚礼
   Wedding
2. 饭店外景
   Hotel Exterior View

1. 厅房
   Private Room
2. 下午茶
   Afternoon Tea
3. 咖啡套餐
   Coffee Set
4. 外卖服务
   Outside Catering
5. 空间 3 酒吧
   Bar 3

meeting facilities. The Hotel is located in the heart of the provincial capital, between Chengdong Road and Jin Shui Road which is the centre of the financial and shopping district of Zhengzhou. Only 10 minutes to the Zhengzhou Economic Zone, 15 minutes to Zhengzhou's Railway station and 30 minutes to Xinzheng International airport. The Provincial Government Offices are located nearby. It is located close to many local attractions such as Zijingshan Park, Jinshui River or Henan Museum. The city of Zhengzhou houses the best museum in China outside the capital and is close to the world famous Shaolin Temple, Yellow River scenic spots, Longmen Grottoes – UNESCO World Heritage site, as well as the ancient capital cities of Kaifeng and Luoyang.

Sofitel Zhengzhou International is a luxury five star hotel with 240 guest rooms and suites. Furthermore there are 129 luxury rooms, 25 Club Sofitel rooms, 2 superior special access rooms, 44 suites, 1 presidential suite and private a Club Lounge. The Hotel provides 24 hour reception & concierge, 24 hour room service, business center, limousine service, in-room broadband and Wi-Fi access from all public areas.

Sofitel Zhengzhou International is widely recognized for its professional and experienced Conference and Catering team available at every stage, from planning to execution of your special event. With its exclusive glamorous atrium area which can hold a banquet for 2,000 persons. Sofitel Zhengzhou International is the best place to hold any kind of event. Furthermore the hotel offers 7 individually styled meeting rooms from 54 to 448 square meters which can host from 14 to 500 people. There are also 12 private VIP banquet rooms designed in various styles. The different meeting & conference rooms undertake many different events such as weddings, media events, various forums, cocktail parties, etc. All venues are supported by a line-up of ultra-sophisticated equipment including LCD projectors, digital surround sound, audio-visual system and close-circuit camera. In addition ample car parking space and a beautiful garden square is available group

photo taking. The business centre offers comprehensive office-away-from-office services. All the meeting & conference rooms can be set up in different set ups such as theater, classroom shape, U-shape, banquet or cocktail style.

Exit 3 Bar offers a sumptuous variety of cocktails as well as a wide selection of local and imported beers and wines. Other hotel facilities are the Indoor Heated Pool, Computerized Gymnasium Equipments, Aerobic Room, Billiards, Sauna, Night Club and a shopping gallery with international brand names.

So many couples get weighed down by the pressures of creating a memorable wedding day for their guests. We are here to take the pressure off and remind you that this is your day. It should be one of the most important days in your life and we want you to enjoy the occasion at Sofitel Zhengzhou International. Our dedicated and experienced team will ensure that your day runs effortlessly and in the way you always dreamed it would be. We have the enviable reputation of providing the finest facilities for your wedding reception. We created a luxury "Dream Package" priced from RMB 1,699 to RMB 2,299 per table, which is includes complimentary overnight accommodation in a deluxe suite with breakfast buffet, wine, menus, floral decoration, seating arrangement, disco and any other special requirements you think of. We can even arrange all the little touches such as a red carpet or musical accompaniment. Sofitel Zhengzhou International will take care of your most precious occasion by ensuring your wedding is a memorable day for everyone.

Sofitel Zhengzhou International offers "Club Sofitel" floors on the 18th and 19th floors. The Club rooms and suites on these two floors are the most distinguished in Henan. The Sofitel Club Lounge on 20th floor is only accessible for Club Sofitel floor guests. There they can enjoy breakfast, afternoon tea with home made snacks, chatting with friends and also a well equipped meeting room for small business gatherings. The Guest Relations team are specially trained to deliver luxurious service to all guests.

1、6. 宴会厅房
　　Banquet Room
2. 会议厅
　　Meeting Room
3. 圆顶阁西餐厅
　　Dome Brasserie
4. 会所酒廊
　　Club Lounge
5. 宴会厅
　　Grand Ballroom

1. 外卖服务
   Outside Catering
2. 水疗
   SPA
3. 游泳池
   Swimming Pool
4. 健身房
   Recreation Center

1. 索菲特会所客房
   Club Sofitel Room
2、3. 总统套房
   Presidential Suite
4. 精英套房
   Elite Suite

武汉香格里拉大饭店是武汉市第一家国际五星级豪华酒店,位于汉口商业中心地带,25分钟即达天河国际机场,10分钟即达汉口火车站。

武汉香格里拉大饭店拥有442间空间宽敞、布置精美的客房和套房,装修风格既现代又不失中国特色,入住的客人在享受市区美丽景色的同时,还可体验到香格里拉闻名遐迩的热勤服务。客房配有豪华床上用品及现代化的卫浴设施,舒适、松软的大床及各种供客人挑选的枕头,保证您享受舒适的睡眠,令客人感觉宾至如归。

豪华阁客房为公务繁忙的旅客提供更体贴入微的服务、更舒适方便的环境,例如延迟退房时间、宽带及无线上网、私人礼宾员等。

武汉香格里拉大饭店套房拥有现代化的宽敞空间,独立起居室及高品位的亚洲风格装修。所有套房均提供室内传真、打印机、大屏幕电视、DVD娱乐系统、立体声音响系统、宽敞的浴室及多项特色洗浴用品。部分套房还带有专用的小厨房、书房或独立就餐区。

酒店同时还为希望停留较长时间的客人准备了服务式公寓。公寓拥有舒适精致的配套家具,全配套厨房和浴室,以及来自饭店的各种体贴服务。在这里,您不仅可享受到酒店的方便,更可体验家的温馨。香格里拉公寓共44套,

1. 酒店外景
   Hotel Exterior

有4种设计布局。提供一室（72~108平方米）、二室（108~160平方米）的公寓套房供客人选择。公寓拥有设备齐全的厨房器具、壁橱、保险箱、中央采暖系统、卫星电视、熨斗熨板等设施。另外，客人还可享受酒店的各类服务，如定期房间清扫、客房送餐服务、前往各餐厅用餐、大堂酒廊、健身中心等。

酒店还是享受美食的好去处，粤菜、淮扬菜、西餐，各种风味满足客人的就餐需要。香苑咖啡厅充满了时尚华丽的现代气息，整体用餐环境温馨典雅、轻松惬意。全日提供零点服务，更有选择多样的自助餐点，包括欧陆式风味、亚式精选和本地特色等。香宫中餐厅设施现代，环境幽雅，古风灵韵的风格中透出最新的时尚元素。该餐厅以精致的粤菜闻名，同时也提供正宗湖北、扬州、四川、湖南等地的特色小吃和每天午餐的点心。大堂酒廊拥有两层挑高玻璃窗，是酒店内最受欢迎的场所之一。大堂酒廊晚间有现场音乐演奏，供应种类齐全的饮料和鸡尾酒，是朋友欢聚或商务洽谈的绝佳场所。

酒店提供设施高档的健身中心，包括大型室内游泳池、室外网球场、桑拿、蒸汽浴等。先进的健身房配备齐全的心血管功能锻炼设备及卫星电视。酒店还提供室外网球场和各类SPA、按摩服务。

武汉香格里拉大饭店拥有1,600平方米无柱式大宴会厅，堪居全城之最，可同时容纳多达2,500人，是国际顶级商务及休闲活动的不二选择。同时，宴会厅可分隔成多个小型场地，以便举行小型聚会。酒店另有10多个高雅华丽的多功能室，满足客人的多种需要。专业的会议统筹团队也将随时为您提供高效优质的服务，保证您会议的顺畅进行。

1. 香宫
Shang Palace

The first true luxury hotel in the city, the Shangri-La Hotel, Wuhan is located in the heart of the Hankou business district, just a 25 minutes drive from Tianhe International Airport and a 10 minutes walk from the Hankou Railway Station.

Rooms

Shangri-La Hotel, Wuhan has 442 spacious, well-appointed guest rooms and suites, each with a contemporary Chinese decor and dramatic city views. Comfortable beds and a pillow menu ensure a good night's sleep. With every guest receiving the gracious service for which Shangri-La is known around the world, each room is elegantly appointed with luxurious bedding, modern bathrooms and the fine touches that make guests feel welcome and at home.

Horizon Club

Horizon Club rooms offer an enhanced level of service, comfort and convenience for busy travellers, including late check-out, complimentary wired or wireless broadband Internet access and a personal concierge.

Suites

Shangri-La Hotel, Wuhan suites offer spacious modern living quarters with a tastefully Asian spirit. All suites include separate sitting areas, in-room fax/copy/printer, large-screen televisions, DVD entertainment and stereo sound systems, and beautiful bathrooms stocked with designer bath amenities. Some suites offer a separate kitchenette, study or dining area.

The hotel also offers fully serviced apartments for guests wishing a longer stay. Shangri-La Hotel, Wuhan apartments are fully furnished to a five-star luxury standard and feature fitted kitchens and bathrooms as well as a host of services and facilities. There

1. 中式婚宴（大宴会厅）
Ballroom Chinese Wedding Setup

are 44 apartments with four unit layouts. You can select one-bedroom (72 – 108 square metres) or two-bedroom (108 – 160 square metres) apartments. Each furnished apartment is fitted with a full range of choice furniture, complete kitchen fittings, built-in wardrobes, a safe deposit box, air-conditioning, central heating, satellite television and ironing board. In addition, apartments offer all the services guests enjoy at the Hotel, such as regular housekeeping and room service, and full access to all restaurants, lounges and the fitness centre.

Restaurants and Entertainment

The Hotel is a destination for fine dining, offering Wuhan's the best Cantonese and Huaiyang cuisine as well as Western-style restaurants. The recently refurbished Café Wu at Shangri-La Hotel, Wuhan has a new look and new additions to the buffet and a la carte menus. Café Wu is an exciting and fresh dining destination for international travelers and local patrons alike. Shang Palace serves Wuhan's finest Cantonese home style cuisine in a modern, picturesque setting. Not to be missed are the specialties or the daily dim sum lunch. Surrounded by double-storey glass windows, the Lobby Lounge at Shangri-La Hotel, Wuhan is one of the hotel's most inviting and enjoyed areas. A fine place to meet for a drink, the lounge delivers live entertainment in the evening and a full range of beverages and cocktails.

The Hotel offers a superbly equipped Fitness Centre with a full-size indoor swimming pool, outdoor tennis courts, sauna and steam bath.

The state-of-the-art gymnasium is equipped with an array of cardiovascular equipment along with satellite television. The Hotel also offers an outdoor tennis court and a menu of indulgent SPA and massage services.

Meetings

The superb Grand Ballroom is the largest in Wuhan, accommodating up to 2,500 people, which makes the hotel a preferred destination among Wuhan hotels for the world's most discriminating business events. The Grand Ballroom can be subdivided for gatherings that are more intimate. As Wuhan's first luxury hotel, Shangri-La Hotel, Wuhan is the city's premier venue for conferences, business meetings and social occasions. Regardless of the event you host at the hotel professional staff are on hand to help make it a resounding success. Complementing the ballroom are 10 elegant function rooms.

1. 香苑
   Cafe Wu
2. 功能厅
   Function Room VIP Reception
3. 健身中心游泳池
   Health Club Swimming Pool
4. 健身中心
   Health Club

多功能的国际商务空间

会议·酒店·展览·演出

广州白云国际会议中心作为广州岭南国际企业集团的成员企业，是中国华南地区规模最大、设施最先进、配套最完善的综合性会议中心。集会议中心、五星级标准酒店、展览中心、演出中心于一体，地处中国广州现代化、生态型商贸文化中心——白云新城核心地段，距广州白云国际机场25分钟车程，距中国进出口商品交易会展馆20分钟车程。

中国进出口商品交易会、16届亚运会举办地——广州欢迎您！

五星级标准观景酒店

1,080间观景客房和豪华完善的酒店配套设施，为您打造白云山下五星级的家。

客房设施：免费高速宽带上网、免费拨打国内和31个国家和地区的长途电话、迷你酒吧、数码E房等。

配套及设施：外币兑换、租车服务、洗衣服务、票务服务、阳光泳池、健身馆、电影放映厅、东方美术馆、娱乐会所、美容美发中心、花店、商场、空中花园。

餐饮设施：18间风格各异宴会中心和餐厅，荟萃亚洲及世界美食。无论是朋友聚会，抑或千人宴会、喜庆婚宴，均能为您精彩呈献。

会议中心

具国际会议服务水准的服务团队，确保您的每次会议完美成功。

规模庞大的会议中心，拥有66间专业标准会议厅，配备电子报到和表决系统、会议音视频采集编辑系统、同声传译系统、智能化电子信息屏蔽系统、记者采录接口系统、中央控制系统、专业扩声系统、大屏幕显示系统等当今最为先进和专业的会议设施，可同时举办多场20~2,500人不同规模的会议。

6万平方米展览场地

是中国华南地区举办专业展览的最佳平台，距广州白云国际机场最近的大型综合性展馆。30,000平方米多功能展场间隔灵活，可同时举办各类展会。24,000平方米户外展场，适合举办大型机械、汽车试驾、庆典仪式等各类展览活动。拥有1,200个停车位。

三大顶级剧院

国际及国内专业演出团体到访广州首选之地。世纪大会堂（2,500座）：1,700平方米超大舞台，配置5个升降平台、8个车台、80根吊杆，最大声压级、座位不均匀度均达到国家一级标准，是大型芭蕾舞剧、音乐剧、歌剧、综艺晚会的尊贵之选。岭南大会堂（1,200座）：采用左中右三声道（L、C、R）布局，音响效果达到国家音乐扩声一级标准，是专业音乐会、戏曲、话剧演出的理想场所。广东大会堂（500座）：面积613m²，配备专业舞台和电影放映设施，适合举办戏剧、曲艺、杂技及电影放映等。东方厅、露天剧院及大型户外广场，提供多样化选择。

五大亮点

广州最佳景致；世界水准的服务；荟萃亚洲及世界美食；免费拨打31个国家和国内长途、免费高速宽带、无线上网，助您驰骋无限商务空间；交通便捷，连通国际。

1. 全景
   Grand View
2. 夜景
   Night View
3. 1号楼大堂
   Lobby in Block 1

1

International Multifunctional Business Space

Convention · Hotel ·Exhibition ·Performance

Guangzhou Baiyun International Convention Center (GZBICC) is a subsidiary company of Guangzhou Ling Nan International Corporate Group, which is the largest international comprehensive venue with most advanced establishment and perfect supporting facilities in South China, which integrates convention center, five-star standard hotel, exhibition center and performance center. Located in the core area of the Baiyun New District, which is the modern ecologic commercial, and culture center, besides Baiyun Mountain.

To New BaiYun International Airport 25 minutes by Taxi, To China Import & Export Fair Complex 20 minutes by Taxi.

Welcome to Guangzhou—the host city of China Import & Export Fair and the 16th Asian Games.

Five-star Standard Mountain View Hotel

1,080 Mountain view guest rooms and luxury hotel facilities to create a five-star home for you in Baiyun Mountain.

Room Facilities: Free broadband internet access, free domestic calls and international calls to 31 countries and regions, mini Bar, E-home.

Hotel Facilities and Services

Swimming pool, Gymnasium, Tennis court, Outdoor garden, Cinema hall, Painting and Calligraphy Gallery, KTV, Beauty & hair Salon, Florist's shop, Foreign currency exchange and luxury car rental services.

Foreign currency exchange, luxury cars rental service, Laundry/press service, tickets services, swimming pool, gymnastics center, cinema hall, Oriental Painting and Calligraphy Gallery, Night Club, Beauty & hair Salon, Florist's shop, Prestige boutique, Outdoor garden.

You can enjoy the Asian & world gourmets foods in our 18 banquet rooms & restaurants in all occasion .

Professional Conference Rooms

The professional team provides the high-level service standard to ensure your meeting every time.

1. 细节见尊贵
   Our Details Make You More Honorable
2. 外景
   Outdoor Scenic

The largest convention center with 66 professional and standard conference rooms that is contained the advanced meeting facilities such as electronic registration & voting system, meeting audio & visual collection & edit system, synchronized interpretation system, intelligent electronic information screened system, record & gather system for reporters, central control system, professional amplify system, grand screen monitor system and etc. which can hold any scale of the conferences from 20-2,500 persons at the same time.

60,000m^2 Exhibition Venue

The best professional exhibition platform in South China of China

The nearest complex exhibition venue to Guangzhou Baiyun International Airport

30,000m^2 Multi-purpose exhibition space for any types of the exhibition with flexible interval space. 24,000m^2 outdoor exhibition venue, adapt to hold the grand machinery exhibition, cars test-driving. There are 1,200 parking spaces.

The hall is equipped with 8 business conference rooms.

3 Top Theatres

The 1st choice for the professional performance team to hold the performance in Guangzhou.

Century Hall (2,500 seats): the most prestige venue for large-scale ballet, musical drama, opera and variety show with the 1,700m^2 super large stage, 5 elevating boards, 80 swing hangers and 8 mechanism of stage. Sound pressure level and seating equality level are reached international first level standard.

Lingnan Hall (1,200 seats): Ideal venue for professional concerts, operas and modern dramas with the national music amplifiers first level standard system.

Guangdong Hall (500 seats): 613 m^2, with professional cinema projection equipments and stage equipments, adapt to hold opera, concert, acrobatics and cinema projection .

Oriental Hall and outdoor plaza supply you with more choices.

Five Unique Experiences

Best view in guangzhou,international services, worldwide gourmets, Asian & world gourmets foods, free international calls.

1. 东方厅
   Oriental Hall
2. 一号楼西餐厅连空中花园
   Western Restaurant with Outdoor Garden in Block 1
3. 清和厅
   Qinghe Hall
4. 优雅的西式摆台
   Banquet Table Decoration

1. 岭南大会堂（1,200座）
   Lingnan Hall (1,200 Seats)
2. 国际会议2厅
   International Conference Hall No. 2
3. 世纪大会堂（2,500座）
   Century Hall (2,500 Seats)
4. 广东大会堂（500座）
   Guangdong Hall (500 Seats)
5. 中型会议室 深圳厅
   Medium Conference Room Shenzhen Room
6. 越秀华堂（250座）
   Yue Xiu Conference Hall (250 Seats)

1. 世纪大会堂（2,500座）
   Century Hall (2,500 Seats)
2. 演出《罗密欧与朱丽叶》
   Show *Romeo & Juliet*
3. 演出《云南的响声》
   Show *What Birds Dream*
4. 网球场
   Tennis Court
5. 展览厅
   Exhibition Hall
6. 健身房
   Gym Center

1. 1号楼总统套房
   Presidential Suite in Block 1
2. 5号楼总统套房
   Presidential Suite in Block 5
3. 双床房
   Double Room
4. 大床房
   King-size Bed Room